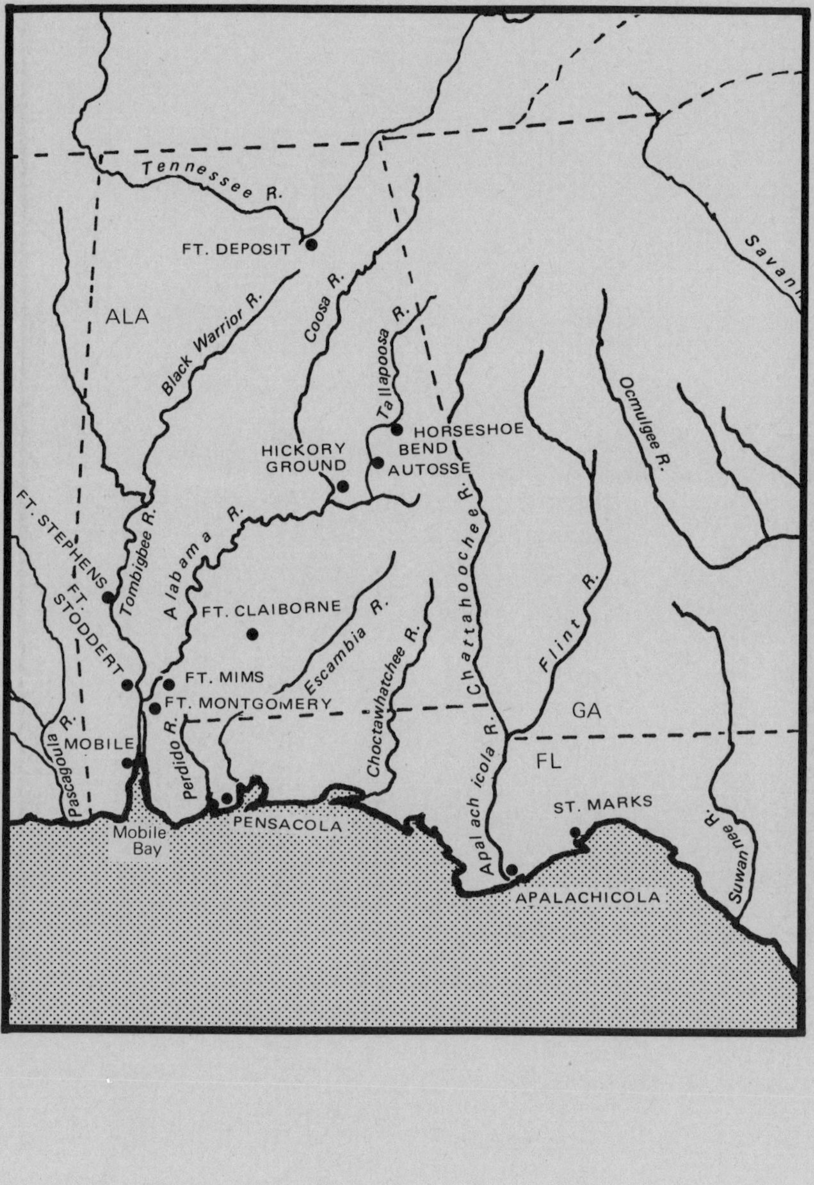

Tennessee R.
FT. DEPOSIT
ALA
Black Warrior R.
Coosa R.
Tallapoosa R.
Savann
Ocmulgee R.
HORSESHOE BEND
AUTOSSE
HICKORY GROUND
FT. STEPHENS
Tombigbee R.
Alabama R.
Chattahoochee R.
FT. STODDERT
FT. CLAIBORNE
Escambia R.
Choctawhatchee R.
Flint R.
FT. MIMS
FT. MONTGOMERY
GA
FL
Pascagoula R.
MOBILE
Perdido R.
Apalachicola R.
ST. MARKS
Suwannee R.
Mobile Bay
PENSACOLA
APALACHICOLA

Struggle for the Gulf Borderlands

Struggle for the Gulf Borderlands

The Creek War and the Battle of New Orleans 1812-1815

Frank Lawrence Owsley, Jr.

A University of Florida Book

University Presses of Florida

Gainesville

To my wife, Dorothy Sellers Owsley, and my mother, Harriet Chappell Owsley, and to the memory of my father, Frank Owsley, this book is lovingly dedicated.

University Presses of Florida is the central agency for scholarly publishing of the State of Florida's university system. Its offices are located at 15 NW 15th Street, Gainesville, FL 32603. Works published by University Presses of Florida are evaluated and selected for publication by a faculty editorial committee of any one of Florida's nine public universities: Florida A&M University (Tallahassee), Florida Atlantic University (Boca Raton), Florida International University (Miami), Florida State University (Tallahassee), University of Central Florida (Orlando), University of Florida (Gainesville), University of North Florida (Jacksonville), University of South Florida (Tampa), University of West Florida (Pensacola).

Library of Congress Cataloging in Publication Data

Owsley, Frank Lawrence, 1928–
Struggle for the gulf borderlands.

"A University of Florida book."
Bibliography: p.
Includes index.
1. United States—War of 1812—
Campaigns and battles. 2. Creek War, 1813–1814.
3. Gulf States—History. 4. New Orleans,
Battle of, 1815. 5. Jackson, Andrew, Pres. U. S.,
1767–1845. I. Title.
E355.1.097 973.5′238 80–11109
ISBN 0–8130–0662–7

Printed in U.S.A.

Acknowledgments

IT IS impossible to name all the people who helped in the preparation of this book. When I was a graduate student, my late father, Frank Owsley, suggested that a study of the Indians in our country would be a worthwhile specialization. My first endeavor in this area was my master's thesis on Benjamin Hawkins, Indian agent, followed by a doctoral dissertation on Albert J. Pickett's *History of Alabama.* Through the latter study I became familiar with source materials on the Creek Indian War. By the time I had finished my dissertation, I knew that I wanted to write a history of the Creek War.

My research for this book was made possible in part by research grants-in-aid from Auburn University. I wish to express appreciation to the University of Alabama Press for permission to use portions of articles on Jackson's attack on Pensacola and on the Fort Mims massacre which have previously been published in the *Alabama Review.*

Several historians gave me valuable advice and suggestions: John K. Mahon, author of *The War of 1812;* Robert V. Remini, whose most recent book is *Andrew Jackson and the Course of the Empire 1767–1821;* Jack D.L. Holmes, author of many works on the Spanish-American borderlands; William Coker, editor of the Panton-Leslie-Forbes Papers; Jane de Grummond, author of *The Baratarians and the Battle of New Orleans;* J. Leitch Wright, Jr., author of several works on the Indians, including *Anglo-Spanish Rivalry in North America;* Alfred B. Thomas, a specialist in Spanish borderlands; and Paul Ghioto, historian of Horseshoe Bend National Military Park. I am greatly indebted to Melvin and Marie Bradford for their advice and critical reading of the manuscript.

Of those who aided me with the research, I wish to express my appreciation especially to Sara Dunlap Jackson of the National Historical Publications and Records Commission and to George Chalou and Dale Floyd of the National Archives. Margaret Franklin helped with the research in the British Public Record Office and in the National Maritime Museum at Greenwich, England. Others I would like to thank are staff member of the Mobile Public Library; the university libraries at Alabama, Auburn, Florida (Gainesville), South Florida (Tampa), Georgia, Indiana, Louisiana State, and Oklahoma; the Manuscript Division of the Library of Congress; the departments of Archives and History of Alabama, Georgia, Mississippi, and Tennessee; the Louisiana State Museum; the State Historical Society of Wisconsin; the Military Records Division of the National Archives; the National Library of Scotland; and the British Public Record Office.

I wish to thank the National Library of Scotland for permission to reproduce portions of letters from the papers of Alexander Inglis Cochrane and the British Public Record Office for permission to reproduce portions of manuscript materials having a Crown copyright.

There is no way I can ever fully express my thanks to my wife, Dorothy Sellers Owsley, who typed this manuscript and performed editorial and numerous other tasks, or to my mother, Harriet Chappell Owsley, who has read the manuscript in numerous drafts and has given me advice on both research and writing.

Frank Lawrence Owsley, Jr.

Contents

List of Maps

Introduction

THIS STUDY was originally planned as a history of the Creek Indian War, one of the few major Indian conflicts about which there is no recent or complete work. While there are a number of accounts of Andrew Jackson's campaigns against the Creek Indians, not any one of them covers the entire war. Three books, all of which are over eighty years old — A. J. Pickett, *History of Alabama,* J. F. H. Claiborne, *History of Mississippi,* H. S. Halbert and T. H. Ball, *The Creek War of 1813 and 1814* — contain information about the Indian conflict; but they deal with it as local history and are entirely inadequate in their coverage of Jackson. With the exception of the Jackson biographies and some general accounts, little has been done to integrate the Creek hostilities with the War of 1812. It is the major purpose of this study to make this connection and to emphasize the importance of the Indian war in bringing to the front on the Gulf Coast a trained army and an experienced general in the person of Andrew Jackson.

It is increasingly apparent after a thorough examination of the Creek War and its sequel on the Gulf Coast that scholars have overlooked the significance of the War of 1812 in this area. Only the Battle of New Orleans has been given adequate treatment. Because of this omission, the importance of the Gulf theater has been underrated. This is unfortunate because it was this section of the country, along with the northwest and southeast, which led the nation in demanding war in 1812. Such neglect probably resulted from the fact that most early scholars were New England or Canadian oriented and were not acquainted with the activities that occurred in the Gulf region. With few exceptions, southern historians have been so completely submerged in the period *circa* 1861–65 that they have paid little attention to the earlier war.

Most of the original research on the War of 1812 was done a number of years ago by scholars who did not have access to manuscripts more recently located. As a result, a considerable amount of erroneous information has found its way into the accepted works on the subject. Aware of these errors, this researcher began with a return to the sources. An examination of manuscripts discovered since earlier works were written, together with a re-examination of the sources used by the early authors, led to the conclusion that this study was needed. The first draft of this volume was written almost entirely from primary sources, and only after it had been completed was a study made of existing scholarly works in order to discover and reconcile conflicting views. While this manuscript was under way several new books, especially those by Robin Reilly, John K. Mahon, and Robert Remini, were published. These authors have also re-examined the original sources, and in a number of cases their conclusions are similar to this author's.

The war in the Gulf region can properly be divided into two parts—the Creek Indian War, reaching its height at the Battle of Horseshoe Bend, and the British offensive against the Gulf Coast with its climax at the Battle of New Orleans. American records pertaining to the Creek War are, as a whole, woefully inaccurate as to the origin of the hostilities. Many earlier studies have insisted that Tecumseh was acting as an agent of the British government when he aroused the Creeks to war. While he had English support, his appeal to the Indians was for the rejection of white culture. The first result of Tecumseh's agitation was civil war between the "pro" and "anti" white factions of the Upper Creeks. The civil war ended, and the Creek War began with the massacre at Fort Mims of a large number of whites, mixed bloods, and their Indian allies. Contemporary United States leaders believed that the Indians were receiving large amounts of arms from the British through the port of Pensacola in Spanish West Florida. An examination of English official documents in the Public Record Office casts doubt on these conclusions.

Most previous studies of the Creek conflict give some attention to Spanish aid to the Indians but contain no real insight into Spain's course in the war. Correspondence between the Spanish governor of West Florida and his superior, the captain general of Cuba, supports the conclusion that Spain was a major participant in the struggle. Also letters from Spanish officials found at the captured Indian town of "Holy Ground" contained encouragement for the Indians and offered congratulations to the Creek chiefs for their victory at Fort Mims. These letters, together with the observations of the Innerarity brothers and other officials of the John Forbes

Company, which controlled most of the Spanish-Indian trade, provide a clear and accurate record of the role of Spain in the southern campaign of the war. When one considers that the only territory gained by the United States during the War of 1812 was seized from Spanish Florida, the position of Spain in the conflict assumes much greater significance.

Most scholars have heretofore not utilized British and Spanish documents relative to the Creek hostilities. With the exception of brief accounts in some of the most recent general studies, which include Harry Coles' *The War of 1812*, Reginald Horsman's *The War of 1812*, John K. Mahon's *The War of 1812*, and the biographies of Andrew Jackson—Marquis James' *Andrew Jackson: The Border Captain* and Robert Remini's *Andrew Jackson and the Course of American Empire, 1767–1821*—few narratives have attempted to correlate the British and Indian operations on the Gulf Coast. Of these, Mahon's, Horsman's, and Remini's works employ British manuscripts; only Remini has examined the Spanish documents.

As for the second part of the war—the British offensive on the Gulf Coast—there are a number of excellent studies of the Battle of New Orleans. Charles B. Brooks' *Siege of New Orleans*, Wilburt S. Brown's *The Amphibious Campaign for West Florida and Louisiana, 1814–1815*, Jane de Grummond's *The Baratarians and the Battle of New Orleans*, and Robin Reilly's *The British at the Gates* are well done in their special areas of research. With the exception of Reilly's work, all the other books fail to employ extensive manuscript material from both sides of the engagement and are limited in scope to one or two aspects of the subject. Only Reilly's account makes any effort to relate the Battle of New Orleans to the war on other fronts and to evaluate its significance to the overall conflict. He does not, however, develop the Spanish role in the war or understand the impact of blacks and Indians in the British plan. He also assumes that the war objectives of the South and Southwest were the same as those of the Northeast. Although Reilly is one of the few historians to grasp the importance of the successful defense of the American claim to Louisiana, he is little interested in the annexation of Mobile and the total defeat of the southern Indians. These factors caused the South to conclude that it had won a smashing victory over the British.

This study is not intended as another biography of Andrew Jackson; but exhaustive research has shown that, while the Tennessean played little part in the early events of the War of 1812, the scope of his activities grew until he completely dominated the southern front. Creek hostilities, which did not end after Horseshoe Bend, merged into the British offensive against the Gulf Coast. When Jackson assumed overall leadership of the American forces in this area, Admiral Alexander Inglis Cochrane eliminated the Spanish influence among the Creek Indians and became Jackson's principal adversary. As part of the British attack on the Gulf Coast, Cochrane reorganized the Indians and recruited the pro-British Lower Creeks, who were supposed by the Americans to be peaceable. This relatively unknown second part of the Creek War eventually evolved as the First Seminole War.

Another important part of the British offensive which has been largely ignored by historians is the extensive efforts of the British to recruit black troops from among the slave population in the South. Cochrane and other British leaders believed black troops would arouse so much fear in the South that this section would force an immediate peace. Cochrane proposed using black troops to occupy New Orleans if the British were able to capture the city. In addition to his Indian and black allies, Cochrane also tried to recruit other dissidents in the South and join them with a massive amphibious assault on the area. The struggle eventually developed into a contest between Jackson and Cochrane.

Sir John Fortescue in his history of the British army has implied that Cochrane deliberately missed the rendezvous with General Pakenham at Jamaica because he feared the general would cancel the planned operation against New Orleans and Cochrane would not get any prize money or plunder. Cochrane's real reason for hurrying to New Orleans was the hope that he would arrive before Jackson and capture an undefended city. He was only about ten days late. His plans were basically sound, and with all the admiral's advantages of mobility, supplies, and manpower, he should have been victorious. Cochrane, like nearly all naval officers, especially Scotsmen, was certainly interested in prize money. New Orleans offered much plunder, and the admiral undoubtedly wanted his part of this wealth. The capture of New Orleans was a very worthwhile objective and one calculated to hurt most the South and the West—those parts of the United States that had demanded war. Jackson succeeded in foiling the British time after time. The American general is usually characterized as a tough and aggressive fighter who had little military training and a large amount of luck. Jackson was lucky. Any commander with a small force who successfully counters an amphibious landing with its infinite mobility must have a great deal of luck. He also must have skill, good military judgment, and, in Jackson's case, an excellent intelligence service. His espionage system kept him well informed of all the major British operations in time for him to counteract them. The general throughout both the Indian war and the campaign against the British exhibited an iron will. He had the ability to drive himself and his army through almost any kind of hardship, to maintain good discipline in his militia units, and never to lose confidence that he would win in the end. He did win, and he clearly emerges from the contest not only as being a tough, aggressive fighter but also as having a first-rate military mind. He was probably the ablest general in North America in 1815.

Jackson won the war on the Gulf Coast. Had there been a general with Jackson's military attributes on the northern frontier, the United States might very well have had a clear-cut victory there. Cochrane was a tenacious foe, and even after the defeat at New Orleans he launched another major offensive against Mobile, which was ended only by the arrival of news of the peace treaty. The threat of Indian and black hostilities was not finally concluded until Jackson invaded Florida in 1818.

This study is concerned primarily with the Indian conflict and subsequently the War of 1812 in the Gulf states. An attempt has been made to explain the actions of various participants and their motives. Only an examination of British and Spanish manuscript records makes possible a true evaluation of the extent of Jackson's victory in the South.

1

The Beginning of Hostilities on the Gulf

THE EUROPEAN struggle for possession of the Gulf of Mexico and Florida is older than British colonization of North America. Even before the British settled at Jamestown, English adventurers, official and otherwise, had used these regions as temporary bases in their constant raids on Spanish commerce. After the settlement of Jamestown, the colonists soon pushed southward and westward, only to meet and fight the French in the Mississippi Valley and the Spanish in Florida.

In an area beyond the Appalachian Mountains extending west to the Mississippi River, north to Canada, and south to the Gulf Coast lay a sort of no-man's-land inhabited by numerous tribes of Indians. The intrigues and conflicts in the northern territory, well known to students of American history, concern the struggle between Britain and France for possession of Canada. Both adversaries used Indians as pawns in this great international engagement.

In the South the conflict, though not as well known by historians, was just as intense and probably more important. The nation that held the Gulf Coast controlled the entire interior of North America south of the Great Lakes and had an excellent base from which a strong naval power could dominate the West Indies.[1] The Gulf Coast commands the mouths of the Mississippi and smaller rivers, through which nearly all travel and trade with the interior was conducted in the early period of American history. Florida and the Gulf Coast are close to Cuba and Hispaniola, which in colonial times were considered to be among the greatest prizes of the Western Hemisphere. France held the Mississippi Valley, Spain held Florida, and Britain held the east coast.

Military districts, 1813–1815

In the area which now comprises Alabama, Mississippi, Florida, Tennessee, and western Georgia, there were five major tribes of Indians: Creeks, Chickasaws, Cherokees, Seminoles, and Choctaws. All three European powers courted them, for control would be a tremendous asset to any power that hoped to dominate this strategic area. In any case, the Indians were a valuable ally for offense or defense. They usually cooperated more closely with France and Spain because British settlers demanded ever increasing amounts of their lands. The exception was the Chickasaws, who, because of their enmity with the Choctaws, allied with the British.

In 1763 the picture changed drastically. The Treaty of Paris eliminated France from North America, and Spain, which lost all Florida, remained only in the West and in Louisiana. Britain now made peace with all the Indians and gained possession of their valuable trade. Such a feat was accomplished by the establishment of a very elaborate system of agents and merchants, who were to keep the Indians friendly and conduct a profitable trade. Charleston and Savannah had originally been the British bases for this trade, but after the annexation of Florida, Pensacola and Mobile became more important. In an effort to maintain Anglo-Indian harmony, Parliament established the Proclamation Line of 1763. This act was designed to prevent colonial settlers from encroaching on Indian land and thereby to protect British trade. The English doubtless were preparing for the next step in their own plan of conquest, which was to take Louisiana or Cuba.

As it turned out, the American Revolution wrecked British plans. The British efforts among the Indians, however, were not unrewarded, for nearly all of those led by the British merchants and agents remained loyal to King George and in fact fought well against the revolutionaries. British defeat during the Revolution led to the restoration of Florida to Spain, but it did not by any means end British influence with the southern Indians. Although most British merchants were loyalists and were forced to leave the United States, they continued to trade both legally and illegally with the Indians long after the Revolution. The great British trading house of Panton, Leslie, and Forbes was permitted by the Spanish to continue in operation. Because of a close association with Alexander McGillivray, the powerful Creek chief, this firm at one time had almost complete control of the legal Creek trade. Other smaller mercantile houses continued to operate legally through outlets in Spanish Florida.[2]

Legal trade was not the only commerce conducted by British merchants. The relatively thin settlement and weak control by Spain enabled many of the old British merchants to continue an illegal trade by smuggling.

There were also numerous British adventurers who continued to agitate the Indians, and, as in the case of William Augustus Bowles, to have the unofficial support of the British government.[3] In addition to the trade, there were also kinship ties. Men like Alexander McGillivray, William Weatherford, David Tate, and other Indian leaders were the half-breed descendants of British agents and traders.[4] Because of this continuing relationship with the southern Indians, especially the Creeks and Seminoles, the British made special efforts to maintain their Indian friendships in case of war with the United States.

During 1811 and 1812, when war with Britain appeared inevitable, many American leaders believed that there was an army of British agents stirring up hostility among the Indians in the Gulf region. There seemed to be a contradiction between these American reports and an official British "hands-off" policy. The probable truth was that many individual British traders were agitating the Indians. The official English position did not change until the War of 1812 commenced, but there seems little doubt that the governments of the British West Indies knew of, and winked at, the activities of their merchants. A thorough knowledge of the affairs of the southern Indians was widespread among British colonial officials, but the London government seemed uninformed concerning these activities.[5]

It should be noted that this situation in the South is a close parallel to the trade and agent relationship that the British were enjoying with the northern Indians from their bases in Canada. There is little doubt that the British would have liked to use the firm of John Forbes and Company, formerly Panton, Leslie, and Forbes, to continue their control over the Indians through trade. This firm had the right under its British charter to operate under any flag of convenience, and the partners even had the right to hold dual citizenship. They did in fact become citizens of Spain when they felt it desirable.[6]

When war seemed imminent, it was natural that the British would consider the southern Indians as their allies against the United States. This alliance was clouded by two factors. First, the Indians themselves had few real grievances against the United States; but of greater importance, the conservative element of the Creek Nation bitterly resented the acceptance of the white man's civilization by their brother Creeks. This dislike of white culture, when stimulated by Tecumseh, would probably have caused the Creeks to go to war regardless of the British influence. Second, the Spaniards in Florida, in an effort to protect their weakly held frontier, had long cultivated the friendship of the southern Indians. The Spaniards had for many years encouraged the Indians, especially the Creeks and Seminoles, to resist American encroachments on their lands, and had indicated to these tribes that they could expect Spanish assistance with arms and supplies in the event of war.[7]

In any study of this conflict the various sources of friction between the Americans and the southern Indians are difficult to differentiate since they are thoroughly enmeshed. Florida, with or without Spanish permission, was used first as a base of operations for smuggling goods to the Indians and to the frontier. Later it was used as a regular British base for military operations.[8] The British, Spanish, and Indians each had grievances against the Americans and felt threatened by them. Because of these multiple complaints and viewpoints, it is not possible to establish any single cause of Indian-American hostility in the South.

Between the whites and Indians on the Georgia frontier there had always been a number of grievances. Parties of whites were continually trying to settle on Indian lands, and groups of Indians were often found hunting and stealing horses and cattle belonging to the whites. After the appointment of Benjamin Hawkins as the Creek agent in 1796, these issues were usually settled to the satisfaction of all parties, at least until about 1809.[9] Around that time there were many American raids on Indian cattle, and always there were attempts to extend the Georgia frontier into the Creek Nation.[10] Most Creeks, especially the older chiefs, were reasonably well pleased with the manner in which Hawkins settled these difficulties, but among the younger Indians there was a surge of unrest.[11]

Although Spanish interest in the Creek Indians was not a new development, rumors were prevalent during the period after 1810 of extensive activities on the part of the Spanish agents to win the loyalty of the Creeks. One such project was an attempt by the governor of West Florida to have a pro-Spanish chief made speaker of the nation. This endeavor, apparently supported by gifts and bribes to important Creek leaders, created even more unrest.[12]

Apart from the visit of Tecumseh, what caused the greatest alarm among the more conservative Creeks was the white settlements being made on the Alabama River. When these appeared, the Creeks found themselves facing the white man's frontier not only to the north and east but now to the west as well. Their only remaining retreat was south into Spanish Florida. This feeling of being surrounded was undoubtedly accentuated by the increasing number of travelers who pushed through Creek territory from Georgia west to the Alabama River. When the United States proposed to build a regular road from the Georgia frontier to the new settlements in Alabama, many of the Creeks were strongly opposed.[13] Even the more responsible chiefs considered that opening the rivers to travel and building roads would increase hostile incidents and an undersirable whiskey trade.[14]

The road was completed in 1810, and though the Creeks were allowed to make considerable profits from trade with the travelers, the unrest continued. The sight of dozens of wagons going westward every day convinced the chiefs that their lands would soon be taken. With this prospect facing them, there is little wonder that the old chiefs were alarmed by the possibility of their young men committing depredations along the road.[15] One of the first unfriendly acts of the Indians was to charge the travelers illegal tolls for crossing the bridges along the road. The Indians used this means to harass the settlers, and Hawkins found the practice very difficult to stop. Reginald Horsman believed that the new roads were the main source of conflict between the Creeks and whites.[16] Certainly they were a significant source of trouble.

This Creek hostility, although blamed on the encroachments of the white man, was probably more influenced by Indian resentment of white culture. On the western frontier along the Alabama River there had been considerable intermarriage, and a great many Indians were living like white men. John K. Mahon correctly suggests in *War of 1812* that Benjamin Hawkins' policy of assimilation was itself a major cause of Indian hostility. Much of the resentment in the nation was against the assimilated Indians and mixed bloods rather than against the white man.[17] It was this sentiment that provided fertile ground for the appeals of Tecumseh, the Shawnee leader, and his brother, the Prophet, who arrived in Creek country in October 1811. Tecumseh's plan was to create a great confederation by banding together the tribes of the Old Northwest, the South, and the eastern Mississippi Valley. This union would be for the protection of the Indian and the recovery of his lands and to encourage the redmen to reject white civilization.[18]

During 1811 Tecumseh traveled through much of the territory of the southern Indians, but he met his only real success among the Creeks and Seminoles. It might well be supposed that the Creeks and Seminoles were willing to accept the emissaries from the North because they had experienced more immediate grievances than had the other Indians. Along with 24 warriors, Tecumseh and the Prophet arrived at Tookaubatchee in time for the annual Creek council, which was also attended by Hawkins and his advisers.[19] These government representatives did not take Tecumseh seriously. They believed the visitors were from the group of Shawnees who had lived among the Creeks about twenty years before. Their talks seemed absurd to the white men, and Hawkins was advised to take no notice of them.[20]

The Shawnee warrior delivered his dramatic hour-long speech to the 5,000 assembled Creeks after Hawkins and his men had left the meeting.[21]* His voice rang out in defiance against the white man. He told the gathering that he had come from the great lakes of the North and had passed through the settlements of the whites "like the wind at night. No war-whoop was sounded, no track was made, no fire was kindled," but, he said, "there is blood on our war clubs."

Great resentment was proclaimed against the race that had made women of their warriors and harlots of their women: "They have seized our country, and our fathers in their graves reproach us as slaves and cowards." He appealed to their pride by telling them that the Muscogees were once a mighty people:

> The pale faces trembled at your war-whoop, and the maidens of my tribe, on the distant lakes, sung the prowess of your warriors, and sighed for their embraces. And when our young men set out on the war-path the Shawnee sachems bade them "be brave like the Muscogees!" But now your blood has become white; your tomahawks have no edge; your bows and arrows were buried with your fathers. You sleep while the pale face ploughs over their tombs, and fertilizes his fields with their sacred ashes.

Tecumseh rose to great heights of oratory, according to reports of his speech, in his effort to stir the redmen to action:

> Oh, Muscogees! Brethren of my mother! Brush from your eyelids the sleep of slavery, and strike for vengeance and your country! The red men have fallen as the leaves now fall. I hear their voices in those aged pines. Their tears drop from the weeping skies. Their bones bleach on the hills of Georgia. Will no son of those brave men strike the pale face and quiet these complaining ghosts? Let the white race perish! They seize your land; they corrupt your women; they trample on the bones of your dead! Back whence they came, upon a trail of blood, they must be driven! Back—aye, back into the great water whose accursed waves brought them to our shores! Burn their dwellings—destroy their stock—slay their wives and children, that

*Although there is no exact copy of Tecumseh's speech, Historian J. F. H. Claiborne produced the text given here by reconstructing the talk from eyewitness accounts. The Indians of the Creek Nation were descendants of the Natchez-Muscogee, and they were often spoken of as Muscogees or Miskogees.

> the very breed may perish. War now! War always! War on the living! War on the dead! Dig their very corpses from their graves. The redman's land must give no shelter to a white man's bones!

The Shawnee warrior promised that arms would be sent from across the sea. In the North they would be received at Detroit and in the South at Pensacola. He told the Creeks that he would leave his prophets with them to stand by their sides and "catch the bullets of their enemies."

Tecumseh's last appeal was an attempt to arouse the Indians' fear of the supernatural. Before he had left Canada, the British informed him that, according to reports, a comet would soon appear in the sky, and he made good use of this information. It had also been noted that all during 1811 earthquakes had recurred throughout the southeastern part of the United States, and his predictions were not without substantiation. He told the assembled Creeks that the Great Spirit had spoken in the ear of his brother, the Prophet: "When the white men approach your towns the earth shall open and swallow them up. Soon shall you see my arm of fire stretched athwart the sky. You will know that I am on the war-path. I will stamp my foot and the very earth shall shake."[22]

The speech apparently had great effect on the Creeks. Big Warrior, one of the Creek leaders, and a number of the older chiefs, though temporarily swayed by Tecumseh, had seen the power of the United States, and probably out of fear rather than love they soon withdrew their support.[23] But the Shawnee warrior found his true mark among the younger Indians and among the older groups who resented the encroachment of the white man's culture. They were joined by members of rival factions of the Creek government. Tecumseh's prophecy that he would stamp his foot and the whole earth would shake won many more of the superstitious Indians when, a few weeks after his departure, an earthquake severely damaged the town of Tookaubatchee.[24] The appearance of the comet, which he had predicted would be his "arm of fire stretched athwart the sky" beckoning them to the war path, added still more to his prestige.[25]

In the past, efforts to bring about joint uprisings by allied Indians had sometimes failed because of poor timing. One tribe would go to war, and then weeks or months later another would attack. Thus the white armies were able to put down the revolt piecemeal. Tecumseh solved this dilemma by distributing among his followers small bundles of sticks painted red. When his friends saw his sign, presumably the comet, they were to throw away a stick. They were then to throw away another every morning until the sticks were gone, at which time they were to attack. In this way

Tecumseh's uprising was to be coordinated so that all Indians would attack at once. The use of these sticks and red war clubs by the hostile faction of the Creeks was the origin of the term "Red Sticks" by which they were called.[26]

As previously noted, Tecumseh and his followers had been traveling through the country of the southern tribes for many months before they arrived in the Creek country. The war dance and war songs of the Shawnees were being performed in many of the towns on the Tallapoosa River, even before he made his famous speech, indicating that he had already made some converts. There were also indications that some of the Indians in the Tallapoosa towns were hoarding supplies of lead and powder well before the council meeting, and that one of the largest supplies of powder belonged to Big Warrior, who at one time had seriously considered joining the war party.[27] Tecumseh's tactics persuaded a large number of Creeks to join his crusade. These people were so certain that he was endowed with supernatural power that they became complete fanatics. In addition to inciting the Indians, he and his party trained a number of Creeks as prophets and also persuaded a party of Creeks to return to Canada with them, where they were given presents by the British.[28]

If he had been left to his own devices, Tecumseh would probably have provoked a war with the United States in 1811. The British, who later allied themselves with the Indians, did not encourage war at this time, and their efforts to prevent it were partially successful. Tecumseh continued to recruit tribes to his cause but avoided making an immediate attack.[29]

The Creek Nation during this period was in a state of confusion and near civil war. Tecumseh's followers soon caused trouble among both whites and Indians. The more immediate problem came from the prophets who remained in the nation. Those who had been trained by Tecumseh, and presumably endowed with some of his power, set about persuading the people to accept their leadership and to follow the Prophet. Persons who were not willing to support the war party were often murdered in their sleep by what seemed to be supernatural means. Others, including many who were disposed to peace, were tied to trees and burned alive. It was said that this purging was done for the common good, but certain hostile leaders gained much from these executions by eliminating rivals.

The leading prophet was Josiah Francis, a half-breed whose tricks convinced many that he possessed great supernatural powers. He devoted much of his time to communing with the river gods and sometimes spent days in the stream, apparently under water.[30] He must have accomplished his river act by swimming under water to a hidden spot where he would surface and hide in the woods. Several days later he would emerge from the river, greatly impressing the other Indians.

Many of the prophets appear to have believed in their own power and in the reality of their cause. In their dances, they often went into convulsions. Samuel Manac, a half-breed Creek who witnessed the war dance as performed by High Head Jim, an important prophet, described it, "He shook hands with me and immediately began to tremble and jerk in every part of his frame, and the very calves of his legs would be convulsed and he would get entirely out of breath with agitation."[31] From such a description one might suspect that the Red Sticks were using some sort of drugs, but there is no mention of anything like this in the records.

With this kind of excitement, trouble could not be long in coming. On March 26, 1812, a party of whites was crossing Catoma Creek, when it was attacked by several Indians. During this assault an Indian chief named Mamoth killed Thomas Meredith.[32]

Hawkins took quick action on the Meredith murder and promptly called the Creek Council. Mamoth was an old and respected chief, but under prodding from Hawkins the council agreed to act. Within a short time five Indians who had taken part in the murder were executed.[33] Unfortunately, punishing Meredith's murderers did not end the incident, and a short time later a white man named William Lott was killed only a few miles from his own home. Lott was considered to be a friend of the Creeks, and his murder was without provocation. The Indians apparently agreed that Lott was not their enemy because, as in Meredith's case, they wasted little time in catching and executing the men who had killed him.[34]

Hostility inside the limits of the Creek Nation was not the only difficulty. In the spring of 1812 the party of Indians led by Little Warrior, leader of the Creek war faction, returned from Canada. While on their way, Little Warrior and his band received erroneous information that hostilities had already started. Having been stirred to a fever pitch by Tecumseh and possibly by the British while in the North, this group began to engage in serious atrocities, even before they reached Creek territory. Their first attack on the whites occurred when they reached the mouth of the Duck River in Tennessee. It was at this place that the blood lust overcame them, and they attacked a small settlement. The Creeks killed a man, a woman, and five children. In addition they took as prisoner Mrs. Martha Crawley, whom they carried south into Creek country. Mrs. Crawley was held captive for several weeks, but she finally escaped into the woods. After wandering for a number of days, she was rescued by a white trader. In compliance with the demands of Hawkins, the Creeks sent a party of warriors to punish the hostiles. The murderers, including their leader, Little Warrior, were found within a few days and put to death.[35]

Another such incident was the attack by a mixed party of Creeks and northern Indians in February 1813 on a group of whites at the mouth of the Ohio River. This action, which included murdering seven families, was accompanied by extreme brutality, doubtless aimed at terrorizing the white population. In one case, a woman was cut open and her unborn child taken out and stuck upon a stake for all who passed to see. This act had the desired effect—panic on the frontier.[36]

By the spring of 1813 Creek depredations were numerous, and the pressure for counteraction had become almost overpowering. Although Hawkins demanded satisfaction from the Indians, he hesitated to call for any outside help. He believed that the sending of troops into the Creek Nation would certainly lead to a demand by the United States for the cession of more Indian land. He felt that a war could be averted at this time; but if the demand for a land cession was added to the existing unrest, a major Indian conflict would be unavoidable. He advised that the safest course of action would be to use the Indians as long as possible to enforce peace in their own nation, and then to call troops only as a last resort.[37] If the situation deteriorated to the point where troops had to be sent into the nation, he wanted them to be a force of United States regulars, under his orders.[38]

In spite of the fact that some of his critics were extremely angry with him for his refusal to move sooner, Hawkins acted in good faith in trying to avert war. He was guilty of underestimating the strength of the war party, but he had been concerned about the likelihood of an Indian uprising ever since the visit of Tecumseh. He was also apprehensive about the incursions of the Spanish and British agents who he believed had been active among the Creeks.[39] Another of his concerns was the possibility of hostilities with the Seminoles, who were already fighting the whites in East Florida.[40]

Hawkins believed that too much active white intervention in the conflict would drive the friendly Indians into the ranks of the war party.[41] A great deal of the information he received played down the hostile faction because the Indians most influenced by Tecumseh were the Upper Creeks, who were farthest removed from Hawkins' agency. The Lower Creeks, who were closer to him, seemed to be loyal in the early part of the war.[42] Until late June 1813 Hawkins believed the Indians would put down their own troublesome elements.[43]

Hawkins' apparent unwillingness to take any kind of action led to severe criticism by a large number of Georgians. Both the *Augusta Chronicle* and the *Republican and Savannah Evening Ledger* questioned the agent's ability and even his loyalty.[44]

The state of affairs among the Indians had gradually worsened. In the beginning Tecumseh had influenced only a relatively small part of the Creek Nation. But the domination of the war party gradually increased until the spring of 1813, when large parts of the nation seem to have been willing to take the warpath. The execution of Little Warrior brought the war party into the open, and very soon this group began a large-scale campaign of murdering the chiefs and warriors who had tried to keep the peace.[45] The climax of this campaign of murder was an attempt to kill Captain Isaacs, an influential Indian who had gone to Canada with Tecumseh but had decided to remain friendly to the whites.[46]

This action was almost immediately followed by a hostile attack on Tookaubatchee, which was placed under siege. Big Warrior, one of the main leaders of the friendly Creeks, held the fortified part of the town, but he was in serious need of weapons. He called upon the whites to furnish him with troops and guns. The siege of Tookaubatchee made it apparent that war could not be averted, and Hawkins at last asked for troops.[47] The hostile Indians, also aware that war was imminent, began a major campaign to collect arms. They sent delegations to Pensacola and other places for this purpose. Feelings on both sides were aroused to fever heat, and the war quickly became a reality.[48]

2

The Role of Britain and Spain in the War in the South

THE AGITATION of the southern Indians by Tecumseh has received considerable attention in histories of the Creek War, but the role of the so-called British and Spanish agents has scarcely been noted. British merchants continued to trade with the southern Indians long after 1783, and various freebooters and filibusterers, such as William Augustus Bowles, considered taking Florida from the Spanish. This was to be done by creating an Indian state, which would presumably be loyal to the British. The battle for control of the Indians was an old one, reflected in the long-standing interest of the British in the Creeks and Seminoles and their accelerated activities among these tribes as the War of 1812 approached.[1]

Although American observers considered the influence of Tecumseh the most important factor in Creek hostility, they were not unaware of the work of the agents of both England and Spain. They believed that the British government itself was actively engaged in promoting an Indian War, and they regarded the Gulf Coast as extremely vulnerable to attack. Pensacola was undoubtedly the best potential base for British aid to the Indians, though there were other likely places. The area was almost inaccessible from the land but could be approached with relative ease from the sea.[2] Most Americans assumed that it would be nearly impossible to repel a British attack on the Gulf Coast. Before the War of 1812 there were rumors that the British had actually landed black troops at Pensacola and at other points on the gulf and that they planned to incite a slave uprising. The rumors existed long before there was any action by the British, and the stories became more and more numerous after the war began.[3]

The Americans believed that the British were furnishing aid to the Indians even before the war started. In support of this charge the southern

Indians had requested arms and aid from the British in Nassau as early as 1811, but they had been refused and advised to remain at peace. This belief of the Americans may have been based on the knowledge that certain Indians frequently visited Nassau.[4] It was fairly common for British warships to come into Pensacola and Mobile, and it was not unusual for dissatisfied Indians to visit with the officers of these ships.[5]

The visit of Lieutenant James Stirling of H.M.S. *Brazen* to Pensacola and Mobile during September 1812 was the cause of further rumors of Indian aid and the possibility of joint Spanish-British actions against the Americans. Stirling reported the vulnerability of the Gulf Coast to naval-supported action. He also suggested that one way to oppose the Americans "would be to engage the Indians of the Creek Nation in the contest," and this he was certain might easily be done: "They still have the highest attachment to the English, and the greatest hatred to the American name. . . ."[6]

According to Reginald Horsman, the British in Canada had organized Indian resistance to American frontier expansion.[7] However, English dealings with the southern Indians had been somewhat neglected since the loss of British Florida, though communication and trade with them still existed from the Bahamas. British leaders understood the strategic value of the Gulf Coast; and if there had been any questions about it, they were well answered by Lieutenant Stirling's report and by communications from their colonial governors, merchants, and naval officers. They expected to be able to use the area for supply bases with which to support the Indians in the event of war with the United States.

Tecumseh and his prophets told the Creeks that weapons and supplies could be obtained at Pensacola, St. Marks, and other Florida ports. It was believed by the British and Americans that the Spaniards would cooperate in this venture and that the latter were already using their agents to incite Creek hostilities.[8]

Most of the so-called British agents were merchants and lesser governmental authorities, acting without orders. The largest portion of the British traders operated around Apalachicola* with their main bases at Nassau, although a few came from Jamaica.[9] Because of the trade, the British had more direct influence among the Lower Creeks and Seminoles than they did with the Upper Creeks, who were located farther inland.

*There was no town of Apalachicola at this time, but the area around the mouth of the Apalachicola River is frequently called Apalachicola in contemporary records. Since this is the location of the present-day town of that name, the area is frequently referred to as Apalachicola in this book.

Alexander Durant was still another type of unofficial British agent. He was a mixed-blood Indian countryman. Persons spoken of as Indian countrymen were whites and mixed bloods who lived among the Indians as traders and interpreters. Durant, a nephew of Alexander McGillivray, dwelled among the Creeks and made his living by trading. In late 1812 he bought a schooner of his own and became one of the main communication links between the Indians and the British at Nassau. He was not officially encouraged to stir up hostilities, although he probably talked to British officials on one or more of his trips. In any case, once war commenced, Durant, along with Thomas and William Perryman, became spokesmen for the war faction of the Lower Creeks and Seminoles.[10] When belligerency seemed imminent, these men promptly looked for British aid.[11]

Much of the British trade with the Indians was illegal, according to the Spanish, and they wished to stop it or to regulate it. Some idea of the size of the trade can be had from the fact that the Spaniards constructed a fort at San Marcos de Apalachee near Apalachicola in order to "cut communications between the Creeks and the Bahama Islands." The fort was weak and largely ineffective, but such an installation would never have been built if commerce had not been extensive.[12]

The Spanish officials were from the outset more involved with the Indians than were the British. In order to understand Spain's position on the Gulf Coast, it is necessary first to realize that the Spanish holdings in Florida were not Spain's most valuable possessions but were in fact small military outposts that had been established as a defense for the holdings in Cuba and Central America. These buffers had first been erected against the British North American incursions and later were used as a bulwark against the United States. When the Spanish homeland was overrun by Napoleon, there was little military force left for defense of such a distant post as Pensacola. This problem was further complicated by revolt and unrest in the more important parts of Spain's possessions in America. Obviously, any system of priority in Spain's defense arrangement would of necessity leave the holdings in Florida near the bottom in importance.

Spanish policy in Florida for many years had been to prevent the United States from planting strong settlements in the Mississippi Valley and in the area that is now Alabama and Mississippi. This strategy was enforced in the period before 1795 in three ways. First, the rivers were kept restricted or closed so that the settlers would be unable to market their crops. Second, attempts were made to undermine the position of the United States in the West and perhaps to detach the western states and join them to Spain. Spanish officials spent considerable amounts of time and money to win over or to buy the loyalty of some of the leading citizens of the West and for a time even encouraged westerners to settle on Spanish lands and to take Spanish citizenship. Third, the Spanish defense stressed the maintenance of alliances with the southern Indians; and, after it became necessary to open the western rivers to navigation, the friendship of the Indians became even more valuable.[13]

The Spanish policy with regard to the Indians was to keep them strong enough to defend themselves but not so powerful as to risk an attack on the Americans. Spain rightly assumed that this balance was necessary; if the Indians were hostile to the United States, there would be a major war and the Indians would be destroyed. Spain wished to keep the Indians as a force in being, to be used only in the event that the United States planned direct action against Florida.[14]

By 1812 the war in Europe and the revolts in South America had caused the Spanish position on the Gulf Coast to deteriorate to a point of total weakness. American filibusterers and adventurers of all nationalities were engaged in full-scale military campaigns in Texas and in East Florida. In the latter place the Americans in the Patriots' War had taken Amelia Island and were in 1812 actually laying siege to St. Augustine, where they were supported by some forces of the regular army and navy and several units of Georgia and Tennessee militia.[15]

In addition to these activities, the United States had already "illegally" (so the Spanish claimed) purchased Louisiana from France and on February 24, 1804, passed the Mobile Act, claiming that Mobile belonged to the United States as part of the acquisition. No direct action was taken to seize Mobile at that time, and although Spain protested bitterly, the only real result of the act was to create a Mobile customs district with headquarters at St. Stephens. In 1810 American filibusterers seized Baton Rouge and tried to capture Mobile.[16]

As a part of this continuous gnawing process, the United States Congress on April 14, 1812, had again claimed Mobile as a part of the Louisiana Purchase and had incorporated the town and surrounding land as far as the Perdido River into the Mississippi Territory. This claim was presented without Spanish consent and led to an extremely unusual and dangerous situation. The governor of the Mississippi Territory appointed American officials for the Mobile district and quickly organized the area as American territory. Meanwhile, a Spanish garrison of 130 men continued to occupy Fort Charlotte in the town of Mobile. Their troops were not strong enough to drive the Americans out or to enforce Spanish law, but the Americans for a full year made no effort to expel the Spaniards.[17]

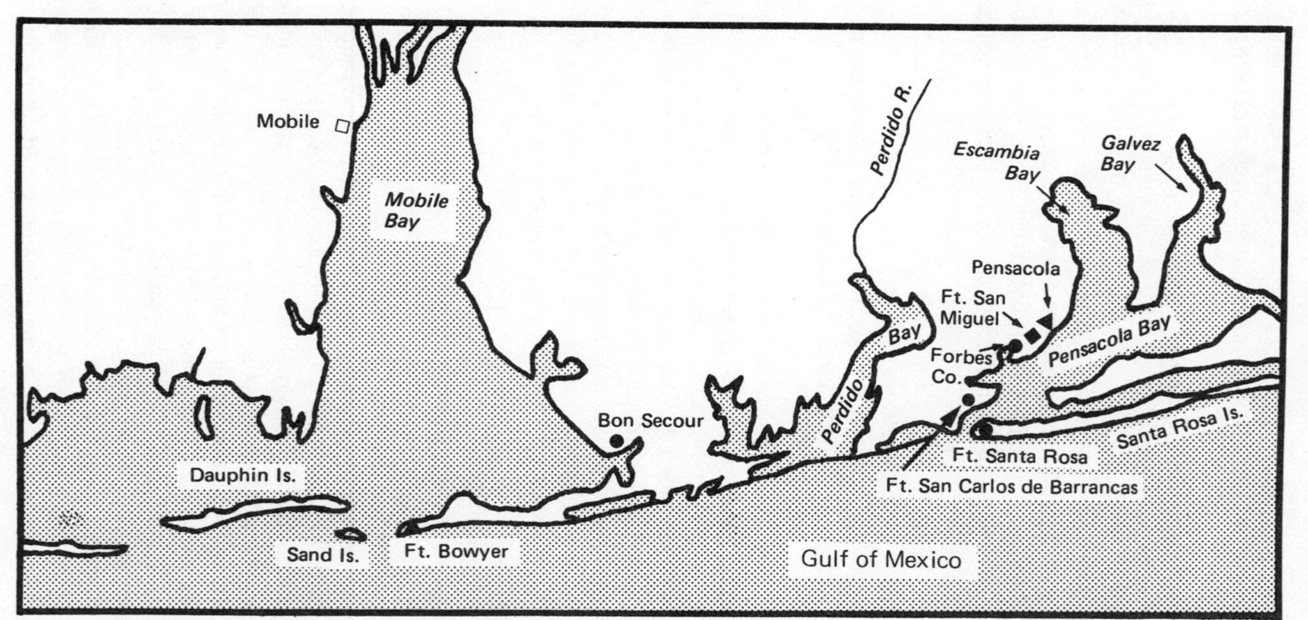

Pensacola-Mobile area, 1813–1815

During this period of joint occupation, the Spaniards were in no position to take any offensive action; and since the American troops were not ordered to move, a kind of uneasy truce existed between the two factions.[18] After nearly a full year of delay, Secretary of War Armstrong in February 1813 ordered General James Wilkinson to occupy Fort Charlotte and dispossess the Spanish garrison.[19] The orders to take full possession of Mobile were apparently a compromise, since Wilkinson, along with nearly all of the remaining American officials in the Gulf Coast area, wanted to take both Mobile and Pensacola. The Washington government was unwilling to go further at this time and directed Wilkinson to take only Mobile and the Mobile district as far as the Perdido River.[20]

The capture of Fort Charlotte took place without bloodshed. On April 11, 1813, Wilkinson arrived in Mobile Bay with 800 men and 5 gunboats, cutting off any sea communication between Pensacola and Mobile. Another 400 men marched from Fort Stoddert to a position across the Tensaw River from the Spanish installation, thus making impossible any relief from Pensacola. Having isolated the Spanish garrison, Wilkinson on April 12 demanded the surrender of the fort.[21] Spanish Commander Cayetano Pérez was nearly out of supplies and surrendered the fort on April 13. Wilkinson allowed the garrison to evacuate to Pensacola, carrying their own weapons and personal belongings. They were not permitted to remove the cannon or any of the munitions from the fort.[22]

This seizure was perhaps the most flagrant attack on the Spanish territory up to that time. At least in the past, annexation of Spanish territory had usually been cloaked with the character of unofficial filibusters. This action was taken by regular United States forces acting with authority from Washington. In addition it was widely believed that the United States planned to occupy all of West Florida soon, by force if necessary.

The communications among the various Spanish commanders at the time of the seizure of Mobile indicated a high degree of frustration and anger. Cayetano Pérez was made a scapegoat. He had absolutely no chance of defending his post, and no doubt most of his superiors knew this.

Luis de Onís, the unrecognized Spanish minister to Washington, believed that Spain's only hope of holding Florida was through diplomacy instead of military force. Following this idea, Onís objected to any efforts to defend Florida, either by Spanish action or by alliances with the Indians, or even with British military help. His attitude is demonstrated by his protest concerning the capture of Mobile, a very mild document considering the nature of the offense against Spain.[23]

There were only two choices open to the Spanish if they wished to have any chance whatsoever of keeping Florida. One method would follow the Onís idea of depending on diplomacy to hold, or at least to restore, Florida. The other method would require military defense.

Juan Ruiz Apodaca, the captain general of Cuba, whose province included East and West Florida, was convinced that the Americans planned to attack Pensacola shortly. While under no illusion that the Floridas could be defended with the forces available, he wished his commanders to make a good showing for themselves.[24] Obviously hesitant and dubious of the results, Ruiz Apodaca decided to follow the policy of defending Florida with military force. The Spanish lack of all necessities was demonstrated in the report of a council of war on December 18, 1813. The officers of the Pensacola garrison reported that their men had been fifty-six months without pay, were at the time on half-rations, and were short of every form of clothing and military supplies.[25]

Immediately after the fall of Mobile, Ruiz Apodaca attempted to improve the military situation by dispatching Lieutenant Colonel José de Soto and his Cuban regiment, composed largely of Havana Negro militia, as a reinforcement to Pensacola. The captain general realized that de Soto's troops were only a minor addition to the military strength of West Florida.[26] He thought the main defense of the area would be conducted by the English and Indians, but both of these groups offered serious barriers against Spanish cooperation. He and almost every other Spanish official were suspicious of the British and did not want the responsibility of calling the British lion to the aid of the Spanish lamb, Florida. They would summon them to help only as a last resort. On the other hand, if the British landed in Florida anywhere except in the Spanish towns, Ruiz Apodaca had no plans to interfere.[27]

An alliance with the Indians, therefore, was the only possibility left to the Spanish for the defense of Florida. Mauricio Zuñiga, the governor of West Florida, was apprehensive of an immediate American attack, and this fear was responsible for his decision to provide as much support as he could for the Indians and to encourage their hostility to the United States. It was too late to save Mobile. The governor knew that an attack by the Indians on that city would lead to the loss of many Spanish subjects. On the other hand, a general Indian uprising in the Mississippi Territory might cause the Americans to evacuate the city. The worst problem faced by the Spaniards in their efforts to gain real support from the Indians in 1813 was the lack of supplies with which to arm them.[28]

It was believed that the British and Spanish were both in favor of an attack by the Indians on the United States and that both countries (so the Indians thought) had promised to supply them with arms at Pensacola. Several things had helped to confirm this belief of the Indians. Little Warrior, the Creek chief who had gone to Canada with Tecumseh, had been given a letter to the Spanish commander at Pensacola by the British officer who had entertained him. It was mistakenly assumed by the Indians that the letter was a request for the Spaniards to furnish the Indians with arms and ammunition.[29]

The second event which caused the Indians to believe that they would be given immediate support for their war with the United States was Governor Zuñiga's request that they come to Pensacola.[30] The governor denied, or never admitted, making this invitation, even to his own superiors, but there were too many statements to the contrary. Several Spanish letters admitting such a proposal by the governor were captured among the various groups of Indians.[31] In addition to these reasons, the Indians had Tecumseh's word that arms and other war supplies could be had at Pensacola.

These expectations of the Indians were premature and resulted from a very confused set of circumstances. While it is apparent from the correspondence of the Spaniards that they had decided to support an Indian attack on the United States, they obviously were in no position to provide immediate aid for such hostility. Certainly, the Spaniards would not have aroused the Indians to war with the United States and promised them arms at Pensacola, only to turn them away empty handed and angry. Since this was essentially what happened, it is clear that there was much confusion within the Spanish command. Governor Zuñiga had probably invited the Creek chiefs to meet with him at Pensacola in order to make plans for future action against the United States. Unfortunately for the Indians, they interpreted the Spanish invitation as a call for immediate hostilities.[32]

A short time after the invitation was issued, Zuñiga was replaced by Don Mateo González Manrique.[33] The new governor decided at first not to continue the policy of encouraging Indian hostility. When in May the first group of about 60 Indians came to Pensacola seeking aid, he sent them away without giving them arms.[34] After due consideration, however, González Manrique reached the same conclusion as Zuñiga, that the Americans were planning to attack Pensacola in the very near future and that Indian support represented the only possible Spanish defense. He reported this conclusion to Ruiz Apodaca and asked for his approval. In addition the governor made urgent requests for supplies from Cuba, for his own men as well as for the Indians. Unfortunately for him, the second and larger group of Creeks arrived, demanding arms, before he had received any new supplies or any approval of his plans.[35]

The first reaction of the hostile elements of the Creek Nation after receiving the Spanish invitation was to lay siege to Big Warrior's fortified encampment in the early summer of 1813. At this time the Red Sticks were nearly without arms, lead, or powder. Since these items were essential to the war, a group of between 280 and 300 hostiles set off for Pensacola, bringing with them packhorses for transporting these necessary munitions. This party was led by Peter McQueen, Josiah Francis, and the prophet, High Head Jim, all of whom were major leaders of the Upper Creeks.[36]

The reception given to the McQueen party was considerably more friendly than that accorded the earlier group. There is no question that the size of this second delegation of Indians, together with the great likelihood that more were close by or would soon join them, caused González Manrique considerable anxiety lest the Indians become enraged and decide to attack Pensacola. The Spanish garrison was strong enough to deal with the 300 or so Indians, but a fight would have been extremely costly. All reports of his meeting with the Indian chiefs indicate that González Manrique was of divided mind and showed some reluctance in his dealings with them. After some hesitation, however, he furnished the Indians with about 1,000 pounds of gunpowder, a quantity of lead, and a quantity of food and blankets, but no guns and no repairs for those they brought with them.[37]

This refusal to supply guns enraged the Indians, as González Manrique had feared, and they threatened to destroy the town. These threats induced the governor to call out the entire garrison and militia. With this show of force, the Indians became considerably more peaceable and accepted the gifts that had been offered them. In addition to the supplies they obtained from the Spanish, the Indians, who had brought with them all their goods and captured booty, bought or were given war supplies by some of the Pensacola merchants. They probably obtained a few stands of arms in this manner.

Of the merchants operating in this area, the John Forbes Company was by far the largest and the most influential. This English trading firm was very much opposed to an Indian war and, because of this opposition, had been called traitor by some British leaders.[38] John Innerarity, a British citizen who was manager of the firm's Pensacola store and an old Creek trader, was strongly opposed to an Indian war. He refused to provide supplies for the Indians, and he also tried to persuade González Manrique to turn them away. Innerarity convinced the Indians that the store had no arms or powder to give or sell by showing them the empty powder barrels.[39] The Indians were unaware of police regulations in Pensacola which did not allow large quantities of powder to be stored in the city, and they did not know that the Forbes Company at that time had a large quantity of powder stored at Fort Barrancas, only a few miles away.[40] The company had far more war matériel than did the Spanish government, and by failing to gain the company's support the Indians lost their best source of supply.

Upon the departure of the Indians, González Manrique immediately reported his actions to Captain General Ruiz Apodaca and requested approval of a policy for arming the Indians. Ruiz Apodaca's reaction was considerably stronger than González Manrique's. The captain general not only approved arming the Indians; he ordered the governor to give them all the arms and supplies he could spare in the future. He did not, however, encourage González Manrique to use Spanish troops, except in actual defense of the city.[41] Ruiz Apodaca's decision to arm the Indians and to make a strong stand against the expected American advance was supported by the Spanish government, and his plan was approved by royal order of the Regency on December 9, 1813. It is clear that whatever the orders, the Spaniards were unable to furnish the Indians with any sizable amounts of supplies.[42]

This was the situation when the third delegation of Indians, composed of Seminoles and Lower Creeks, descended upon the Spanish town. They arrived in September after the McQueen party of Upper Creeks had gone. They were led by Thomas Perryman and Alexander Durant, and they too had received the Spanish governor's invitation to come to Pensacola, presumably to receive arms.[43]

This group of Lower Creeks not only met with the Spanish authorities but also communicated with the British officer Lieutenant Edward Handfield of H.M.S. *Herald*, a warship which happened to be in the harbor.[44] Handfield landed at Pensacola around September 18, conducted extensive talks with the Indians, and probably supplied them with some arms. He had been dispatched, on the authority of Governor Charles Cameron of Nassau, with orders to determine the condition and attitude of the southern Indians. In his report, Handfield stated that he had missed by several weeks the visit of Peter McQueen and his group of Indians but that there were many Creeks in Pensacola at the time of his arrival. This latter group, led by William and Thomas Perryman, claimed that because they were at war with the United States they were in dire need of British aid.[45] In support of their request for aid, Handfield carried several of their letters to Governor Cameron at Nassau.[46]

The Indians sent Henry Durgen, one of their interpreters, to Nassau aboard the *Herald* to discuss their needs with Cameron. These Lower Creeks were not under the influence of the prophets, but they believed that without British assistance the Americans would soon destroy them. In a letter written by Alexander Durant and signed by William Perryman, head of the Creek Nation, his brother Thomas Perryman, and several other prominent Creeks, their reasons for fighting the Americans were given: "We hope you will eade and asist us as your alis and friends Sir you know that our four fathers owned the Lan Wher we now live But and Ever since our father the King of Grate Briton Left us the Americans had Bin Robing us of our Rights and now the americans has maid war against our nations and we aply for armes and amenisun to defend our silves from so Greid a Enemy and as you Know that this nations all ways was frinds to the English we hope you will send us Seplys By Henry Durgen as soon as possible and we hope that you will send sum of our old frind the British troops to eade and asist us a ganst our Enemeys."[47]

A second letter written by Durant was directed to the governor of New Providence. Durant professed loyalty to the British crown and asked for a commission in the British service.[48] Governor Cameron forwarded these letters to Earl Bathurst, British secretary of state for war and colonies.[49]

As a direct result of the Durant, Perryman, and Cameron letters, Bathurst sent orders to the British naval forces to aid the Indians. The communication with the British started the long sequence of events that led to the establishment of a British base for the Indians at Apalachicola and greatly affected British plans on the southern coast. It appears that until early in 1814 no high-ranking British official had been engaged in aiding the Creek Indians, and that all supplies they had received had come from junior officials acting on their own, from private individuals, or from the Spaniards.[50]

According to all available evidence, it is safe to conclude that the American suspicions were wrong and that the British government was not officially involved in any massive efforts to incite the Creeks before 1814. It is clear from the fact that it took the British eight months to respond to the Creek request for aid that the London government had had no advance plans to encourage an Indian war in the South. The Indians were sorely lacking in arms and other war supplies. Probably not more than one Indian in three had any firearm during the Creek War. Neither the Spanish nor the British had been able or willing to supply them. It was not until after Andrew Jackson had dealt the Creeks a major defeat at Horseshoe Bend that the British moved with their full force to reorganize, resupply, and regroup the Indians who had survived the Creek War.

3

Burnt Corn and Fort Mims

THE DELEGATION led by Peter McQueen received some powder and shot from the Spanish. These supplies were loaded on packhorses, and the party set out for the villages of the Upper Creeks. It is not clear whether McQueen intended to store the supplies and wait for further aid or to attack the whites immediately. In any case, the action of the Americans forced him to make a decision.

McQueen's expedition had been promptly reported to the Americans. The Spanish town of Pensacola contained many inhabitants who took the side of the United States, and these men constantly supplied intelligence of Indian activities. So effective was the American intelligence network in Pensacola that it is likely United States officials knew of McQueen's visit before the Creeks left town.[1]

The wisest course for the Americans, in order to prevent a major Indian war, was to capture the munitions before they could be distributed, but it would be necessary to act immediately. When news of the Creek activities in Pensacola reached Colonel James Caller of Washington County, Mississippi Territory, the senior officer on that frontier, he called out the militia at once. He was able to muster a force of several small companies, about 180 men. His troops were mounted and armed better than most, but they lacked serious discipline. In this respect they were little better or worse than most militia of the time.

Caller's men were not the only group searching for McQueen's Indians, but it fell to their lot to find them. The morning of July 27, 1813, around eleven o'clock, scouts from Caller's force reported seeing members of McQueen's party encamped on a low pine-barren peninsula formed by a bend in Burnt Corn Creek. Divided into three sections, Caller's men took up a position on a slight rise overlooking the peninsula, and he ordered an immediate charge. Although taken by surprise, the Indians managed to establish a defense and were able to retreat across the creek. The Americans pursued them to the water's edge but made no effort to cross the stream.[2] This group of Indians numbered less than a dozen men, but they had most of the pack animals. The remainder of the Indian party was in the woods and swamp nearby, and probably more warriors were camped down the trail. As soon as the Creeks crossed Burnt Corn Creek, they took refuge in a swamp which had much tall grass and other growth. From this cover, they opened fire on the white men and were able to inflict some wounds. Many more Creeks who were nearby, hearing the noise of battle, quickly came to join the action. Within a short time there were between 60 and 100 Indians in the swamp, firing on the whites.

In the meantime, Caller's men, believing that they had won a nearly bloodless victory, began to take possession of the packhorses. In this way they captured a good part of the powder, lead, and provisions brought from Pensacola. Unfortunately, the white men, with the usual failings of undisciplined militia, became engrossed in dividing up the captured goods and neglected to keep up a fire on the swamp or to watch the Indians closely. This proved to be a serious error. Without warning, the enlarged force of Indians charged out of the swamp, screaming war whoops and doubtless causing the whites to exaggerate their numbers.[3] So surprised were the whites, who believed the battle over, that they fled in panic from the field, and the Indians pursued them for several miles. When Caller's men reached high ground, several officers attempted to rally the men and to make a stand. Less than half of them could be found. This small group of militia held off the main Indian forces for about two hours, enabling the Americans to retreat safely.[4]

The command was never reassembled; the men simply went home by the easiest route. Even Colonel Caller became lost in the woods and wandered several days before reaching home. With such confusion and disorder, an accurate count of the killed and wounded was impossible. Historian A. J. Pickett, who talked to a number of the participants, concluded that 2 Americans were killed and 15 wounded. He made no effort to determine the Indian losses. George Stiggins, a half-breed who knew a number of the Indians in the battle, claimed that 5 Americans were killed and 10 wounded, compared to 2 Indians killed and 5 wounded.[5]

The accounts differ as to Caller's conduct in battle. The Stiggins account and that of Joseph Carson, another militia officer who was nearby but did not actually participate in the battle, insisted that Caller did his best to rally his men and make a counterattack.[6] Most accounts suggest that Caller mismanaged the battle rather badly, and there were some who claimed that he acted cowardly. One description declared Caller to be so afraid that he remained safely out of range in the rear during the whole battle; when the Indians counterattacked, he was one of the first to run, leaving in such a state of fear that he became lost and wandered for a week in the woods.[7]

It is interesting to note that although a number of Indians were nearby they did not join the battle. The panic was caused by a force of only 60 to 100 Creeks, mostly armed with war clubs and bows and arrows. According to Stiggins, only about 13 of the Indians at Burnt Corn had any guns; the rest whooped and made whatever noise they could to add to the confusion.[8] Although the losses were small, this skirmish resulted in a significant victory for the Indians.

The military commanders and officials were most anxious to avoid blame for the battle, just as they would have been happy to take credit for it if Caller had won.[9] David Holmes, governor of the Mississippi Territory, insisted that Caller had acted without authority, but an examination of Caller's orders from Holmes showed that the colonel had been given a good deal of latitude. The governor stated that he had received information which caused him to think "that a considerable portion of the Creek Indians are disposed for war with the United States, and that they are using every effort in their power, to bring the nation generally into their views. Should this party ultimately prevail it is probable that the settlements between the Tombigbee and Alabama will be their first object of attack; in fact the whole of our eastern frontier will in some degree be opened to their aggression. You are therefore ordered to have your regiment in the best condition for actual service that the means within your power will permit." Holmes also ordered Caller to furnish detachments "to act as scouts . . . in aid of the regular forces stationed on the eastern frontier." He told Caller that as commanding officer his patriotism, courage, and vigilance would be required and assured him that he had the utmost confidence in him.[10]

The white forces at Burnt Corn had managed to capture some of the powder and lead which the Indians had brought from Pensacola. The loss may have weakened the Indian fighting power, but the confidence gained by the Red Sticks was worth far more than a little powder.[11] Burnt Corn was after all an unusual defeat. Heretofore, whenever the whites had a force which was approximately equal to the Indians, the whites had won. When the victorious Indians reached the hostile camps, they showed the scalps they had taken and claimed to have routed completely an enormous

American army. This victory, they maintained, proved that they had supernatural power and could not be defeated.

It was during this period that the Red Sticks recruited William Weatherford, perhaps their best leader. There are many reports concerning the manner in which Weatherford was induced to join the war party, and doubtless there will never be any certainty as to their accuracy. George Stiggins, who knew Weatherford, stated that he had not intended to join the hostiles, as indeed most of his family did not join them. Weatherford, who was more than half white and had lived the greater portion of his life as a white man, was forced to join the war party when his wife and family were taken as hostages by that faction. He tried several times unsuccessfully to escape with his family. After the Fort Mims massacre, it was impossible for him to change sides.[12] Pickett claimed that Weatherford was a leader of the hostiles from the beginning, but Thomas Woodward in his *Reminiscences* gives substantially the same account as Stiggins.[13] Whatever the reason, Weatherford was without doubt the Red Sticks' most intelligent leader, and he was apparently one of the few hostiles who placed little faith in magic.

The prophets, now in full control in many towns, ordered their people to kill all the white people and all Indians who refused to join them. The hostiles were also expected to rid themselves of everything that they had ever received from the white men.[14] In addition to destroying their "tainted" property, the Red Sticks abandoned some of their corn crops and killed and dried all of their cattle for use during the war. They considered farming a trick of the white man's civilization, and thought that they should live by hunting in true Indian style.[15] Some of the prophets became so enamored of their own power that they would have cast aside the white man's gun and fought the war with magic, war clubs, and bows and arrows. Fortunately for the hostiles, most of the Indians would not accept such reasoning.[16]

Caller's raid had one useful effect on the frontier. At last the white settlers realized that they were engaged in a real Indian war, and they began to take more serious measures for defense. Some of the militia in the Mississippi Territory had already been on notice for possible duty; but after Caller's defeat most of the troops were called into service, and the white frontiersmen and their families were advised to move into the forts.[17] In turn, the blockhouses and forts were garrisoned and strengthened by militia. Although everyone thought that there was danger from the Creeks, there was also concern regarding the sympathies of some of the other tribes. For example, it was believed that there was hostility among the Choctaws, and a few of them did indeed join the war party.[18]

Overwhelmed with a strong sense of success, the leaders of the Red Sticks decided that the time for action had arrived. Although they claimed that they wished to destroy the white man and his civilization completely, their plans never actually went beyond the annihilation of a few frontier forts. The first Creeks to turn to actual war against the white men were the Upper Creeks. These Indians lived on the Alabama River system in the western part of the nation. They had been most directly influenced by Tecumseh and were also among the first to learn of Caller's fiasco at Burnt Corn.

As one of their first acts against the white man, the Upper Creeks determined to attack and destroy Fort Mims and Fort Pierce in the Mississippi Territory. The prophets especially wanted to destroy Fort Mims, not only to avenge the attack at Burnt Corn but also because of their hatred for the large number of friendly Creeks and mixed bloods living at the fort. The Red Sticks chose Prophet Paddy Welsh as their leader for the attack on Mims, but the man who became the real leader and organized the assault was William Weatherford.[19]

After the Burnt Corn fight, the white settlers in the Mississippi Territory had tried to keep scouts in the field and to maintain intelligence concerning the Red Sticks. On August 23, 1813, only a few days before the fatal attack on Fort Mims, a Choctaw Indian reported that he had seen a large party of Red Sticks.[20]

The Indians moved into a position to attack Fort Mims, as the fort itself was being made ready to protect the settlers. The defense preparations progressed slowly and inefficiently for several reasons. The fort was one of the strongest and largest in the Tombigbee area, and no one seriously believed the Indians would attack such a strong position. All things considered, the Indians would never have met with success at Fort Mims if any real precautions had been taken for its protection or if the garrison had been properly led.

After the defeat at Burnt Corn when the Creek War showed signs of becoming a serious engagement, the entire Mississippi Territorial militia was called out to insure greater protection for the settlers.[21] Brigadier General Ferdinand L. Claiborne commanded the militia. His effort to protect the settlements was to divide his troops into detachments and send them to reinforce the various forts. As a result, Claiborne was left with no troops as a reserve for use in offensive action against the Indians. He requested General Thomas Flournoy, the regular army commander of the Seventh Military District, to reinforce him, but Flournoy had no men to spare.[22]

Claiborne sent Major Daniel Beasley with 170 men to guard the settlements on the Tensaw River. Beasley was a lawyer from Jefferson County, Mississippi Territory, apparently with little military experience. He had been appointed at the request of General Claiborne. Of the troops available to Beasley, only 120 of his command were stationed at Fort Mims; the remainder were assigned to several other posts, including 40 men at Pierce's Mill, about a mile away from Fort Mims.[23] In addition to the 120 militia, Fort Mims was reinforced by a group of settlers. In all, at the time of the attack on the fort there were between 275 and 300 whites, mixed bloods, and friendly Indians in Fort Mims, and probably a number of Negro slaves. Most of these people were able to offer some resistance.[24]

General Claiborne was severely criticized by many of the newspapers and public officials for not having had a stronger garrison at Fort Mims. Still, he had posted enough troops to defend the fort against all the power the Indians could muster, if Beasley had taken even rudimentary defensive precautions. In addition to dividing his troops, Beasley failed to keep adequate scouts and lookouts around the fort, and the few he did send out were poorly trained and careless. An example of the poor quality of his scouts came from the accounts of the hostile Indians themselves. The day before the assault on the fort, August 29, 1813, the whole band of hostiles, about 750 in number, camped about six miles away in a wooded area. They would have been hard to conceal if the scouts had been alert. While resting in the woods, the Indians observed two mounted scouts ride past them on the road. The scouts were engaged in conversation, and they passed the Indians twice without seeing them. The white men even reached a place where the Indians had recently forded a creek but saw nothing unusual.[25]

Beasley had reason to believe that his fort was strong enough to defend itself, even though there were numerous reports of large forces of Indians in the general area. Two days before the attack, General Claiborne reported that there were 1,200 Creek Indians in 3 groups planning to attack the Tombigbee settlements. With this many Red Sticks in the country, there was no excuse for laxness.[26]

Beasley did not believe there was any chance of an attack, and when his scouts failed to see the Indians he refused to consider seriously that there could be any danger to the fort. He reported to F. L. Claiborne on the day of the attack that there had been a false alarm at the fort on the previous day. "Two negro boys belonging to Mr. Randon were out some distance from the Fort minding some beef cattle and told that they saw a great number of Indians painted, running and hallooing on towards Messrs. Pierce's Mill. The conclusion was that they knew the mill fort to be more vulnerable than this and that they had determined to make their attack there first." Captain Hatton Middleton was dispatched with eight or ten mounted men "to reconnitre & ascertain the strength of the enemy, that if they were not too powerful," Beasley would "turn out the most of the men . . . and pursue on to Pierce's Mill; but the alarm has proved to be a false one. What gave some plausibility to the report of the negro boys at first was some of Mr. Randon's negroes who had been sent up to his plantation for corn and reported his plantation to be full of Indians committing every kind of Havoc; but I now doubt the truth of that report." The major commented that he was pleased at the appearance of the soldiers at the time of the alarm "when it was expected every moment that the Indians would appear in sight, the soldiers very generally appeared anxious to see them."[27] Four hours after the report was written, Beasley was dead.

The slaves were whipped for giving a false alarm when the scouts failed to see anything of a suspicious nature. In fact, according to Pickett, at the moment of the attack, one of the blacks was tied to a post to be whipped. General Woodward's account may have located the real trouble with Beasley's behavior. He stated that Jim Cornells rode to the fort on the morning of the attack and warned Beasley that he had seen Indians. According to Cornells, Beasley was drunk and insisted that Cornells had seen only cattle.[28]

The Red Sticks attacked at the noon hour when, with few exceptions, the settlers and the garrison were eating their lunch. The Indians had been hidden in a ravine about a hundred yards from the fort. They jumped from their hiding place and rushed through the open gate into the fort, taking everyone by surprise. The first few Indians were shot by the sentries, who recovered sufficiently to fire their weapons. This slight break in the fighting enabled Major Beasley, whose house was near the gate, to rush to the entrance and try to close it. Unfortunately, Beasley's lack of precautions plagued him again. A large amount of sand had washed against the gate, making it difficult to close. Before the major could close and secure the opening, a larger group of Indians rushed into the fort, killing Beasley.[29]

The Indians knew that the gate would be open, and probably knew that it was jammed with sand. It is even possible that they piled the sand against the gate themselves. The evening before the attack, Weatherford and several other Indians crawled to the walls of the fort and looked through the portholes. These were about four feet from the ground and four feet apart. From these positions, the group was able to scout the fort. The guards, busy playing cards, never saw the Indians, who apparently learned all they needed to know about the interior of the fort.

The prophet leader, Paddy Welsh, suggested that the best way to take the fort would be to surround it without warning. On signal, all of the Indians would charge up and take possession of the portholes. Through them the attacker could fire into the fort just as easily as the garrison could fire out. This part of Welsh's excellent plan was used with great success. It actually turned the walls of Fort Mims into a fort for the protection of the Indians. Welsh planned that four men would rush through the gate and divert the guards, while the remaining Indians seized the portholes. To protect his four, Welsh made them magically bulletproof against the guns of the Americans. These men ran through the gate and all but one were promptly shot down. The lone survivor had the presence of mind to run out of the fort and escape. Although the Red Sticks were not bulletproof, the diversion worked, and the Indians succeeded in capturing a large part of the portholes.[30]

Immediately following this initial attack, the Indians rushed into the fort in large numbers. The people inside now tried to organize a defense for themselves, but their commander was dead and the confusion in the camp was overwhelming. The militia officers gathered whatever men they could around them and prepared to make stands at various places in the fort. A picket wall enclosed the buildings around Mims' house, but most of the interior of the fort was an open area. The people inside took refuge in or behind the buildings, where the various officers made their defense. Captain William Jack defended the south wing, Lieutenant Peter Randon made a stand at the guardhouse, and Captain Dixon Bailey and his men were the only Americans to gain possession of some of the portholes, enabling them to make the best defense. Eventually Bailey came to lead the entire resistance.

If the settlers had been able to unify their forces and establish a defense line, they would in all likelihood have driven off the Indian attack. At 3:00 P.M. a good many of the Indians had become tired of the fighting and were ready to withdraw.[31] The main defense centered on an attempt to hold a partial wall inside the fort. This would have made a good defense line, except that the Indians held most of the portholes in the outer wall behind it and could fire into the unprotected rear of the defenders. The houses at first offered some cover, but the Indians set fire to most of them. Smoke, fire, and close quarters made the defense an extremely difficult task. Soon the fire had spread to all buildings except two, which alone did not give enough shelter to protect the settlers. However, they kept up such heavy fire from these positions that Weatherford and the other hostile leaders had to rally their men again and again to attack. The Indians suffered heavy casualties from these attacks, but it was becoming apparent that victory would be theirs.[32]

Many of the settlers, especially the women and children, were burned alive inside the buildings where they were trapped. The whites tried to concentrate in the shelter of the loom house and in the small area where there was no fire. Bailey mounted a strong defense here, but the area was too crowded and the settlers and soldiers too cramped to fire their weapons properly. The Indians could not miss, so it seemed. Pickett described the defenders at this point as being like "beeves in the slaughter-pen of the butcher."[33]

It now became evident to the defenders that they would be better off in the open, where they might have a chance of escaping to Fort Pierce or to some other place of refuge. To carry out this plan, several pickets in the exterior wall were cut away, and a number of men escaped. These men were too few to make a stand, and all who could ran into the swamp or woods and fled from the Indians. The number who thus survived the Fort Mims massacre has never been determined. Stiggins says that seven soldiers got through the pickets. These were not the only escapees. Some persons hid in the woods for weeks, and many went on to other forts. A few women and a large number of blacks were carried off by the Indians, but most of them were eventually freed.[34]

For those who did not escape, death was not easy. Many were burned in the buildings, but those taken alive in the area around the loom house died awful deaths. Pickett's graphic description was taken from eyewitness accounts and verified by the scouts who later buried the dead. It is an account of Indian warfare at its worst—the final murder at Fort Mims. Every house was in flames. The loom house "was broken down, the helpless inmates were butchered in the quickest manner, and blood and brains bespattered the whole earth. The children were seized by the legs, and killed by batting their heads against the stockading. The women were scalped, and those who were pregnant were opened, while they were alive, and the embryo infants let out of the womb." It was stated that Weatherford had "implored the warriors to spare the women and children, and reproached them for their barbarity; but his own life was threatened, for interposing, many clubs were raised over his head, and he was forced to retire."[35]

The losses suffered at Fort Mims were serious, and their effect was to create panic over much of the frontier. Of the 275 to 300 whites, friendly Indians, and mixed bloods who were in Fort Mims, between 20 and 40 escaped; around 250 to 275 were killed in the battle or carried off as prisoners. Captain Joseph P. Kennedy was sent to Fort Mims three weeks after the massacre to bury the dead. His men found and buried the bodies of 247 white men, women, and children.[36] General Claiborne explained that he could not bury the dead any sooner because he had so few men and he believed the Indians would attack again.

News of Fort Mims was published all over the United States before the official casualty statistics were available. This lack of information about the casualties caused much speculation, and some accounts claimed that as many as 400 to 600 persons had been killed.[37] This incorrect information created fear and consternation on the frontier.[38] A long-range effect has been the acceptance by many historians of these incorrect figures. To add to the confusion of numbers, there was no accurate count of the slaves in the fort. There may have been more than a hundred. The majority of them were carried off by the Indians and recaptured at the end of the war.

The Indians' losses were also very heavy. Captain Kennedy found the bodies of at least a hundred Red Sticks around the area of Fort Mims,[39] and a great many more died later from wounds inflicted during the battle. In fact, it was the heavy losses suffered during this battle that caused the Indians to leave without making any effort to take Fort Pierce or any of the other posts in the area. It is not likely that they would ever again have had the combination of luck that enabled them to capture Fort Mims, and it is probable that an attack on Fort Pierce would have failed. There is every reason to believe, however, that the Red Sticks would have tried more such attacks had they had enough ammunition and had they not been so badly hurt.

Many of the Indians were disillusioned with the prophets who had promised that they could not be killed. The heavy Indian losses in this battle went a long way toward convincing them that the war could not be won by witchcraft. The battle of Fort Mims probably exhausted the Indians' limited supply of powder and lead, and it is doubtful whether they could have sustained more action without a new supply. The hostiles in the western parts of the nation spent the next few weeks recovering from their wounds and enjoying their booty. Without any real plan of action or recognized leader, they attempted little action.[40]

The panic resulting from the capture of Fort Mims had far-reaching effects. No fort of this size and strength had ever been captured by the Indians. Many of the settlers must have believed after this that the Indians did have some magical power. Reports of future plans of attack were numerous. Louisiana Governor W. C. C. Claiborne believed that events at Fort Mims had been not only an Indian massacre but also the result of a slave uprising. This idea can be attributed to the fact that some of the blacks from Mims had joined the Indians, and there were recurring rumors of slave uprisings throughout the frontier area.[41] These rumors had been liberally enlarged by the imaginations of many frontiersmen. From opposite sides of the nation, the stories spread. Benjamin Hawkins reported from his agency in Georgia that Spanish and British influence was being used to agitate both the Indians and the blacks. On the other side of the Creek land, David Holmes, governor of the Mississippi Territory, reported exactly the same thing and added that the British were raising a large force of West Indian Negro troops to invade the country and support a slave insurrection.[42] Although Hawkins' and Holmes' information proved later to be correct, there is no evidence that any slave uprisings actually took place at this time.

The Indian success led some Americans to think that an intelligent Spanish or British officer must have led the attack. This was not the case.[43] At about the same time as the action at Fort Mims, the Red Sticks made a number of smaller attacks against forts and settlements and inflicted a few casualties on the whites. While these smaller attacks were repulsed, they did add considerably to the general state of alarm and increased the credibility of the rumors of widespread attack and destruction. Fear spread throughout the entire Mississippi Territory, preventing offensive action for several weeks.[44] If the fall of Fort Mims did nothing else, it convinced all Americans that it would be necessary to launch a major campaign and crush the Creeks before they could join forces with the British.[45]

Most alarmed by this outbreak of hostilities was Major General Andrew Jackson of theTennessee militia. Even before the Fort Mims attack, he had urged Governor Blount to send the Tennessee volunteers against the Creeks.[46] He wanted to strike immediately with all available forces and destroy the Creeks before they could "be supported by their allies the British and Spaniards."[47] He believed a major British lodgment at Pensacola and along the coast could make it extremely easy for the British to supply and reinforce the Indians. Jackson was perfectly willing to invade Spanish territory if necessary to crush the resistance, since he did not consider Spain a neutral country.

The Spaniards must have anticipated the American reaction to Fort Mims. It was generally known that they had furnished munitions and supplies to the Creeks who attacked the fort, and most Americans believed incorrectly that they had also supplied large quantities of arms. Letters from the governor of West Florida to the Creek war chiefs were captured at the Holy Ground. These letters congratulated the hostiles on their success at Fort Mims and promised them Spanish friendship and future aid.[48]

A different view was held by the Spanish representative to the United States, Luis de Onís, who feared that supplying the Indians might lead to a full-scale invasion of Spanish Florida and possible war between Spain and America. He realized that such a conflict would force Spain to request British assistance against the United States, but he did not think that the Spanish province could be held even with the aid of England.[49]

The long-range significance of the Fort Mims massacre was the drastically changed American relationship with the southern Indians. Before these hostilities, the Creek Indians were living peaceably and in close contact with the settlers of the Mississippi Territory. They were gradually being assimilated into white society. Agitation for Indian removal was not yet strong in the western settlements, and, had it not been for Fort Mims, many of the southern Indians might have been allowed to remain in the Gulf states.[50]

4

The Alabama River Campaigns

IT BECAME apparent with the fall of Fort Mims that the last chance to avoid a real Indian war had passed. Several American governors and some other officials sent out observers among the southern tribes in attempts to obtain some facts. Andrew Jackson wrote his friend John Coffee, on September 29, 1813, that correct information was all-important before making a move.[1]

The regular Indian agents were usually the best source of intelligence, though their reports were not always accurate, as in the case of Hawkins' early misjudgment of the scope of the Creek War. The Cherokees were thought to be friendly, but they might be tempted to join the hostiles if the latter proved successful in their encounters with the whites. In fact, the Red Sticks and northern Indians had already appealed unsuccessfully to the Cherokees.[2] While there were some hostile Choctaws, most of them were persuaded to remain friendly by their respected leaders, Mooshulatabbe Mingo and Pushmataha Mingo.[3]

The Red Sticks tried to tempt the Chickasaws to join their cause by showing scalps as proof of their victories, but there is no record of any number of that tribe becoming hostile. However, James Neelly, the Chickasaw agent, discovered to his horror that an Indian who had formerly been trusted by him was trying to win recruits for the war party. The men most responsible for keeping these people at peace were the Colberts, a family of several brothers. The most influential of them was James Colbert, interpreter for the Chickasaws. He was described by Neelly as "a man of unblemished character, three-fourths white" and with "a tolerable education."[4]

One dominant characteristic of all tribes was the need to be active. It was, therefore, desirable to enroll all able-bodied Indians under the American standard before they could join the enemy. As a matter of fact, the enlisted Indians remained loyal to the United States, thus proving the validity of this policy.[5]

An unusual feature of the Creek War was the unanimity between the various state governors and national officials as to the manner of conducting the war. The Tennessee and Georgia militia were each called upon to furnish at least 1,500 men.[6] There was considerable disagreement regarding the choice of a leader for the expedition against the Creek Indians. For a time, President James Madison favored Governor David B. Mitchell of Georgia, but he withdrew his support when Mitchell prematurely resigned his governorship. Apparently the president had wanted Mitchell to command only as long as the latter remained governor of Georgia. When Mitchell resigned, the president appointed Major General Thomas Pinckney to direct the entire operation.[7] Even this choice was not without problems.

The basic overall plan in the Creek War was modified slightly but never seriously changed. Four armies were to enter the nation from different sides and merge where the Coosa and Tallapoosa rivers flow together to form the Alabama River, near the present town of Wetumpka, Alabama. There were to be two armies from Tennessee, one from East Tennessee under General John Cocke and one from West Tennessee under General Andrew Jackson. These two forces were expected to merge under the command of Jackson in northern Alabama and advance down the Coosa or Tallapoosa to the confluence of the two rivers. The Georgia army under Major General John Floyd was to set up an advance base at Fort Mitchell, near the present site of Columbus, Georgia. These troops were to march from there and join the two armies from Tennessee at the juncture of the rivers. The Third Regiment of United States Army regulars and the forces of Mississippi Territory were to advance up the Alabama River to the meeting place. All units were to attack any Red Sticks they encountered on the way, burn all hostile or abandoned villages, and destroy the crops. Each army was also expected to build and garrison forts about one day's march apart, so that when the central point was reached there would be lines of blockhouses dividing the Creek country north and south, east and west. The advancing armies would build roads between the stockades not already connected by navigable waterways, and each installation would be provided a stockpile of supplies, enabling large armies to move into them rapidly.[8] This was the overall plan at the beginning of the war, and this was

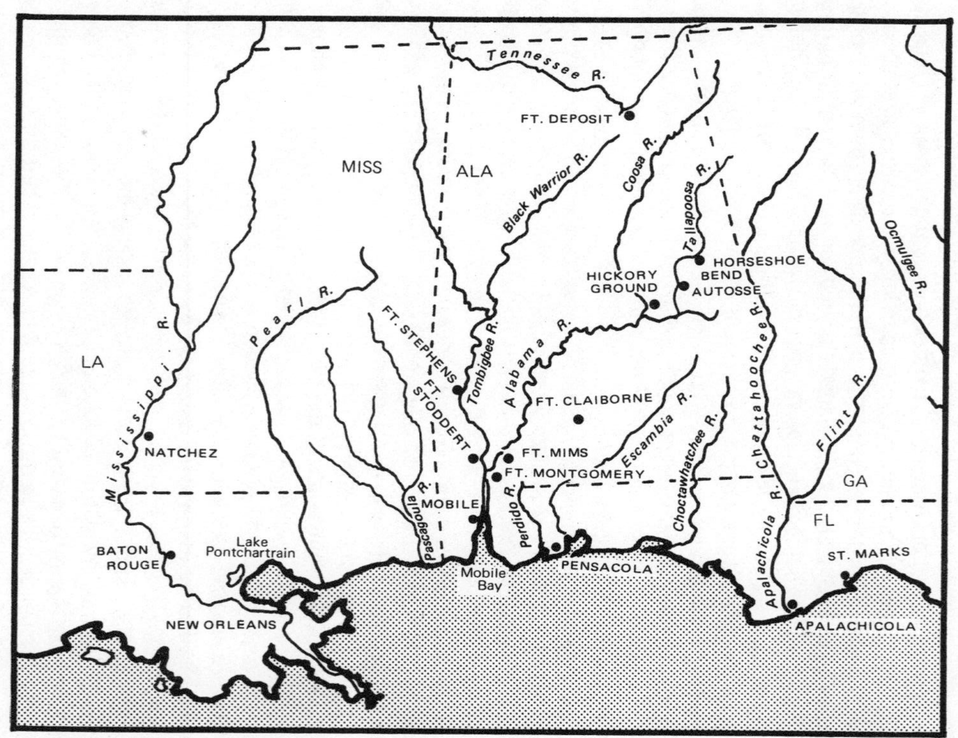

Mississippi Territory, 1810

the way in which the war was eventually won. It took about ten months, however, instead of the projected two or three, to subdue the Creeks. The entire operation against the Indians was plagued with shortages of supplies of all sorts and by a constant turnover of militia. Had there been from the first troops enlisted for the war and a reasonable supply system, the Indians would have been defeated in two or three months.

Another problem which became very serious was the question of command. The Creek Nation lay in two military districts, the Sixth Military District under the orders of Major General Thomas Pinckney, who made his headquarters at Charleston, South Carolina, and the Seventh Military District, commanded by Brigadier General Thomas Flournoy, with headquarters at New Orleans. Communication between these two headquarters was difficult at best, but with the Creek country hostile and the coast blockaded by the British, it became nearly impossible. Dispatches had to be sent all the way around through Tennessee and down the Mississippi River, or by way of the Natchez Trace road. Because of this problem of communication, Secretary of War John Armstrong believed that the Creek War should be under one commander. Overall control of the armies was given to General Pinckney of the Sixth District.[9] Such a system of unified command was logical and necessary, but placing the entire war under the direction of Pinckney obviously infringed on Flournoy's authority.[10] Eventually, when he realized the confusion he had created by giving Pinckney possession of part of Flournoy's district, the secretary tried to rectify the situation by explaining that Pinckney was to concern himself only with the Indian conflict and that the rest of the activities of the Seventh District were to remain in Flournoy's hands.[11] This action served only to increase the friction, and Flournoy eventually resigned his command.

The first real outbreak of the war at Burnt Corn and Fort Mims was in Flournoy's district. Not knowing that he was to be removed from command, he began to organize his own offensive operations. The expedition was led by General Ferdinand L. Claiborne, who commanded the Mississippi militia. The first objective was to advance with about 800 militiamen northward to the fork of the Alabama and Tombigbee rivers and to attack and defeat the enemy believed to be encamped in that area. After this had been accomplished, he was to establish a fort and wait for Flournoy's main force, the Third and Seventh regiments of the United States infantry.[12]

Claiborne set out from St. Stephens on October 12. The army advanced very slowly, carefully scouting the countryside. There were several skirmishes with the Indians but no encounter with any large parties of Red Sticks.[13] One of these contests was the famous canoe fight in which Sam

Dale, Jeremiah Austill, James Smith, and a black named Caesar, fighting from a canoe, killed the nine Indians in another large canoe, with no loss of any of Dale's men. The skirmish was significant in that it was won by force and cunning rather than by an advantage in firearms on the part of the whites; they administered this defeat to the Indians by using gun butts and boat paddles as clubs. Even though this was a small encounter, it was witnessed by a number of the adversaries of both sides. It gave the whites two things which they badly needed: a hero in the form of Sam Dale, who could obviously defeat the Indians with their own weapons, and a victory which, though small, was decisive enough to restore their sagging morale.[14]

On November 6 General Flournoy received orders to turn over the Third Regiment to General Pinckney, now in command of all Creek War operations. Flournoy considered that this directive relieved him of any responsibility for the conflict, so he took his remaining regular troops and returned to New Orleans. Claiborne, camped at Pine Level, only ten miles from St. Stephens, expressed a wish to continue the expedition despite his loss of support. He believed his men, if combined with the Choctaws under Pushmataha, could capture Weatherford's town on the Alabama.[15]

The effective strength of Claiborne's forces was seriously undermined at this critical time by General Flournoy's suprising decision to dismiss Major Thomas Hinds' Mississippi Dragoons from the service. Claiborne considered the dragoons excellent troops and wanted to use them on the expedition.[16] Flournoy had a great dislike for the militia, and in his opinion Major Hinds' detachment lacked discipline and was therefore useless.* While it was no easy task to get proper service from militia units, the United States military establishment, as it was then constituted, was dependent on them.

Despite his warning to Claiborne not to "enter into any rash enterprise," Flournoy was apparently impressed by the militia general's desire to fight. He ordered Claiborne to capture Weatherford's town and to establish a depot for supplies near by. In pursuance of this order on November 13, Claiborne finally left his camp at Pine Level. About two weeks later his command was joined by Colonel Gilbert Russell and the Third Regiment,

*Apparently the difficulty lay in the fact that Major Hinds and his men, most of whom came from the aristocratic element of the territory, had been assigned to guard the civilian population and to garrison several forts in the territory. His men wanted a more active campaign and requested that General Flournoy assign them to offensive operations. Flournoy apparently interpreted this request as insubordination and ordered the force dismissed. Claiborne's effort to clear up this misunderstanding and rectify the situation led Flournoy to reprimand Claiborne himself for questioning his orders dismissing Hinds.

increasing his army to 1,200 men.[17] The combined force advanced about 80 miles up the river, where they erected a stockade. Using this base some 20 miles south of Weatherford's town called Holy Ground, Claiborne set out December 23, 1813, to attack the Creek town.[18] The Indians, aware of Claiborne's approach, sent their women and children across the river, where they secured them in the thick forests.[19]

According to the prophet Josiah Francis, the Holy Ground had been made sacred by the Great Spirit. Francis claimed that the ground had been consecrated especially for the Indians and that it was surrounded by an invisible barrier which would strike dead any white man who tried to pass through it. When the prophet received word that General Claiborne's army was advancing toward the town, he showed little concern. The Indians fired a few rounds at the advancing troops, then waited for them to march into the barrier and fall dead. The Indians' faith was badly shaken when this did not happen. Francis, though no warrior, had a good escape route planned, and after his barrier failed, he and his party escaped from the area in great haste.

The only real defense of Holy Ground was made by William Weatherford and about 30 of his followers. They fought in the style of the white man. From the start they had never believed in the prophet's barrier, and they did not panic when it failed.[20] The village on the Holy Ground was fortified, in addition to the magic barrier, with stakes and fallen logs and located on high ground surrounded by wooded ravines. The town was in a strong position, and it is possible that the Indians could have saved it from capture if Francis' men had waged a real fight.

Claiborne's army advanced in three columns.[21] Major Joseph Carson's column reached the Indian village about noon and was promptly attacked. Almost immediately the Third Regiment, commanded by Colonel Russell, charged in support of Carson's force. Russell's action broke the spirit of the enemy, who fled from the field in all directions, many so distraught that they threw away their arms.[22] Major Henry Cassels, commanding the third column of Claiborne's army, a small mounted force, was ordered to take a position on the far side of the town to cut off the retreat of the Indians. A miscarriage of plans prevented Cassels' being in position when the attack was made, and most of the Indians escaped.[23] About 33 Red Sticks were killed, 12 of them were Negroes fighting as allies of the Creeks, and a number wounded. Claiborne's loss was only one man killed and 20 wounded. The Americans were in immediate pursuit but were unable to catch either the fleeing hostiles or their women and children.[24]

Weatherford remained in the fight as long as he could. Then he made a dramatic escape: he rode his horse down one of the ravines to the river, and then leaped ten or fifteen feet into the water. He and the horse swam the river and escaped.[25] Since Weatherford was seen riding at a full gallop toward the high bluff and was later seen in the water, it was reported by many that he had jumped over a 60-foot bluff and lived.[26]

The town of Holy Ground, about 200 houses, contained a large quantity of provisions and property, all of which was carried off or burned by the Americans. Three hundred scalps, most of which had been taken at Fort Mims, were found on a pole in the middle of the public square.[27] Perhaps the most significant prize captured in the town was the correspondence of the Pensacola governor, González Manrique, with the chiefs of the Creek Nation. The Spanish governor congratulated the chiefs on their victory at Fort Mims but declined their offer to help restore Mobile to the Spanish. González Manrique reminded the Creeks that Spain hoped to get the return of the town without such an attack. The Spanish governor enjoined the Indians, "I hope that you will not put in execution the project which you tell me of, to burn the town: Since those houses and properties do not belong to the Americans but to the Spaniards."[28]

The day after the capture of the Holy Ground another town of 60 houses, about eight miles up the river, was also destroyed after a brief skirmish. In this last incident several Indians, including three Shawnee prophets, were killed. Even though most of the Indians escaped, the Battle of Holy Ground reduced their strength and proved conclusively that they were not invincible.[29]

Perhaps the most important result of Claiborne's campaign was his construction of forts on the Alabama River, thereby making more difficult any communication between the hostile Creeks and Pensacola. Once he had destroyed Weatherford's village, Claiborne marched his army back to Fort Claiborne and in January 1814 discharged the men because their terms of service had expired.[30] Colonel Gilbert Russell and the Third Regiment were garrisoned at Fort Claiborne. These were the only forces on the Alabama still active against the Creeks. General Pinckney had received reports of the large quantities of foodstuff available at this time in the area of Mobile and St. Stephens. He ordered General Claiborne and Colonel Russell to stockpile large amounts of provisions in a fort on the Alabama River so as to be ready to supply Andrew Jackson's Tennessee forces and John Floyd's Georgia troops when they reached the river.[31]

The best invasion route into the Creek Nation was by way of the Alabama River. Had there been a substantial army in this sector, the Indians might have been defeated quickly. With the loss of Claiborne's troops, however, only the Third Regiment remained available, and its activity was greatly restricted by General Flournoy's lack of cooperation. Showing his usual pettiness, he would not allow Colonel Russell to use the boats which were decaying at Mobile and New Orleans. At first he would not permit Russell to use tools or draw quartermaster or camp supplies from the Seventh Military District, arguing that since the Third Regiment had been taken from his command, he was not obliged to cooperate with it in any way. As far as Flournoy was concerned, General Pinckney could send across the hostile country whatever provisions Russell might need. By March 1814 he had softened his position and allowed Russell to have supplies.

General Pinckney did not expect Russell with his small force of 600 men to take offensive action on the Alabama River. Jackson's and Floyd's armies were to be the main striking force. Russell's orders were to build or secure a large number of boats, to load them with provisions, and to take them to the confluence of the Coosa and Tallapoosa rivers. He was cautioned to exercise care with his small force and his boats.[32] Soon after Claiborne's departure, the energetic Russell began planning an offensive of his own. He believed with good reason that there would be even more serious danger from the Creeks if the British reached them with large amounts of supplies. Prompt action against the Red Sticks was essential. He agreed with Jackson and Pinckney that in order to defeat the Creeks it was mandatory that he carry large amounts of foodstuffs so that his army could remain in the field for an extended period.

Russell believed that he could launch a major offensive and break the back of the hostile Creeks if he could collect 900 men and enough boats to carry 90 days' supplies.[33] Unable to construct or borrow the necessary vessels because of Flournoy's refusal to cooperate, Russell was only able to make a series of short raids into the territory near the forts.[34] In January 1814 he received considerable reinforcement from a group of Choctaw and Chickasaw Indians who had been recruited under the supervision of John McKee. These Indians were of great help in searching the countryside for bands of hostile Creeks.[35] With the addition of the friendly Indians, Russell believed that he was strong enough to start a major offensive. With this objective in mind, he set out about February 1, 1814, with 600 men. He planned to advance up the Black Warrior and Cahaba rivers and destroy the hostile towns located there. He sent Captain James Dinkins up the river with 2 armed boats, 70 men, and a large amount of supplies. He was to meet the main force with the supplies at a point near the Cahaba towns.

Russell soon realized that his guides had been wrong; either the distance was much greater than had been reported or his army had taken the wrong trail. There seemed to be no way to communicate with Captain Dinkins, and Russell was forced to push on and try to find the Cahaba towns. After seven days of forced marches, he reached the towns, only to find that the Creeks had recently abandoned them. He was by this time completely out of supplies, and he did not know Dinkins' location. He dared not wait for the boats, so it became necessary for Russell to return to his base by forced marches without provisions. After burning the towns, he sent Lieutenant James M. Wilcox and three men down the Cahaba River to meet Dinkins and turn him back. Two survivors of the Wilcox party, after harrowing experiences with great hardship, eventually reached Dinkins.[36] Russell's own force reached camp near starvation, having had to eat their horses to survive.[37] Aside from burning the towns, Russell discovered as a result of the campaign that it was much farther than he had believed to the confluence of the Coosa and Tallapoosa and that more boats would be needed to provide for Jackson's and Floyd's armies.[38]

By February, Russell's army was composed of the Third Regiment, a small force of militia, and about 300 Choctaws and Chickasaws.[39] The Indian detachment, commanded by General William Colbert, a Chickasaw of mixed blood, had increased in numbers to 661 by the end of March. By improving their armament and training Russell was able to convert his Indians into a formidable fighting force.[40]

The combined action of Claiborne, Russell, and the friendly Indians during the early stages of the Creek War cleared most of the lower Alabama River of Red Sticks and made it difficult for the Indians to communicate with Pensacola. Ultimately Russell's greatest contribution to the war effort was the large quantity of supplies that he brought up the Alabama River to the Georgia and Tennessee armies, making it possible for them to remain in the Creek country. Because of its access to New Orleans and Mobile, Mississippi Territory was the one area that had on hand the abundant food supplies essential for any large military action. The unfortunate aspect of the whole Alabama River campaign was General Flournoy's refusal to cooperate. Russell's advance was thereby postponed for many weeks, and this delay extended the war four or five critical months.

5

The Georgia Campaign: Autosse and Calabee Creek

THE STATE of Georgia, like Mississippi Territory, was one of the first areas to be affected by the Indian war. However, before the massacre at Fort Mims many Georgia leaders doubted the seriousness of the Red Stick menace. Once it became a certainty that there was to be a real conflict, Georgia and Tennessee became the main focal points. They were able to furnish large forces and were in better communication with Washington than was the Mississippi Territory.[1]

The main Georgia army was under the command of John Floyd. These troops, numbering between 2,000 and 3,000, were supposed to advance to the junction of the Coosa and the Tallapoosa rivers. There they would join Jackson's army and divide the Creek Nation on an east-west line.[2] Floyd was expected to build a series of forts along his route and to sweep the countryside, destroying hostile Indians, their villages, and their crops.[3] In addition to Floyd's army, a number of Georgia militia and volunteer units were called out to guard the frontier.[4]

Governor David Mitchell and later Governor Peter Early were especially concerned about the protection of Jasper and Jones counties, located in an exposed position near the hostile Upper Creeks. Spies' reports confirmed the danger to these unprotected portions of the state. For this reason, it was decided to raise a regiment of 500 to 1,000 Georgia militia volunteers under Major General David Adams, to conduct offensive operations against the Indians in the sectors directly north of General Floyd's army.[5] General Adams' force fought several skirmishes against the Red Sticks. His advance did not result in killing many hostile Indians, but it did succeed in burning the village of New Yaucau and disrupting the Creek food supply. In the long run, the lack of food was a major cause of their defeat.[6]

By mid-September 1813 Floyd's army had increased to 2,364 men, more than had originally been called out by the federal government.[7] Sickness, food shortages, and other disabilities reduced the army by December to the point where there were only 950 militiamen and 300 to 400 friendly Indians in the field. For various reasons Floyd's fighting force was probably never larger than 1,500 men.[8]

The main difficulty the Georgia army faced was not a shortage of manpower but the enormous problem of collecting enough rations and getting them to the troops in the Indian nation. The problem of supply collections arose from a lack of foresight. The Creek hostility had been recognized for several months, but it was not until July and August that the gravity of the war was admitted. To buy foodstuffs in the quantities needed by the army, the contractors would have had to have been among the farmers making their purchases by August or earlier. The Georgia troops were not called out until late August and September, and it was after that time that the contractors started buying rations.

Floyd's army was assembled at Fort Hawkins in September, but the serious supply shortage prevented him from starting his campaign for several months. Finally, in November, Floyd was given the authority to requisition his own supplies without having to deal with a middleman, an unusual procedure, but in this manner enough rations were eventually obtained to launch the campaign.[9]

The extra time spent in camp near Fort Hawkins did permit Floyd to train and organize his army, but the delay itself created serious new problems. The militia companies were reorganized, and discipline improved. Reorganization of volunteer and militia units was not popular; it was considered by some of the militiamen to be a violation of their terms of service, and it led to a morale problem in Floyd's army.[10] Many people condemned him for his inactivity and believed that the Georgia forces were afraid of the Indians.[11]

Before Floyd's army entered the field, the only real offensive action against the Red Sticks in Georgia was taken by the friendly Creeks. Around the first of October, a group of these Creeks, led by Big Warrior, Little Prince, and William McIntosh, defeated 150 Uchees who were on their way to join the hostile faction. In addition, the friendly Indians burned several Red Stick villages and destroyed their crops over a large area before retiring to their base at Coweta.[12]

In mid-November Floyd finally believed that his army had enough supplies to commence operations. He had only twenty days' rations of flour and a very small amount of beef, but he hoped to increase the beef supply

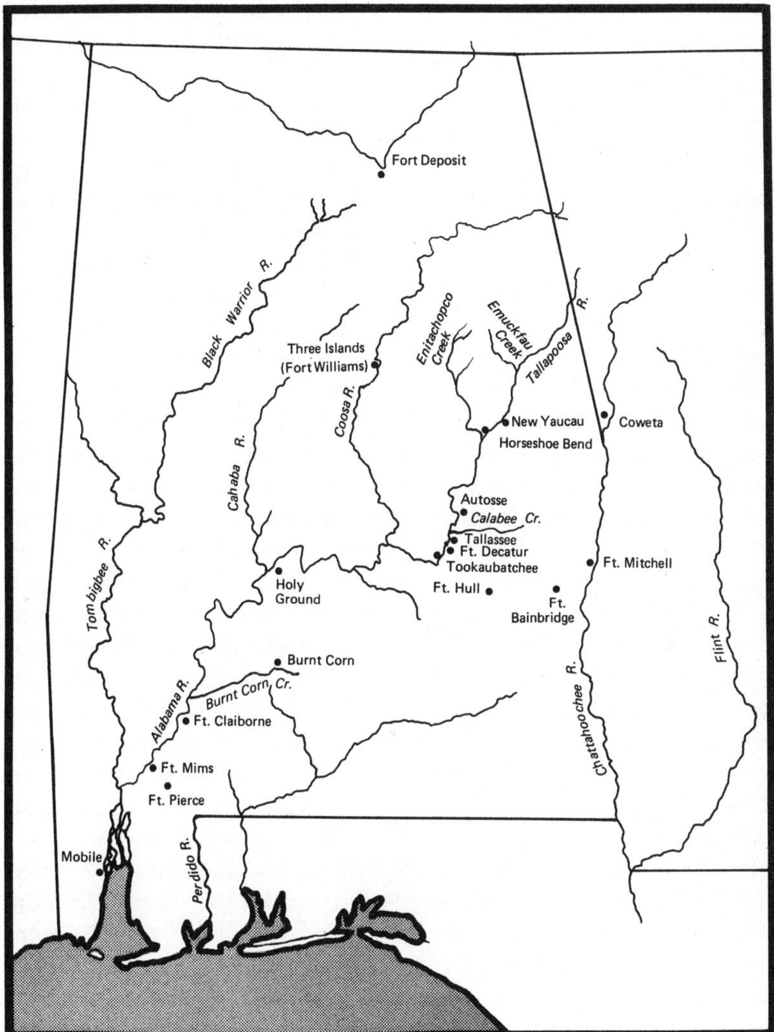

Floyd's campaigns

on the march. A campaign under these conditions was risky, but he thought he could advance his base to the Chattahoochee River and thereby place his army in easy striking distance of the Red Stick towns across the river. He also hoped to be able to help the friendly Coweta Indians, who were under siege by the hostiles and were dangerously short of arms and ammunition.[13]

Upon reaching the Chattahoochee, Floyd constructed Fort Mitchell, the first fort of the series he was expected to build along his line of advance to the headwaters of the Alabama River. He was joined by 300 to 400 friendly Indians. Taking 950 of his men and the Indian allies, he began an advance toward the hostile town of Autosse, about 60 miles away. This town, supposed to be one of the main centers of the hostile Creeks, was located on the southern bank of the Tallapoosa River about 20 miles above its junction with the Coosa. The Georgians reached a point near Autosse just before daylight on November 29, 1813.

Autosse was thought to be located on the Tallapoosa near the mouth of Calabee Creek. Basing his plans accordingly, Floyd formed his army into two main columns with his rifle companies on the flanks. He hoped to surround the enemy by extending his right flank to Calabee Creek and his left flank to a point on the river below the town. The friendly Indians were to cross the river and take up a position opposite the town, blocking escape in that direction. The river proved to be so cold and the ford so deep that the friendly Indians could not get across the river. They were then ordered to cross Calabee Creek and cut off escape in that direction.

Floyd's intelligence concerning Autosse was fairly accurate as to its size and location; but when he reached the river, he learned that there was a second town about 500 yards from Autosse. The Georgians wanted to destroy both towns, so Floyd modified his plans. He extended his left column so as to surround the lower town as well as Autosse. Soon after the advance started, the battle became a general one. The hostile Indians fought frantically but were driven back into the woods at the rear of the town. Floyd had hoped to surround the hostiles, but the area covered by their towns proved too extensive, thus permitting most of the Red Sticks to escape. The battle was closely fought; the deciding factor was Floyd's artillery. He fired a heavy barrage at the town and followed it with a bayonet charge, which broke the Indians' line.

By 9:00 A.M. the Indians had been driven from the area, and the houses of both towns were burned. Although most of the hostiles escaped, the Battle of Autosse was a substantial American victory. At least 200 Red Sticks were killed and many more wounded. The chronic food shortage forced Floyd to return to his base on the Chattahoochee and prevented him from pursuing the demoralized Red Sticks. The white army sustained 11 killed and 54 wounded, including General Floyd, who was seriously disabled. The friendly Indians also suffered heavy casualties.[14]

General Pinckney interpreted Floyd's retreat to the Chattahoochee River as a defeat for the Georgians, but this was not the whole truth.[15] The retreat had been planned in advance by Floyd, who knew that he was too far from his base to establish a permanent post before an intermediate fort could be built.[16] The campaign was undoubtedly planned as a search-and-destroy mission rather than an effort to occupy land. Floyd was well pleased with the outcome of the battle. He had defeated a major body of Indians and had partially avenged Fort Mims. The Old Tallassee King and the Autosse King, two important Red Stick leaders, had been killed, and Peter McQueen had been chased from the field.[17]

The white soldiers captured no Indian women or children at Autosse. The approach of the army had been seen by an Indian who was out hunting turkey, and the alarm had been given. Women, old men, and children were sent to a place of safety before the battle.[18] After the destruction of Autosse, the hostile Indians began bringing their forces together in the area of the horseshoe bend on the Tallapoosa River.[19]

Returning to his main camp at Fort Mitchell on the east bank of the Chattahoochee, Floyd found himself troubled with the same old problem, lack of provisions. Food would have been scarce in any event, but the situation was made worse by the refusal of the contractors to deliver supplies to the Chattahoochee. They claimed that the river was beyond the Georgia frontier. This difficulty arose over different interpretations of the contract. Floyd thought supplies were to be brought to the army whatever its location, and the contractors thought they were to deliver them only to the frontier. In any case, because of this disagreement the vouchers had not been signed, the provisions had not arrived, and the army was starving.[20] Supplies were not received at Fort Mitchell until December 29, at which time it had been planned that the army would take the field again in a few days. Floyd's wound was thought serious enough that some consideration was given to his removal from command; but by the time a replacement was decided upon it was nearly January, and Floyd had recovered sufficiently to exercise his duties.[21]

The future campaign of the Georgia army was further complicated by the necessity to furnish food for the friendly Indians. Their crops had been completely destroyed, and Floyd was certain that if he did not feed these people, a large part of them would join the hostiles. He suspected, with good reason, that many of the so-called friendly Indians were loyal only so long as they were receiving supplies.[22]

Cavalry would have been useful in fighting the Indians; but because of the large amounts of corn needed for horses and the great difficulties of bringing supplies into the Creek country, Floyd preferred to keep only a small detachment of cavalry with the army.[23] General Pinckney, who feared that the Indians would soon be receiving British aid, was anxious for Floyd to get his troops into action as soon as possible. There were rumors of British arms going to the Indians and reports of British landings at Apalachicola and other points on the coast. While these rumors were premature, Pinckney's anxiety was understandable.

Another serious problem lay in the expiration of enlistments in Floyd's army on February 22, 1814. At the time the Georgia troops were called into service, no one could have anticipated the countless delays ahead; in fact, it had been assumed that the Creeks could easily be defeated in six months. General Pinckney wanted to accomplish something with these troops before the termination of their enlistments, and he pressured Floyd with orders for an early advance.[24] By the middle of January enough supplies had been collected, and Floyd determined to take the field again. He advanced his army from Fort Mitchell to a point 41 miles west of the Chattahoochee. Here he erected Fort Hull. His force at that time was composed of approximately 1,100 militia and volunteers and 600 friendly Indians.

After the defeat at Autosse, the Red Sticks found their powder supply completely exhausted. This shortage combined with the defeat had caused some of the hostiles to flee into the swamps with their families or make their way to Pensacola, where they hoped to find safety among the Spaniards. With morale at a low ebb, the hostile chiefs and prophets held a meeting at the Othewalle camps to determine their future course. William Weatherford was summoned to counsel with them. The decision was made to send Weatherford and a small party to Pensacola to obtain more powder. Spanish Governor González Manrique was unable to furnish any military supplies from his own stocks at this time, but Weatherford did obtain three horseloads of powder from British and private sources. While this was not a great deal of ammunition, it was enough to raise the confidence of the Indians once more.[25]

The party had barely returned from Pensacola when the Indians received word that the Georgia troops were on the road again, advancing deeper into Creek territory. Scouts reported that the Georgians were building a fortified camp on the west side of Calabee Creek. Spurred on by this information, Red Stick leaders quickly agreed to an immediate attack on the camp before the Americans could complete their fortifications. The Indians set out with around 1,300 warriors led by four men: Paddy Welsh, High Head Jim, William Weatherford, and William McGillivray, probably a relative of Alexander McGillivray.

There was disagreement among the leaders as to strategy. Paddy Welsh and High Head Jim wanted to attack the camp at night while the troops were sleeping. The encampment of the whites was laid off in two squares. Paddy Welsh's plan was to attack on all sides in the dark, getting as close to the camp as possible before being discovered. By this means he hoped to gain the greatest advantage from war clubs and tomahawks. He would withdraw the forces at daylight, when the enemy's superior firepower would be more effective.

Weatherford and McGillivray also wanted to make a night attack, but they did not want to be committed to any advance plan of retreat. Weatherford believed that a force of about 300 men could slip close to one of the squares during the night. Then, once they were discovered, they would rush to the center of the square where the officers were encamped and kill them. Once that was accomplished, the raiding party would withdraw and join the main body of Indians. As soon as the small party made its thrust, the remaining Indians would attack all sides of the encampment. An attack at close quarters with tomahawks and clubs against half-asleep, disorganized men would completely confuse the whites, Weatherford thought. These tactics, if successful, would mean the complete destruction of Floyd's army as a fighting force, even if some of the men were able to reach the frontier.

Weatherford's plan probably would have worked exactly as he thought; had it been carried out, Floyd's army would have been badly mauled, if not destroyed. But Welsh was jealous of Weatherford, and he construed the latter's plan as an attempt to undermine his authority. He was able to thwart Weatherford's plan by persuading the Indians that they would all be killed. Weatherford and McGillivray were so angered at Welsh's opposition to their plan that they left the camp.[26] McGillivray later had second thoughts and decided to remain under Welsh's orders, but, according to George Stiggins, Weatherford returned to his home. Other versions of this episode contended that Weatherford also relented in his determination to return home and rejoined the attack. Whatever happened, the Battle of Calabee fought on January 27, 1814, was one of the best planned attacks the Creeks had made since Fort Mims.[27]

Even General Floyd's report admitted the success of the Indian attack, which was a severe blow to the morale of the white army. He described the battle in a report to General Pinckney as a desperate attack on the army under his command by a very large body of hostile Indians: "They stole upon the Centinels, fired on them, and with great impetuosity rushed upon our line; in 20 minutes the action became general . . . but the brave and gallant conduct of the field and line officers, and the firmness of the men, repelled them at every point. . . . The enemy rushed within thirty yards of the artillery." Floyd said that as soon as it became light enough to distinguish objects, he ordered preparations to be made for the charge, which "was promptly obeyed and the enemy fled in every direction before the bayonet." There were 37 dead on the field, and it was believed "from the effusion of blood, and the number of head dresses and war clubs found in various directions, their loss must have been considerable. . . ."[28]

Whether or not Weatherford returned to the battle remains uncertain. Evidently someone with a great deal of intelligence, perhaps William McGillivray, if it was not Weatherford, persuaded the Indians to try to capture Floyd's artillery. The Georgians had two pieces of artillery mounted on trucks "navy style" rather than on wheels. The battle had been under way only a short time when a large number of Creeks crawled up the slope to the cannon, which were firing over their heads. They were not seen by the whites until they were within a few yards of the cannon and almost succeded in the maneuver. Once these men were discovered in the open directly in front of the cannon, Floyd's guns were depressed and fired several rounds of grapeshot at close range, slaughtering the Indians. This awful destruction of such a large number of Indians proved too much for the hostiles, and at that point the attack was broken.[29]

Weatherford's astute prediction that the white army would be utterly confused by the assault was accurate. The camp at the moment of attack was in a state of panic. Many soldiers lost their shoes and in the dark did not know in which direction to fire their guns. The initial Indian onslaught drove the soldiers from part of their camp and left Floyd's two fieldpieces poorly protected. Each side took its heaviest loss in the battle for control of the cannon, but Floyd managed to retain possession of them and to rally his forces for a counterattack at daylight.[30] The Georgia army would doubtless have been completely routed and probably destroyed, as Weatherford had foreseen, if his plan had been followed.[31]

Floyd's losses in this battle were 17 white men killed, 132 wounded (of which 4 died within a few days), 5 friendly Creeks killed, and 15 wounded. Including those bodies found the day after the battle, the hostiles apparently lost 49 men.[32] While the Indian casualties were heavy, the proportion of losses in this battle was much more in favor of the Indians than usual. Floyd's men had been badly mauled, and their morale was low.[33]

In the midst of such deteriorating morale, with the army on half-rations and rumors of mutiny, Floyd decided to withdraw to Fort Hull. He realized that the fort was deep in hostile country, but he believed that since it was a protected position his men might be willing to hold it. If he could not make a stand, he had no alternative but to retreat to Fort Mitchell.[34] His main worry was that when his troops reached the stockade, they would find no supplies and would refuse to remain there. His anxiety was relieved when they reached Fort Hull and found twelve supply wagons awaiting them.[35] Even with the supplies in hand, Floyd was concerned that the Indians might cut him off.[36]

It was apparent that the army was no longer willing to take offensive action. The men's enlistments would be completed on February 22 and they believed it was their right to be discharged at their mustering points.[37] In the meantime, General Pinckney planned to replace Floyd's army with a newly raised force of South Carolina militia. These troops were on the march and were expected to reach the frontier within a few days. The American commander must somehow hold the valuable position at Fort Hull until the replacements arrived.[38] The general had 352 sick or wounded out of an army of almost 1,500, but none of his men deserted while deep in Creek country.[39] Floyd was able to hold the troops at the fort until February 16, but at that time his militia threatened to march back to Georgia as a body, with or without orders from their leader. Faced with these problems, Floyd turned over the command of Fort Hull to Colonel Homer V. Milton. The colonel believed that he could hold this position with his force of regulars and 140 militia who had volunteered to remain until relief arrived. Milton's troops were provided with twelve days' rations, and Floyd marched the remainder of his army back to the Georgia frontier.[40]

Within a few days Milton began to receive supplies and was reinforced by small detachments of regulars. Conditions improved considerably when the South Carolina troops reached the frontier. According to plan, Milton was to remain in command of all of the troops until the large forces from North Carolina and South Carolina should arrive, at which time command was to be given to one of their generals. In the meantime, Pinckney ordered Milton to move against the hostiles and clear the area near the fort as soon as he had sufficient troops. Pinckney also ordered Milton to be ready to make a junction with General Jackson and Colonel Gilbert Russell as soon as either of their armies reached the confluence of the Coosa and the Tallapoosa.[41]

Even after Milton's force was increased, it continued to be difficult to get enough supplies shipped to his post deep in Creek country. To ease this problem, Milton decided to erect a stockade between Fort Mitchell and Fort Hull. Fort Bainbridge, the new installation, was located 16 miles east of Fort Hull. Supply wagons could now travel between the forts in one-day stages.[42] Milton reported that there had been a heavy snowstorm while the fort was under construction and that he was well pleased with the quality of his South Carolina troops, who had endured considerable hardship while building the fort.[43]

Milton's operation against the Indians was much more systematic than Floyd's had been and reflected his regular army training. Instead of moving his entire army out to the most advanced post, where supply was difficult, he kept most of his troops at Fort Mitchell until he had built a secure position at Fort Bainbridge. Once the fort was finished, his supply line was protected and he manned Fort Bainbridge and Fort Hull with garrisons of 100 to 300 men. His next step was to move large quantities of provisions out to his most advanced post at Fort Hull. Milton eventually put together at Fort Hull a force of 600 troops, mostly regulars, and a substantial number of friendly Indians.[44] In late March and early April Milton was heavily engaged in searching the country for hostiles, as well as in collecting supplies at his most advanced base. He had been ordered by Pinckney to have 50,000 rations ready for the use of General Jackson's army when the latter reached the junction of the Coosa and Tallapoosa rivers.[45]

During the last days of March 1814, the Georgia army was heavily reinforced with North Carolina militia troops; and being a good soldier, Colonel Milton wanted to take a more active role and push deeper into Creek country. Early in April he moved his army to the bank of the Tallapoosa opposite the town of Tookaubatchee, where he and Benjamin Hawkins surveyed the land and erected Fort Decatur. This stockade was to serve as the new base of operations, and the last link in the chain of forts stretching from the Georgia frontier to the junction of the Coosa and Tallapoosa rivers.[46] Although this regular army colonel wanted action, General Pinckney had ordered him to continue his chores as a supply collector and to build boats so that he could complete his final task of delivering rations to Jackson's army.[47]

6

Jackson's First Creek Campaign: Tallushatchee and Talladega

THE NEWS of the Fort Mims massacre circulated widely in Tennessee, where there was already considerable ill feeling toward the Creek Indians. The Tennesseans had been shocked by several depredations committed in or near their territory.[1] The state had no direct boundary with the Creeks, but the nation was close to Tennessee soil and there was danger that the Chickasaw or Cherokee Indians might join the hostiles. For this reason, Governor Willie Blount and General Andrew Jackson maintained a constant vigil on the activities of the Creeks. The settlements around Huntsville in the Mississippi Territory were composed largely of former Tennesseans. They had ties with friends and relatives in their native state, and it is not surprising that Jackson and Blount continued to be well informed of the Indian movements.[2]

Once an Indian war became likely, Blount arranged to send a major expedition into Creek country. He was certain that if the Indians were not crushed at once they would be reinforced by the British, and the situation might become impossible.[3] All the governors in the area were cognizant of the possibility of British and Spanish intervention, but Blount, who was being advised by Jackson, appeared to be more aware of the necessity for quick action than any of the others. Blount and Jackson were made conscious of the danger of British intervention by the many Creeks and northern Indians who had crossed Tennessee on their way to and from Canada, and by the skirmishes fought with them. In Georgia and Mississippi the presence of the northern Indians was rumored, but none had actually been encountered.[4]

Reports of the Fort Mims massacre reached Andrew Jackson at the

Hermitage, where he lay wounded as a result of a gun battle in Nashville with Tom and Jesse Benton.* Though unable to leave his bed, as major general of the state militia he advised Governor Blount to move quickly. Acting on his own authority and without waiting for federal authorization, Blount asked his legislature in September 1813 to call out the 3,500 men. That request was granted with little disagreement, indicating the irate feelings of many citizens.[5]

The first unit ordered into action was General Coffee's volunteer cavalry. It was sent immediately to Huntsville to prepare a camp for General Jackson's main army. Coffee was joined at Huntsville by a detachment of Choctaw Indian scouts. Jackson had ordered the cavalry officer to spread the story that his volunteer company was planning to advance to Mobile, hoping that the rumor might confuse the Indians. In the meantime, the cavalry and other troops, as they arrived, were ordered to scout the Upper Creeks near Huntsville.[6] Coffee was further ordered to cross the Tennessee River if it seemed safe and to create a base on the south bank near Colbert's Ferry.

Almost as soon as he reached Huntsville, Coffee found himself facing a drastic food shortage. The contractors could find little or no flour, and suitable corn was also very scarce in Tennessee. Old corn, hard enough to grind, was in short supply, and new corn had to be kiln dried. The contractors would have needed several months' advance warning to supply adequately an army as large as General Jackson's.[7]

Not only supplies but also manpower for Jackson's forces had to be assembled. The Cherokees were one source from which it was hoped to recruit the necessary troops for the Tennessee army. It was believed that it might be possible to enlist about 750 Indians, but this number would depend on the size of Jackson's forces. According to the reasoning of the Cherokees, if the white army was small the Indians would have to leave more men to protect their homes against the hostile Creeks.[8] In order that the white troops might recognize the Cherokees and other tribes who were friendly, such Indians were ordered to wear white plumes or deer's tails in their hair.[9]

Jackson's first genuinely aggressive action was to send General Coffee to destroy the Black Warrior towns just south of the Tennessee River. Possibly they could capture or destroy the stock and crops of the Creeks;

*Jackson acted as second for William Carroll in a duel with Jesse Benton, brother of Thomas Hart Benton, on June 14, 1813. This angered the two brothers and resulted in an encounter in Nashville on Sept. 4, in which Jackson was wounded in the shoulder and arm.

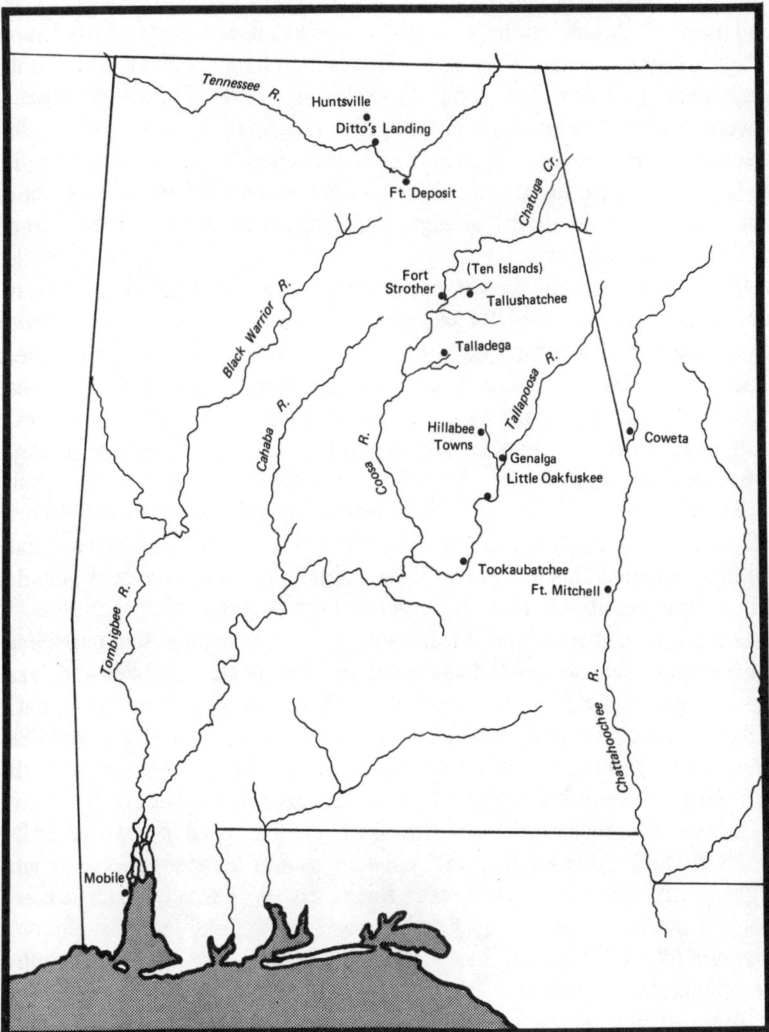

Coffee's routes

thus even if the Indians should escape, they would be eliminated as a fighting force.[10] This was total war, and white armies had used it to fight the Indians from the earliest times. Coffee left camp near Ditto's Landing on the Tennessee River on October 15 with between 600 and 700 men.[11] He had no regular guide on this expedition and was not able to find the Black Warrior towns at once. After three days of marching, Coffee found a small abandoned Indian village about 80 miles from the Tennessee River. Twenty miles farther, after passing through another empty village, he reached the main town. All its inhabitants had fled, except one or two old Indians. Coffee captured some 300 bushels of corn and burned the council house and about 50 other buildings, thus destroying the main town of one of the larger hostile tribes.[12]

The fact that he attacked and destroyed these villages with no opposition caused both Coffee and Jackson to believe that the hostile Creeks would not fight.[13] Encouraged by this weakness, Jackson was more willing than ever to take the offensive. Despite his eagerness, however, the constant shortage of supplies delayed his move for many weeks. It was not until near the end of October that the whole army could be moved south into Creek country.[14]

About October 22, 1813, even before Coffee's return from the Black Warrior settlements, Jackson marched his army to a point 24 miles above Ditto's Landing. This movement placed him on the southernmost point of the Tennessee River. Here he erected Fort Deposit, a stockade which was to serve him as a depot for his supplies. After establishing himself at the new fort, Jackson waited several days for expected supplies and reinforcements that never came.[15] He received a report there from Path Killer, a Cherokee chief, that a large number of hostile Indians were assembled in the area of Ten Islands on the Coosa River for the purpose of attacking the friendly Creeks at Coweta and probably Talladega.[16]

Jackson began his march southward toward Ten Islands on October 24 or 25. He had barely six days' rations; even though his men collected some Indian corn on the march, this was a thin margin with which to start a campaign.[17] Jackson expected daily to be joined by General James White and General John Cocke from East Tennessee, with whom he was in regular communication.

Approaching Ten Islands, Jackson learned that a considerable body of the enemy had encamped at the nearby town of Tallushatchee. Believing this to be an important objective, Coffee was dispatched to destroy the place.[18] Coffee arrived on November 3, 1813, at a point near the town, located about eight miles from Ten Islands. He divided his army into two columns and, marching one on either side of the town, he encircled it. This maneuver was accomplished with little difficulty, and Coffee, finding that the Indians had not fled, advanced on the town from all directions. Two companies were detached from his circular lines and moved into a position inside the circle in plain view of the enemy. When the Indians saw this small force firing on them, they broke from the cover of their buildings and made a wild charge on it. They pursued the retreating whites until they ran into Coffee's main line. They realized their error and attempted to retreat. Many Indians were killed in the open as Coffee's troops charged them. The hostiles who reached the buildings made a stand there, but their organization was completely destroyed. American forces were able to kill them all in a very short time. Coffee was concerned over the fact that when his men ran into the Indians' houses, many women and children were slaughtered. He counted 186 enemy dead and estimated that they probably had killed around 200. Coffee's losses were 5 killed and 41 wounded. He reported that the Indians were very poorly armed, a large part of them having only bows and arrows. All the men at Tallushatchee were killed, and 84 women and children were taken prisoners.[19] This action proved that if the white armies could reach the Creeks, it would be easy for the better armed Americans to annihilate the Indians.[20]

Jackson was entirely too short of supplies to feed his prisoners, so he promptly dispatched them to Tennessee.[21] He then built Fort Strother near Ten Islands. Here he waited in vain for the East Tennessee troops and their supplies.[22] The inaction and a serious shortage of provisions caused a severe deterioration in morale.[23]

On November 7, while still waiting for General White, Jackson received a messenger from the friendly Creek village of Talladega, about 30 miles from Fort Strother. Talladega, which had been fortified, was completely surrounded, and the friendly Indians were being starved out. Jackson realized that this was an excellent opportunity to destroy a large hostile force, and he resolved to move his command at once. Expecting White's momentary arrival, Jackson left his baggage, his sick and wounded, and a small guard force at Fort Strother. By midnight of November 7, he had an army of 1,200 infantry and 800 cavalry ready to march. The army advanced, according to Jackson's custom, in three columns, in such a way that if it were attacked on the march it could quickly be thrown into a hollow square. On the evening of November 8 Jackson camped about six miles from Talladega, while his scouts located the enemy's position. Just after the scouts returned, a runner brought word from White that General Cocke had ordered White to change his course and to join Cocke's army at Chatuga

Creek. Without White's support, Jackson was in a weak position. Fort Strother was not well enough protected to withstand a heavy Indian attack, yet he did not intend to abandon his campaign for the relief of Talladega. The only course left was to attack Talladega and destroy the hostiles as quickly as possible.[24]

The Red Sticks with a force of almost 1,100 men were attacking about 160 friendly Creeks, the latter protected by a fort. Placing his cavalry in front, Jackson advanced his army in two columns to the right and left of the enemy camps, eventually encircling them. Once the Americans closed the circle, the entire force was to face inward and advance toward the center. The plan was sound, but in the advance a large opening was left between the rear of the right wing of the cavalry and General William Hall's brigade. After about twenty minutes of heavy fighting, the Indians found the opening and through it most of them made their escape. When the battle ended, the bodies of 299 Red Sticks were found on the field, and probably many more died of their wounds. The whites lost 14 killed and 81 wounded.[25] Coffee's first engagement with the Creeks had made him lose respect for their fighting ability, but the Battle of Talladega changed his mind. He believed, however, that the superiority of weapons would enable the Americans to defeat the Creeks easily. It was estimated that in the two battles fought against the Creeks, their losses had been 1,000 warriors killed and wounded.[26]

General James White's failure to obey Jackson's orders and march his men to Fort Strother had left that post in a dangerously weak condition. The danger necessitated Jackson's hasty return to the fort, thus making it impossible for him to follow up his victory at Talladega.[27] Had Jackson been able to spend several days in searching for the Indians, it is probable that Talladega would have been decisive in breaking the morale of the hostiles.

General Cocke, not wishing to enhance the reputation of his political rival, decided not to join forces with Jackson immediately. Instead, Cocke moved his army against the Hillabee towns. These towns of the Upper Creek Nation had furnished many of the hostiles at the Battle of Talladega, and their inhabitants were supposed to have been among the first Creeks to join the war party.[28] Acting under General Cocke's orders, White took up his line of march against the Hillabees with his mounted men and a small group of Cherokees under command of Colonel Gideon Morgan. Between November 11 and 17 he destroyed the towns of Little Oakfusky and Genalga, capturing 5 Red Sticks and burning 123 houses. In preparation for their attack on November 18, White sent part of his white troops and Colonel Gideon Morgan with the Cherokee forces to surround the town. These troops moved into position in the darkness, and at daylight they surprised the enemy. In the short disorganized battle that followed, the enemy lost 64 warriors killed. Twenty-nine were taken prisoner, along with 237 women and children. So quickly was the attack completed that a large part of White's army was not able to get into action. There were no American casualties.[29] The small detachment of Cherokees under Colonel Gideon Morgan's command fought extremely well in this battle, and it was the Cherokees who led the assault and killed or captured a large part of the Creek hostiles.[30] Because of this organization of the attacking forces, the victory was in reality a defeat of the Creeks by the Cherokees.

Jackson had hoped to continue an immediate offensive against the Creeks, but the failure of Cocke's army to arrive with fresh troops and supplies made it impossible for him to move.[31] There must have been considerable rivalry between Cocke and Jackson, since they commanded the eastern and western divisions of the Tennessee militia. It does not appear, however, that they had heretofore been bitter enemies. The relationship between the two men changed radically at this time. Jackson, the overall commander, had depended on supplies from Cocke, but the latter had barely enough to feed his own troops. Concluding that Jackson needed food rather than men, Cocke felt justified in disregarding Jackson's orders.[32]

To add to the confusion while the disputatious correspondence was being conducted, Cocke destroyed the Hillabee towns and felt that he had won a great victory. If the two armies had been in closer touch, Cocke would have known that the Hillabees had sent Robert Grierson, a released prisoner, to ask Jackson for peace. Grierson reported that the Hillabees and Fish Pond Indians, the most hostile tribes of the Creek Nation, had been so badly defeated at the Battle of Talladega that they were ready to abandon the fighting. Grierson advised Jackson that the whole Creek Nation was disheartened and would be ready to make peace if the Tennesseans could march quickly into the heart of their country.[33]

Jackson agreed on November 17 to make peace with the Hillabees if they would deliver the instigators of the war and restore all property which they had taken from the whites.[34] A message was promptly sent to General Cocke informing him of the peace with the Hillabees, but the message was sent on November 18, the day that Cocke's army attacked and destroyed the Hillabee towns.[35] The Hillabees, thinking themselves betrayed, determined thereafter to fight to the death. This tribe was indeed one of the last of the Creek groups to make peace with the Americans.[36]

In the midst of his trials Jackson received instructions from Major General Thomas Pinckney to advance as soon as possible to the confluence of the Coosa and Tallapoosa rivers. Although he already had a similar plan, formed before receiving these orders, Jackson decided that this advance was to be his foremost objective. Pinckney suggested that once Jackson reached the junction of the rivers, he could obtain all the supplies he needed from New Orleans.[37]*

After his return to Fort Strother following the Battle of Talladega, Jackson discovered that none of the expected supplies had arrived. The place, except for a few beeves, was without food. Many of Jackson's officers and some entire units petitioned him to allow them to return to the frontier so that they could get food and replenish their supplies. The pressure to do this was great, and had not a few small shipments been forwarded by the contractors, there would undoubtedly have been a mutiny.[38]

The general put off his men's demands as long as he could. Eventually hunger became too strong an influence, and the troops decided to march back to civilization with or without their leader. Jackson's army was composed of two brigades of Tennessee one-year volunteers and one brigade of militia. The militia brigade was the first to decide to march home in defiance of orders, but Jackson deployed part of his volunteer troops across its path to prevent the departure. The stratagem worked, and the disgruntled militia returned to camp.[39] The next day the volunteers themselves determined to march back to Fort Deposit and probably for home. This time Jackson used his militia to prevent the volunteers from leaving camp.[40]

Jackson realized that this situation could not continue indefinitely, and he called his field officers and captains into a meeting. He explained that to move at that time would cause the death of several of the wounded and the loss of all baggage because the wagons had been sent for supplies. He wanted to wait two days, and he promised that if provisions had not arrived by that time the whole army would march to Fort Deposit. They could lay the blame on the contractors. Each brigade was ordered to hold a meeting of its officers and determine a course of action. In answer to the general's request, Coffee's volunteer cavalry voted to remain with him as long as they were needed. General Isaac Roberts' militia agreed to stay for three or four days until it could be ascertained whether or not supplies would

*Historian John Spencer Bassett has suggested that these instructions given by Pinckney were "singularly inept." He considered the idea of supply from New Orleans out of the question. Actually, most of the supply for the Gulf Coast region came through New Orleans. Had Colonel Russell of the Third Regiment had enough boats, there was no reason why his 600 regulars could not have moved up as far as the confluence of the Coosa and the Tallapoosa. The Creeks had nothing capable of stopping a force of well-armed boats.

arrive. General William Hall's brigade of volunteers decided to march at once.[41] Jackson had expected his officers to agree to remain at Fort Strother, and he was visibly disappointed at the action taken by Hall's brigade.[42]

After two more days without supplies Jackson was unable to put his men off any longer, and he agreed to start the march back to Fort Deposit. In a last-ditch effort to save Fort Strother and the baggage, he is reported to have said that "if only two men would remain" with him he "would not abandon this position."[43] As a result of this appeal, 109 volunteers agreed to remain at the fort. Jackson began his march on November 18, 1813, but before the troops had gone more than twelve miles, they met a supply column herd of beeves and nine wagons of flour.[44] The general at once ordered his men to kill and eat their fill. When they had eaten he detached the number of men that were absolutely necessary to escort the sick and wounded back to Fort Deposit, and he ordered the army to return immediately to Fort Strother.

Though they had agreed to return to their post as soon as they were supplied, many of the men were determined to continue their march home. Jackson, some of his staff, and officers from Coffee's command took a stand across the line of march and threatened to fire on the mutineers if they continued to advance. This action stopped the troops for a time, but a little while later Jackson found the entire brigade about to march home. This time he placed himself alone in front of the column. His left arm was still unusable as a result of the wound received in the Benton encounter. Still he laid his musket on the neck of his horse and, according to one of his officers, made a speech to the mutinous soldiers. "You say you will march," Jackson shouted. "I say by the Eternal God you shall not march while a cartridge can sound fire." He was soon joined by General Coffee and Major John Reid, and the column after a little hesitation agreed to return to camp.[45]

When his brigades returned to Fort Strother, Jackson himself went to Fort Deposit to expedite the sending of supplies to his army.[46] Jackson rejoined his troops at Fort Strother on December 2, 1813. He now held high hopes of starting a real offensive against the Creeks. But this time General Hall's brigade had again decided to go home, claiming that their term of enlistment would end on December 10, 1813. These men had been first recruited on December 10, 1812 for a term of one year. They had gone with Jackson on his expedition to Natchez. They had been released early in 1813 after the Natchez service and recalled in September 1813 for duty in the Creek War. They now insisted that the time spent at home counted toward their year's enlistment and that their service would soon be over. Coffee's brigade had already been allowed to go to Huntsville to fatten its horses and obtain remounts. Without these troops Jackson would have had only one brigade of militia, a command entirely too small to undertake an offensive against the Creeks.[47] Despite Jackson's best efforts, the volunteers were determined to have their discharge on December 10; and although he tried to shame the officers and men into remaining in camp, they left at the appointed time.[48] While Coffee's brigade was being allowed to fatten its horses, his officers and men requested permission to go home to obtain remounts and winter clothing, pledging to return when they had accomplished these things.[49]

With his force reduced to less than 1,000 militia, Jackson learned with some relief that General Cocke would arrive December 12 with 1,450 men. After his defeat of the Hillabees and some rather strong notes from Jackson, Cocke had at length decided to join the latter with his full force. The arrival of Cocke's army and some additional supplies caused Jackson to believe that he might soon be able to start the offensive which Pinckney had ordered.[50] These plans too were short lived. As soon as the East Tennessee army arrived, he discovered that its term of service was also nearly at an end. In fact, Cocke's army was not due to serve much longer than his own militia. One of Cocke's regiments was to be discharged December 1, 1813, another January 1, 1814, and another January 14, 1814.[51] There was little use to start the much needed campaign with this army nearly ready for discharge. He ordered Cocke to take his men home and to raise a new force of at least 1,500 men as quickly as he could. This loss reduced Jackson's army to 400 effectives.[52]

Soon after, General Roberts and his militia reached the end of their enlistment and marched back to Nashville. This loss left Jackson's army far too weak to make another offensive and seriously undermined his ability to hold Fort Strother. Governor Blount, upon hearing of his losses, suggested that he withdraw, at least to Fort Deposit. His position was made even more critical when General Coffee's men, also volunteers, discovered that Hall's brigade was in full retreat. Coffee himself and a company made up mainly of his officers were the only men of his brigade who were willing to remain in Creek territory. When fresh troops were finally received, Fort Strother had only 130 men for its defense.

This first campaign quite possibly would have resulted in much greater success, if not in complete victory, had it not been plagued first by supply shortages and then by short-term enlistments. The expiration of enlistments was not unique to Jackson's army and was, in fact, a major difficulty in nearly all of the American offensives of this time.[53] By the end of 1813 the lack of supplies and the constant turnover of troops had prevented any American army from making a decisive blow against the Creeks. This situation undoubtedly caused most contemporary Americans and many historians to overrate the Red Stick menace. Creeks with firearms were very good warriors, but in 1813 and early 1814 nearly all of them were poorly armed. Only when they had an equal number of men and arms were they any match for an American army. Unfortunately for the Red Sticks, the American armies usually outnumbered them by at least three to one, and the Indians were always poorly armed. Despite the difficulties which the Americans suffered, the battles of 1813 were not without success. A good part of the Creeks' food supply was destroyed and about 1,000 of their warriors killed.

7

Horseshoe Bend

JACKSON'S ARMY had reached a state of complete disintegration by the end of December 1813. Nearly all his militia and volunteers had returned home, claiming that their terms of service had expired. Jackson was greatly disheartened; he had believed that the terms of enlistment of his volunteers would not expire until spring. There remained only a few volunteers and a company composed mostly of officers under General Coffee.[1] Coffee had been ordered to discharge all the men who demanded their release and to reorganize the remainder into a company, a regiment, or whatever their numbers would permit.[2] In so doing, Coffee was left with one company. The only unit of any significant size in Jackson's army was a force of 60-day volunteers under Colonel William Carroll, which arrived at Huntsville on December 27.[3] Carroll's troops, along with a few small detachments, provided Jackson with about 800 recruits, giving him an army of about 1,000 men. Not willing to be delayed again, Jackson took his small army and made a raid into the heart of the Creek Nation.[4]

One reason for Jackson's difficulty in getting together a new army was reports of hunger and cold, which caused men to refuse to volunteer and whole companies to desert.[5] Perhaps the largest single group to desert was a unit of about 200 men. These men had marched as far as Huntsville when they decided that conditions were too bad to continue. They deserted en masse and went home.[6] The rumors of hunger were well founded. Jackson continued to encounter difficulty in getting food delivered to his army. This situation was never again as critical as it had been during November, and the smaller army made the problem easier to solve.[7] They were frequently hungry during January 1814, partly because the men being discharged were loading themselves with rations for the homeward march.[8]

In January, Jackson once again demonstrated the superhuman will which would eventually propel him to victory. With so few troops and the ever present supply problem, Governor Blount suggested that he abandon the campaign; but Jackson remained at his post and ultimately shamed the governor into calling out another 2,500 men from West Tennessee. Even with these additions, it was hard to keep an army of sufficient size because of the large number of desertions.[9]

The general concluded that to have an effective force he needed a small detachment of regular army troops attached to his organization. This unit would provide him with a corps of dependable men at critical times with which he could keep discipline in his militia forces. He, therefore, requested General Pinckney to assign the Thirty-ninth Regiment of regulars to him.[10] Pinckney granted the request, but the regiment was unable to reach him soon enough to take part in his next campaign into Creek territory.[11]

At the very time when Jackson's army was reduced to its lowest level, persistent rumors were reaching him that there were large numbers of Indians collecting for an attack and, even worse, that the British were preparing to land at Pensacola.[12] These rumors confirmed Jackson's belief that the Indians must be quickly defeated before the British could bring them aid.[13] This intelligence concerning the British was an exaggeration, and later information showed that although three British ships had visited Pensacola, they had not landed troops.[14] There was a possibility, however, that these ships were unloading arms for the Indians.

For several months Jackson had received numerous accounts concerning a very large fortified encampment of Red Sticks located in a horseshoe bend near the mouth of the Emuckfau Creek on the Tallapoosa River. Convinced that this place contained the main force of Creek hostiles, he believed that its demolition would end the war.[15] Need for the immediate destruction of the enemy was not Jackson's sole motivation. He was also certain that his 60-day men would become completely disheartened if he remained in camp much longer. Considering all of these factors, Jackson decided that his advance, which was actually planned as a raid, must start immediately. He crossed the Coosa River on January 15, 1814, with almost his entire command, even stripping his garrison at Fort Strother to the bare minimum.[16]

The army Jackson took to the field was composed of the 800 volunteers and about 130 other men, including General Coffee's company of officers, and some 100 friendly Creek and Cherokee Indians. These Indians were

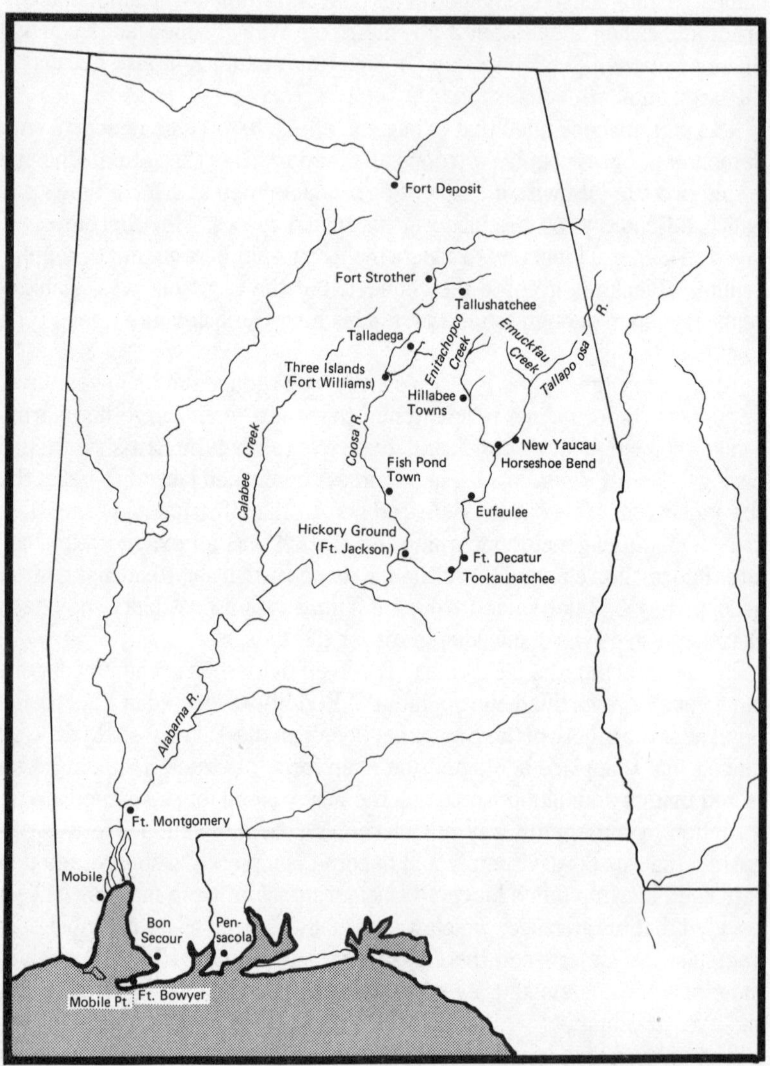

Jackson's operations

poorly armed and somewhat disheartened by the small size of the white army. With this tiny force, Jackson made a daring plunge southward into the heart of the Creek country.[17]

The general had two objectives in executing this raid. He was not only anxious to march again on the Creeks but he was also hopeful of creating a diversion for the advance of General Floyd's army from Georgia.[18] This inexperienced army which Jackson pushed into battle in January 1814 was probably the only American army during the entire Creek War which went on an offensive action against a superior number of Indians. In this campaign Jackson's troops had two advantages—they were better armed than the Indians; they had volunteered for service and seemed willing to withstand the necessary hardships.[19]

On January 18 Jackson reached Talladega, where he was joined by an additional small detachment of friendly Indians. After a three-day march, his raw troops camped for the night at a point about three miles from the Red Stick position at Emuckfau. Being so close to the enemy position, the general expected an attack at any time. About six o'clock in the morning the Indians made their assault on the left flank and rear of Jackson's army and continued the fight for about one-half hour. After daylight his left wing, commanded by General Coffee, charged and routed the enemy.[20]

Thinking the Red Sticks were defeated, Jackson ordered Coffee with 400 of his men and all the Indians to destroy their camp. Upon his approach to the camp, Coffee realized that the enemy's position and numbers were too strong for his troops to destroy, and he retired to his own lines. Within an hour the Indians commenced a new attack. Again Coffee counterattacked the hostiles, this time with 200 men.[21] Coffee's advance moved a considerable distance forward, and his command became scattered. The Indians quickly realized that Coffee had only about 50 men with him, and they immediately brought the white troops under heavy fire. The detachment eventually drove off the Indians, but not before Coffee was wounded and Major Alexander Donelson, his brother-in-law, was killed.

At this point Jackson, with a large number of wounded to care for, decided to abandon the offensive, convinced that his army was not strong enough to capture the Indian town. On his return march to Fort Strother, January 23, 1814, he was burdened with 23 men wounded badly enough to have to be carried on litters, and he constantly expected the Red Sticks to renew their attack.

After a withdrawal of about ten miles, Jackson camped near Enitachopco Creek. The next morning while crossing the creek, the rear of the army was attacked by the Red Sticks. Anticipating this action, the general, wishing to avoid an ambush, had ordered his army to approach the creek in an open area some distance from the usual crossing point.[22] The ferocity of the Red Sticks proved too much for his half-trained troops, and they broke and ran in panic. Luckily, some of the old long-service companies managed to check the retreat. Jackson's six-pounder, firing grapeshot, broke the hostiles' charge, and the Red Sticks fled from the field.

The Americans resumed their march back to Fort Strother with no additional action by the Indians. Jackson listed his casualties on this expedition as 20 killed and 75 wounded. He reported that he had counted 189 dead Indians and that there were probably a good many more. The mission was considered successful because it was believed that the planned diversion, created for General Floyd, had demoralized the enemy during a critical period. Also a good route had been discovered by which the main stronghold of the enemy could be reached.[23] The raid was in reality a reconnaissance in force, and in this respect it was extremely valuable.

The battles of Emuckfau and Enitachopco, while not major victories, came at a time when morale in Washington was at a low ebb and the administration needed good news to report. As a result, these battles were given much praise and probably more consideration than they merited. In any case, they helped to make the name of Jackson a familiar word in Washington and gave considerable stimulus to recruiting in Tennessee.[24]

Jackson's persistence in holding his army together and his determination to continue the Creek campaign to a conclusion also had an important effect on Pinckney. The commanding general had gradually become convinced that Jackson was the best and most energetic general in the field against the Creeks. As early as January 1814 Pinckney had clearly determined to put his main trust in Jackson's army and to provide him with all available resources of men and material. This special regard can be seen in his assignment of the Thirty-ninth Regiment to Jackson's army and by the orders sent to Governor Blount to keep the Tennessee general's ranks filled at all times with new militia as the old terms expired.[25] Pinckney eventually suggested to the secretary of war that the government would do well to consider elevating Jackson to the rank of general in the regular service.[26]

Even before this latest campaign, Pinckney seemed to have agreed with Jackson's appraisal that the Creeks could be defeated with one more strong offensive. In early January the hostile Creeks amounted to about 4,000 poorly armed men. Pinckney thought that Jackson could with little hardship defeat the whole lot with an army of 2,000 men. He doubted that much service could be had from the 60-day men; when Jackson was able to make use of these troops on his January raid, Pinckney was duly impressed with his ingenuity.

The commanding general advised Jackson that the best means of advance would be either to build boats to carry his supplies or to build a wagon road.[27] Previous attempts to carry enough supplies by wagon had convinced Jackson that water transportation would provide a much more satisfactory supply system. In support of this plan, Jackson had his 60-day volunteers perform a final service by building twelve boats. As soon as his boats were finished and the replacements had arrived, he would be ready to start his long campaign.[28]

February and early March were taken up by assembling and training his new army. He also used this time to alleviate the possibility of future supply problems by building more boats and collecting wagons in preparation for his next advance. These winter months were also used to scout the enemy. Never again would Jackson enter an area without knowing where to find the enemy. The scouts reported that fortifications near Emuckfau and the village of Tohopeka were still heavily manned by hostile Indians, but a food shortage had forced some of them to leave.[29]

Jackson's new army grew rapidly but, most important of all, with the Thirty-ninth Regiment he was able to maintain a strong discipline.[30] By February, Jackson's situation with regard to his army was excellent. Governor Blount had called out 5,000 militia troops, perhaps twice the number needed. This surplus of manpower caused Jackson, with the approval of Pinckney, to adopt tough discipline, hoping to diminish his oversized army by driving the soft troops to desertion.[31]

The policy of rigid discipline cost Jackson some popularity. His army was slow to assemble, thus delaying the new campaign at its outset. Harsh discipline forced Jackson to court-martial even several officers, including Isaac Roberts, one of his generals. Roberts had halted his men outside camp and had tried to exact a promise from the general that the men would serve not more than three months. Jackson refused to agree to any terms, and the entire force of about 200 men began their march home. At this point Jackson arrested General Roberts and declared his unit deserters, but he agreed to pardon them and allow the three-months' term if they would return. Eventually most of them came back.

Roberts and his men were not the only troops to be discontented with Jackson's authority. General John Cocke continued to make trouble, even after his disastrous attack on the Hillabees in November 1813. Orders had been given the general to raise a force of men in East Tennessee, and by February he had assembled a number of six-month militia. He was not satisfied to give Jackson complete command of the troops of his division. He complained bitterly before his assembled troops that Governor Blount had been unfair and had acted illegally in calling all the six-months troops from East Tennessee.[32] General George Doherty reported Cocke's words: "If the men were taken to Jackson, they would be placed in a situation he did not like to mention, which he could not endure to witness, as it would not be in his power to extract them, that they would suffer from want of provisions on hand, that those who had a desire to serve a 6 months tour, would be compelled to serve it in Mobile, & those who had not, had better return home now from this camp—that Jackson had the regulars under his command, & would turn his artillery upon them—call to his assistance the 3rd US Infantry commanded by Col. Gilbert Russell, making in all 1500, and would compel them to serve 6 months–9 months and a year if he chose."[33]

Jackson was greatly agitated by this conduct, and he decided to arrest Cocke. Uncertain of his authority, he ordered General Doherty from Cocke's division to make the arrest. However, Cocke had left camp with some of his men before Doherty received the command to make the arrest, and it was not possible to execute the order at that time.

Cocke and the other dissidents were eventually arrested after they had reached Tennessee.[34] Pinckney upheld Jackson's proposed arrest, despite his concern over jurisdictional difficulties.[35] General Cocke was acquitted of the charges placed against him, possibly because most of the witnesses were still with Jackson's army and could not testify. In any case, acquittal was probably inevitable since Cocke was, after all, a powerful politician in East Tennessee.[36]

One incident which won Jackson the undying hatred of many Tennesseans was the execution of an eighteen-year-old private, John Woods, for disobeying orders. This was a legal sentence, but one seldom carried out. Jackson was called a butcher because of this execution, but the example served to reinforce discipline as planned.[37]

With these disciplinary problems settled, Jackson was ready to march into the Creek country and destroy the last major stronghold of the enemy. He found the Coosa River navigable to a place called Three Islands, 27 miles below Talladega. He determined to move all supplies to that point, where he would build a fort. From this new base at Three Islands it was a distance of only 40 miles to the camp of the enemy near Emuckfau on the Tallapoosa.[38]

The march from Fort Strother was begun on March 14, 1814. The regulars were sent down the river with the boats and supplies, and the rest of the army traveled overland to the new depot at Fort Williams.[39] Although the march was difficult and the movement on the Coosa was complicated by low water, Colonel John Williams managed to get the supply boats within a mile and a half of the site of Fort Williams before they finally grounded. The supplies were then carried overland the last, short distance to the fort.[40] Jackson's army, having reached Fort Williams, was ready to make the final assault on the Indians, waiting in their fortified camp.

According to the reports of George Stiggins, the Creeks had been badly disheartened with their defeats at Autosse and Calabee and by Jackson's raid. Although they had damaged the white forces, they had not been able to destroy them and had themselves suffered heavy losses in these attacks. About the only remaining leader of importance who was at Horseshoe Bend was Chief Menewa. This chief had opposed the war party for a long time, but he was now leading the Red Sticks at Horseshoe Bend. He was known as a brave and skillful warrior, and it came as no surprise when he and his men gave a good account of themselves against a greatly superior force.[41]

Jackson's strength at the time of his march into Creek country was 3,500 men. He left about 1,000 of them as guards at the various forts which he had established on his advance. However, he was reinforced by friendly Indians, and American strength was over 3,000 at Horseshoe Bend.[42]

Soon after his arrival at Fort Williams, Jackson was heavily reinforced by William McIntosh at the head of some Creek Indians who had formerly been with Floyd's Georgia army. This addition was most fortunate because McIntosh's Creeks were able to furnish excellent intelligence about the country and the disposition of the hostiles. They did, however, present a serious drain on the dwindling food supply.[43]

After some delay, Jackson left Fort Williams on March 24, 1814, and marched toward Emuckfau Creek. He camped near Emuckfau, the site of his engagement with the Red Sticks two months earlier.[44] From this location he could easily attack the enemy. About 1,000 Indians of the Oakfusky, New Yaucau, Hillabee, Fish Pond, and Eufaula towns had gathered at their camp in the bend of the river. Their fortifications consisted of a breastwork erected across the neck of the bend. The barrier, which ranged from five to eight feet high, was prepared with double rows of portholes arranged in such a way that an army could not approach without being exposed to a double crossfire. Because of the curvature of the breastwork, it could not have been raked by cannon, even if one flank of it had been taken. The engineering of the fort was excellent, according to all observers.

Jackson attacked on March 27,1814. Coffee and his mounted troops, along with most of the friendly Indians, crossed the river about two miles below the encampment and surrounded the bend on the far bank. This maneuver would prevent any of the Indians from making their escape across or down the river.[45] The Indians planned to defend the land side of the bend if they could. In case of defeat, they had provided a number of canoes for an escape either by crossing or by going down the river. Coffee's men were well positioned by the time the Indians realized that a general attack was under way. As soon as they heard Jackson's cannon firing, some of the Indians with Coffee swam the river and seized or cut adrift the enemy canoes, thus destroying the escape route. Part of Coffee's troops crossed the river in canoes and captured the hostile village against little resistance. Having accomplished their first objective, the Americans and friendly Indians were able to advance to a point where they could fire on the enemy breastworks from the rear. Coffee's advance force was never strong enough to drive the enemy from his fortifications, but the charge at the rear made it much more difficult for the Indians to hold their lines against Jackson, who was attacking the front.[46]

In the meantime, Jackson had taken the remainder of his troops and formed them into a position along the point of land in front of the breastworks. He emplaced his artillery, which consisted of a six-pounder and a three-pounder, on a small mound or hill about 80 yards from the nearest point of the works. At about 10:30 A.M., the Americans opened fire on the enemy with both artillery and small arms, continuing the bombardment for approximately two hours. Jackson at this time learned that Coffee's troops were burning the hostiles' village and had reached a position behind the enemy lines. The time had arrived to make the final assault. A charge was quickly organized, and was led by Colonel Williams' Thirty-ninth Regiment and supported by part of General Doherty's brigade on the right and part of General Thomas Johnson's brigade on the left. After heavy fighting, Jackson's troops carried the enemy line. Once their defenses were broken, the Indians were cut into small groups. Many of them continued fighting until darkness in various areas of the 80- to 100-acre peninsula. There were 350 Indian women captured, but only three warriors were taken prisoners. An undetermined number managed to make their escape.[47]

It was noted at the beginning of the battle that part of General Coffee's force crossed the river and took up a position behind the enemy lines. The remainder formed itself around the bend, and a detachment took possession of a small island located along the curve of the bend. From these positions Coffee's brigade was able to prevent the enemy from escaping across the river. Many of the Indians tried to hide under the bluffs formed by parts of the bank, but most of these positions were open on the river side and were easily brought under heavy fire by Coffee's forces.[48]

Other Red Sticks tried to swim down the river or to cross it and break through the American lines. According to Coffee, several hundred Indians tried to cross the river, but almost all of these were killed. Coffee estimated that between 250 and 300 Indians were killed in the water, and their bodies either sank or floated down the river. That loss was in addition to the 557 dead Indians found on the battlefield. This made an estimated total loss to the Indians in this battle of between 800 and 900 killed. Jackson and Coffee did not believe that more than 15 or 20 of the Indians escaped during the night, but it is possible that the number was much larger than this. According to Talwatustunugge, a Hillabee who was wounded nine times in the fighting at Horseshoe Bend, a large number of the Red Sticks, perhaps 200, did escape during the night.

The casualties in Jackson's army were 49 killed and 153 wounded. The loss that grieved Jackson the most was the death of his friend Major Lemuel Montgomery of the Thirty-ninth Infantry, who was killed in the charge on the breastworks.[49] Jackson and the other officers considered the power of the Creeks completely broken with this decisive defeat. Whether this was true or not, their last large concentration was destroyed and their forces were disorganized and scattered.[50]

There was little doubt that the Indians resisted to the bitter end and that their fortification was strongly built. In fact, Jackson and several other observers were most impressed with the strength and military manner with which the Indians had fortified their camp.[51] In terms both of the numbers of persons killed and of its importance to the war, Horseshoe Bend would have to rank high among the major battles of the War of 1812. This defeat of the Indians did not come too soon for the Americans. Within two months the British had landed troops in the South with an enormous arms supply for the Indians. If the Red Sticks had not been scattered and demoralized by the Battle of Horseshoe Bend, they would have constituted a great danger to the entire southern area.

The ratio of Indians killed in the battles with the whites often ran as high as 10 to 1, as it did at the Battle of Horseshoe Bend. It does indeed seem strange that the Indian losses were so high, especially when the whites attacked a fortified position. Why did this happen? It was not that the Indians lacked bravery or that the white forces were better trained. The answer is to be found in three factors: armament, leadership, and numbers.

Most American leaders considered the Creek War to have ended with the Battle of Horseshoe Bend. Early in the war the Creeks never had an adequate supply of weapons. As observed, it is probable that no more than

1 in 3 or 1 in 4 had any kind of gun. It is also likely that those who possessed guns had inferior weapons which would not perform properly and were often without ammunition. The result was that Creeks armed with war clubs, bows and arrows, and spears faced Americans well-armed with guns and cannon.[52]

In leadership, the Creek war chiefs, with the exception of Weatherford and perhaps a few others, had no conception of military objectives and were unable to give any direction to their war. In short, they fought bravely as individuals, but often they merely waited for a white army to come in and butcher them. Thus, they lost all advantage of surprise or concentration of numbers which offensive action might have provided them. The most successful battles of the Creeks were fought on the offensive and had objectives, even if simple ones. Not the least important factor in these fights was the superiority in numbers of the whites, nearly always two or three times more than the Indians.

At Horseshoe Bend, Jackson's army, including Indians, was from two and a half to three times larger than the forces of the hostiles. What, after all, could be expected when a large, well-armed force attacked a small, poorly armed force? All the Americans really had to do was get enough troops, food, and transportation together to reach the Indians deep in their own land. Despite the great losses of the hostiles, with more than half of their warriors killed and the rest scattered, many of them might have been ready to continue the fight but they were starving. In all their fighting and vast sweeps, the white soldiers had destroyed almost the entire Indian food supply.[53]

Jackson's next move after the Battle of Horseshoe Bend was to return to Fort Williams for a fresh supply of provisions. While at the fort, he sent to Fort Talladega the prisoners he had taken. Most of the captured goods and many of the prisoners were taken by the friendly Indians, who probably intended to use them as slaves and servants.[54] The army rested a few days and then set out again from Fort Williams. This time Jackson planned to sweep the countryside and advance to the confluence of the Coosa and Tallapoosa rivers.[55]

Jackson knew that he had dealt the Indians a major blow at Horseshoe Bend, but he anticipated at least one more battle. It would probably occur at the Hickory Ground, a major collecting point for the hostiles.[56] During the last days of the campaign, Jackson's army made a swing down the west bank of the Tallapoosa River, burning and destroying all the hostile villages and property to be found. About 20 miles above the convergence of the Coosa and Tallapoosa rivers, he established communications with Colonel

Homer Milton's army on the east bank; the combined armies were able to make a clean sweep of both sides of the river.[57]

Jackson had planned to carry rations for eight days on this expedition, but he was short of wagons and had enough for only five days. At first this appeared inconsequential. Colonel Milton would be able to supply him with the needed provisions when the two armies met.[58] Milton voluntarily sent Jackson supplies, but he refused to accept any orders from the militia officer, thus creating a serious problem of command.[59] Jackson's army reached the fork of the rivers on April 17 and found that Colonel Milton's men had already arrived. However, the needed provisions had been left at Fort Decatur, several miles up the Tallapoosa. Since there was no road, it was necessary to use rafts or boats to make the transfer of supplies. The delay was minor but doubtless annoying for the tired troops of all the armies. Colonel Russell of the Third Regiment, who was to bring numerous boatloads of supplies up the Alabama River from Mobile, had not yet arrived, and this failure was unquestionably a disappointment to the entire army.

By the last of April 1814 all the armies had converged at Fort Jackson, the new fort built at the confluence of the Coosa and the Tallapoosa rivers. Each of the armies had its own officers, and there was some confusion regarding seniority. Colonel Homer Milton was in command of the Georgia troops; Colonel Gilbert Russell had charge of the troops from Mississippi Territory; General Joseph Graham commanded the North Carolina and South Carolina troops; and General Andrew Jackson commanded the Tennessee troops. Milton and Russell were regular army officers, and they doubtless believed they were better qualified to command than Jackson, a militia officer.[60] The correspondence of Colonel Milton, as well as some of his actions, reveals that he was jealous of Jackson. The cause of this friction was quickly removed by the arrival of General Thomas Pinckney. He came in person to Fort Jackson and took command of the whole army.[61]

Jackson, on orders from Pinckney, sent out detachments of his army to search the countryside for hostile Indians and to destroy their villages. His scouting parties found the towns abandoned and the Red Sticks scattered, indicating that the Indian resistance had been broken.[62] Some were running for Pensacola, but many were hiding in the swamps. There were no signs of preparations for another battle. The starving Indians were coming into the American fort to surrender individually and in groups. They were allowed to return to their homes, and because they were completely destitute, the army supplied them with food where it was available.[63]

The most notorious Indian to surrender at this time was William

Weatherford. He was reported to have ridden directly to Jackson's tent to surrender himself. Writing about three years after the Battle of Horseshoe Bend, Anne Royall described this confrontation:

> The Indians had sued for peace; and Jackson, to prove their sincerity, ordered them to bring Witherford, bound, to his camp. Learning what Jackson demanded, Witherford determined to go and surrender himself voluntarily. He gained Jackson's camp without being known, and desired admittance to the General. Jackson, astonished at his presumption, asked him how he dared to appear in his presence, after acting such a part as he did at Fort Mims? Witherford replied—"I am Witherford: I am in your power. Do with me what you please, I am a soldier still. I have done the white people all the harm I could. I have fought them, and fought them bravely. If I had an army, I would fight them still. But I have none! My people are no more!! Nothing is left me but to weep over the misfortunes of my country."
>
> Jackson, admiring the firmness of his address told him, that he . . . would take no advantage of his situation—that he was at liberty to return to his own camp. "But if," said Jackson, "you choose to try the fate of arms once more, and I take you prisoner, your life shall pay for forfeit of your crimes. But if you really wish for peace, stay where you are, and I will protect you."

According to this report, Weatherford replied with deep emotion: " 'Well you may speak to me in this style, now. There was a time, when *I had a choice*. I have none, *now*—even *hope* is ended: Once I could animate my warriors; but I cannot animate the dead. Their bones are bleaching on the plains of Tallushatches, Talladega, and Emuckfau; and I have not surrendered myself without reflection. While there was the *smallest hope*, I remained firm at my post, nor supplicated for peace. But, my warriors are no more: The miseries of my nation affects me with deepest sorrow:'—His voice was lost in emotion for some minutes, and then he added—'But I desire peace for the few that are left. If I had had none but the Georgia army to contend with, I would have raised my corn on one bank of the river, and fought them on the *other*. But your people are a brave people—you are a brave man; and I rely on your generosity. You talk a good talk: My people shall listen to it.' "[64]

Jackson was so much impressed with Weatherford that he allowed him to go free in the face of many demands that he should be executed. While the Indian leader's bravery is beyond question, there is some indication that Jackson had offered him amnesty if he would surrender.[65]

There are many conflicting stories regarding William Weatherford. According to all accounts, Weatherford thought, fought, and dressed like a white man, and he was the most dangerous leader produced by the Creeks. His success, and that of the Creeks when led by him, supports the idea that the Indians, well armed, well led, and aided by the British, would have been an extremely dangerous adversary. Contemporary accounts give many different reasons for Weatherford's decision to join the Red Sticks. One, mentioned earlier, asserted that he joined the hostile faction because they held his family hostage.[66] According to one of his friends, Weatherford had opposed the war but had joined the hostiles, hoping to prevent atrocities which he believed would destroy the Indian nation. A third reason given for his decision was his dislike of Big Warrior, one of the leaders of the friendly Indians. Weatherford considered Big Warrior a coward and an opportunist. Whatever Weatherford's reasons for joining the Red Sticks may have been, it seems that he later became a good friend of Andrew Jackson. He was reported to have visited him at the Hermitage, where he trained horses for many months.[67]

Indians soon began surrendering in large numbers, and it was necessary to make formal arrangements for dealing with them. An agreement was reached whereby the Indians would be allowed to make military capitulation under which they could surrender in groups or as individuals. It was understood that there would be no territorial settlement until a later date.[68] In the meantime, until the peace agreement became final, Americans were garrisoned at Fort Jackson and other posts in the Indian territory. This garrison duty was to be conducted by the militia for the present, but the militia would eventually be replaced by a more permanent force. General Pinckney wanted to use regulars or long-term volunteers for this purpose, since all parties recognized the necessity of keeping a strong garrison to hold the country. The Indians gave the appearance of being subdued, but it was known that many of them were still hostile.[69]

The arrival of the various American armies at Fort Jackson the last of April 1814 ended the first phase of the Creek War. Both Jackson and Pinckney thought at this time that all the large bands of Creeks had been scattered and that the nation had been subdued. Pinckney believed that it would be safe for him to visit the maritime frontiers of his command, which he had long neglected in favor of the Creek War.[70] This period was the low ebb in the fortunes of the Creek Nation, and it has been considered by many as the end of the Creek War. There were, however, still a number of hostile Indians. They ultimately reorganized and, aided by the British, merged their conflict into the War of 1812.

8

The Treaty of Fort Jackson

EVEN BEFORE the Battle of Horseshoe Bend, the secretary of war appointed General Pinckney and Benjamin Hawkins as commissioners to make a peace treaty with the Creek Indians. The Indians were to indemnify the United States for the cost of the war, and within this guideline General Pinckney was to draw up the terms of settlement at his own discretion. Hawkins was to serve as an advisor but would have no real power. This appointment was very unpopular in Tennessee, where it was generally believed that Pinckney and Hawkins would accept easy terms. Many influential westerners in Washington demanded replacement of these men by persons favoring a harsher settlement. To be more specific, they wanted a very large land cession and feared that Pinckney and Hawkins would not get it.[1]

The concern of the Tennesseans was well founded. In April, almost immediately after assuming his duty as commissioner, Pinckney presented the Indians with the following, relatively easy terms:

> The United States will [retain] so much of the conquered territory as may appear to the Government . . . a just indemnity for the expenses of the war and as a retribution for the injuries sustained by its citizens and by the friendly Creek Indians.
>
> The U. States will retain the right to establish military posts and trading houses, and to make and use such roads as they think necessary, and freely to navigate all the rivers and water courses in the Creek territory.
>
> The enemy must on their part surrender their prophets and such other instigators of the War as may be designated by the Govern-

ment of the U. States, and they must agree to such restrictions upon trade with foreign nations as shall be established by the Government of the U. States.[2]

Pinckney hoped that these rather generous terms would induce the remaining hostiles to bring about a quick end to the war. In spite of western objections to the leniency of these demands, it was not Pinckney and Hawkins who had made them. The items that Pinckney outlined for the Indians were almost an exact copy of his instructions from the secretary of war. If the terms were too conciliatory to satisfy the Tennessee leaders, the fault lay in Washington.[3]

The main spokesman for the western view was Andrew Jackson, who clearly indicated his displeasure with the proposed settlement. He contended that the Creeks should be forced to give up all of their land west of the Coosa and north of the Alabama rivers. The southern boundary could be settled later, but he thought there should be a break in the communication among Creeks, Spaniards, and Seminoles.[4]

On May 22, 1814, Jackson was offered the rank of brigadier of the line and a brevet rank of major general in the United States Army. His command was to be the Seventh Military District. This district comprised Louisiana, Tennessee, Mississippi Territory, and most of the Creek Nation. In the district there was a total military force of only 3,022 regular troops.[5] Before Jackson had had time to reply, Secretary of War Armstrong, assuming that he would accept, ordered him to relieve Pinckney at Fort Jackson and to complete the treaty with the Creeks.[6] Almost as soon as Jackson was appointed to the regular army, his rank in that army increased to major general. He filled the vacancy in that grade created by the resignation of Major General William Henry Harrison.[7]

Jackson, as a representative of the land-hungry westerners, wanted to destroy the power of the Creek Nation once and for all. Therefore, it came as no surprise to anyone when he instituted far harsher demands on the nation than those first proffered.[8] Even before the general could reach Fort Jackson to complete the treaty with the Creeks, he was deluged with a series of dispatches which indicated that there was still a large group of hostiles gathered at Pensacola and Apalachicola under the command of Peter McQueen and Josiah Francis. These Indians had been ready to surrender before the British arrived with massive amounts of arms and ammunition. In addition to the supplies, the British landed a small force of Royal Marines to train the Indians. With the presentation of this aid, the Indians were no longer interested in peace.[9] Many hostiles agreed to continue the war and, worse, there was evidence of serious disaffection among the friendly Creeks.[10]

This activity caused Jackson great concern that the British might reactivate the Indian war on a greater scale, perhaps winning support from most of the southern tribes. In spite of the threats of renewed hostility, he did not reduce his demands for land or moderate the proposed treaty in any way. He was careful to be firm and to keep his word at all times.[11] Jackson hoped to intimidate the friendly Indians while he finished destroying the hostiles.

Benjamin Hawkins, always a friend to the Indians, believed that the peace settlement proposed by Jackson was far too severe, especially in its dealings with the loyal Indians. He believed that there was a real danger of all the Creeks joining the British.[12] This difference of opinion led to a bitter conflict between Hawkins and Jackson.

At first, the United States government placed no credence in the reports that the British were preparing an invasion of the southern coast. The secretary of war did not think that they would attack during the "sickly season" (hot weather), and that would last for another three months. Secretary Armstrong was right in assuming that they had no plans for an attack during the summer or early fall, but he apparently did not realize that the British activity among the Indians was to be the foundation of a major offensive planned for the late fall or winter. Since he did not consider an attack imminent, the secretary ordered Jackson to discharge his militia as soon as possible, leaving only the regulars. Armstrong believed 3,000 regulars would be adequate to defend the area against a few renegade Creeks and for the moment refused to authorize more troops for the Seventh District.[13] Only a few days after the secretary issued this order, Jackson confirmed the landing of the British at Apalachicola.[14]

Jackson was ordered to relieve Pinckney in May, but the delay of communication and transportation prevented him from reaching Fort Jackson until July 10, 1814. Immediately upon his arrival, he called a meeting of the Creek chiefs for the first day of August.[15] He discovered that concessions promised to the Indians by Hawkins and Pinckney had greatly complicated his treaty plans. These assurances led the loyal Indians to believe that land would be taken only from the hostile faction. When it was found that the United States government planned to annex about 22 million acres of land, more than half the area of the Creek Nation, there was understandably great bitterness. Not only was this territory to come from the hostile faction, but there was also to be considerable loss of land by the Indians who had fought on the side of the whites.[16]

The Creeks were shocked and angered by Jackson's terms. No one, including Hawkins, had had any idea that the demands for land would be so unjust. Although Jackson himself had indicated that the lands north of the Alabama and west of the Coosa would be ceded, the only written instructions from Washington were the orders given to Pinckney. These terms, as has been shown, were conciliatory. Jackson was supposed to have been sent a copy of the same instructions, but either he failed to receive them or he would not acknowledge the fact.

The extensive grants demanded from the Indians were almost certainly Jackson's own idea, undoubtedly supporting the views of the Tennesseans.[17] Whatever his authority, he showed himself to be exceedingly firm in his dealings with the Creeks.* Every chief at the meeting was opposed to the treaty and made his objections known. Some were very eloquent with their speeches attacking the treaty, and apparently every person present believed that the Creeks were being treated unfairly, except Jackson, who remained completely unmoved.[18]

Jackson stated in his talks to the Indians that they had allowed Tecumseh to come among them and arouse them to spill blood; therefore, the entire nation was at fault and must pay for the war. The loyal Creeks should have seized Tecumseh when he came to them and sent him as a prisoner to "Their Great Father the President; or have cut his throat." Since they had done neither, they would have to bear the consequences. He told them that if they did not accept his terms, they were free to move to Florida and join the British or the Spanish. He would give any Indian wishing to make such a trip food and ammunition. They could go, but they ought to know that he would soon follow them and invade Florida himself.[19]

John H. Eaton, Jackson's friend and biographer, may have best explained the general's dislike of his Creek allies. According to Eaton, Jackson considered that the friendly Creeks had, when they joined his army, "entered the ranks of an invading army" and were trying to exterminate their own people and destroy their own nation. This made them "as traitors to their country and justly deserving the severest punishment."[20] Jackson apparently considered his Creek allies to be in the same class as the loyalists during the American Revolution.

When at length the Creeks realized that they could not persuade Jackson

*Michael P. Rogin, in *Fathers and Children,* agrees with the conclusion that Jackson's own will and personality forced the Indian cession. However, in focusing most of his attention on Jackson and the development of the general's attitudes, Rogin probably fails to give enough consideration to the fact that Jackson's views were a reflection of prevailing frontier sentiment.

to give up his demands, they signed the treaty and agreed not to block the surveying of the new boundary. As a protest, they insisted that a copy of the mild terms which had been sent to General Pinckney by the secretary of war be attached to the treaty when it was sent to Washington. In an effort to shame the general by their generosity, the Creek chiefs granted Jackson a three-mile-square tract of land. They gave an equal amount to Hawkins and smaller grants to George Mayfield and Alexander Cornells. These parcels were given as a show of appreciation for the services rendered by Hawkins and the others and probably by contrast were expected to embarrass Jackson.[21] The Creeks hoped to save face by making it look as if the treaty had not been forced upon them. The Indian stratagem was somewhat damaged when Congress refused to ratify the grant.[22]

Hawkins viewed the terms of the treaty proposed by Jackson as cruel and unjust and a breach of good faith. Pinckney had discussed generous terms with the Creeks, and Jackson had repudiated them.* Hawkins advised the Indians to sign the treaty but made it clear that he objected to its terms.[23] Indian reaction to the unfair treaty was quick in coming. Almost as soon as it had been signed, there was a raid of some settlements below Hartford near the junction of the Flint and Chattahoochee rivers. If nothing else, this attack proved that there were hostile elements still active in the Creek Nation.[24]

Hawkins protested strongly to his superiors concerning Jackson's high-handed treatment of the Indian allies. His angry attacks on Jackson were logical and probably entirely justified. Unfortunately, the text of his letters remains unknown. The most detailed file was written to the secretary of war, and all Hawkins' correspondence which deals with the Creek treaty is missing from the secretary's file.[25]**

*Numerous recent critics have attacked the policy of Indian removal and assimilation, but certainly in the nineteenth century this was an alternative to extermination. As early as 1803 Thomas Jefferson was promoting Indian removal. He wrote Andrew Jackson that the Louisiana Purchase would "open an asylum for these unhappy people, in a country which may suit their habits of life better than what they now occupy, which perhaps they will be willing to exchange with us" (Thomas Jefferson to Andrew Jackson, Sept. 19, 1803, Andrew Jackson Papers, LC). To condemn the government for following such a policy, in the words of Reginald Horsman, "would be to ask that nineteenth century Americans should have twentieth century values" *(Indian Removal,* p. 18).

**That these letters were deliberately removed is certain. They nearly all dealt with the Creek settlement and were probably all highly critical of Jackson. Hawkins' financial settlements dealing with the Indians, and other letters, are all available; only those letters critical of Jackson are missing. Unfortunately for the Jackson sympathizers, who probably removed the letters, the register of letters

Once Jackson's terms were known to the friendly Creeks, their desire to kill Red Sticks cooled considerably, and grumbling became widespread. Most of the Indians who had fought on the side of the United States remained to be fed by the Americans, and despite their disgust they had nowhere else to turn.[26] Fear rather than loyalty kept nearly all the southern Indians on the side of the Americans, and, as Jackson had believed, the example of hard treatment of the Red Sticks proved to be a good lesson for the Indians.

The treaty that was finally signed at Fort Jackson on August 9, 1814, did not represent a compact between the United States and the hostile Creeks. This extraordinary document was signed by thirty-five friendly chiefs and probably only one who had been a Red Stick.[27] One chief could hardly speak for the war faction of the Creek Nation. The result was that neither the hostiles nor the British ever recognized the validity of the Treaty of Fort Jackson. In spite of its questionable origin, this pact represented a complete victory for the western settlers. If enforced, it would break the power of the southern Indians and clear millions of acres for use by the white man.

At the time the treaty was signed, it was generally believed that, except for the hostiles who had fled to Pensacola, all of the Lower Creeks and Seminoles were friendly. The Seminoles, who had thus far appeared more or less peaceful, were the only remaining large force of uncommitted Indians.[28] They fought briefly during the so-called Patriots' War in Florida, but they retreated rather than fight to the finish and later seemed to follow a policy of neutrality.[29] Many of the Lower Creeks who dwelt on the middle and upper parts of the Flint and Chattahoochee rivers, near Hawkins' agency, did join the war on the side of the United States. The Indians lower down on the rivers and those below the line in Florida had remained quiet, or had furnished a few warriors for the Americans. For the most part, they had not openly participated in the war on either side. In nearly all American reports they were classed as friendly or, more commonly, ignored completely.

The great problem both of contemporaneous observers and of historians of today is to determine which Indians were Creeks and which were

---

received by the secretary of war remained, and in most cases the register gives a brief summary of all letters received. Hawkins' specific criticisms are missing, but it is usually possible to see that the letter was not friendly. For example, on Aug. 16, 1814, Hawkins wrote to the secretary of war asking that Jackson be removed as a negotiator with the Creek Indians. Since this request was made after the signing of the treaty, it is probable that Hawkins hoped to repudiate its terms.

Seminoles. Most of the Seminoles were of Muskogean origin, and in colonial times the Seminoles had been part of the Creek Nation. Because of this close relationship, the Indians themselves frequently did not know whether they were classified as Creeks or Seminoles.[30] About the only sound rule was to say that the Indians living below the boundary line in Florida would be called Seminoles and those living above the line in the United States would be called Creeks.[31] These two groups of Indians, partly Creek and partly Seminole, were relatively untouched by the war. There had been no American troops in their territory. Their crops and towns had not been destroyed, but the large number of refugees from other areas of the Creek Nation caused a shortage of food. Hunger was thus a serious problem, even in Florida. John Floyd, Thomas Pinckney, and Benjamin Hawkins suspected that some of these people were not friendly to the United States, but neither Jackson nor any of his superiors in Washington seemed to realize that the groups existed.

The Lower Creeks and Seminoles probably had the strongest British ties of any of the southern Indians. These people had traded with the English ever since the end of the Revolutionary War and had supported William A. Bowles and other British adventurers. Because of their attachment to the English cause, they had been less influenced by the prophets than the Upper Creeks had been. They had followed the British suggestion and were content to wait for troops and supplies before attacking the Americans. These Indians constituted a sort of shadow force, which was extremely hostile to the Americans but largely unknown to them.[32]

John K. Mahon has suggested that there was so much hatred between the Red Sticks and the Lower Creeks that they could never become allies, and, even though the Lower Creeks lost land by the Treaty of Fort Jackson, they would not fight the Americans.[33] The Lower Creeks were the real friends of the British, and the British alliance was with them rather than with the Red Sticks.[34]

When the British landed supplies at Apalachicola in May 1814, the Perrymans and many others in the area promptly joined them.[35] Existing records show that at about the time of the peace negotiations with the United States, the British sent representatives to the friendly Creeks. Big Warrior was one of the principal leaders of the loyal Indians, and before the end of 1814 his representatives were negotiating with the British.[36] It may have been that Big Warrior's representatives were sent to Apalachicola to spy for the Americans, but their true loyalty will always be an open question. It was observed by Major Edward Nicolls, commander of the British force at Apalachicola, that Big Warrior and his followers had adopted a wait-and-see policy; and if the British had been successful in their efforts to capture Mobile and New Orleans, the so-called friendly Indians would have joined them en masse.[37]

Jackson, while waiting to begin negotiations of the Creek peace treaty, had sent out numerous scouts and spies to discover the nature of the British landings at Pensacola and Apalachicola. His agents were able to provide a sizable amount of information concerning the proposed British expedition against the Gulf Coast. One of the most alarming reports was that the enemy planned to land black troops from Jamaica.[38] Although much of the information was exaggerated, the subsequent British landings and aid to the Indians did confirm Jackson's worst fears.[39]

With this warning constantly being brought to the general's attention, he moved his headquarters to Mobile, closer to the source of his espionage reports.[40] The names and addresses of most of Jackson's informants indicate that they were located either in Pensacola or in New Orleans. They directly or indirectly included John and James Innerarity of the John Forbes Company, along with other well-known residents of the area. Since Pensacola was a neutral Spanish port, it was not under the regular British blockade and received a constant supply of letters and newspapers from the islands of the Gulf and the Caribbean. One such account was published in the *Royal Gazette and Bahama Advertiser* August 17, 1814. This item reported that Lord Rowland Hill was on his way to America with 30,000 veterans. The destination was given as the Chesapeake Bay; but with the obvious preparations in the area by the British, Jackson had good reason to expect that the Gulf Coast was a likely target.[41] An examination of a number of West Indian newspapers available to the Americans through Pensacola indicated that this type of information was contained in all of them.[42]

Jackson had long considered Pensacola as a possible base for British operations, and he believed it should be well scouted. Spain was officially neutral, and his representatives could legally enter the place. In the early summer of 1814 he sent Captain John Jones to Pensacola to study the defenses of the place. As a result of Jones' notes, he was provided with an excellent description of the defenses of the town.[43]

Jackson arrived in Mobile August 27, 1814, and immediately requested that Governor Blount send the entire Tennessee militia to that place as soon as possible. This urgent request was based on information found in Havana newspapers and in reports from Antoine Collin of Pensacola. It was learned that thirteen ships of the line and transports carrying 10,000 men were expected daily for an assault on Mobile and Louisiana. Intelligence also indicated that the Russians had offered the British 10,000 men for this attack.[44] Another, more exaggerated account coming at the same time stated that the treaty ceding Louisiana had been declared null and void by the English, and 40,000 British and 25,000 Spanish troops were ready to go to America to recapture Louisiana. This report was especially interesting because it was written by Pedro Alva, interpreter for Governor González Manrique at Pensacola.[45] Governor Claiborne of Louisiana received the same information in New Orleans.[46]

When these reports first reached Jackson, the strength of his forces was dangerously low to face an invasion. After an initial refusal of reinforcements by the secretary of war, who did not take the threat seriously, Jackson was at last given authority to make a rapid build-up in the Gulf area. This increase in strength was very fortunate, as events soon proved. Even a few more days' delay would have been disastrous.

9

British Arrival on the Gulf

THE TREATY of Fort Jackson, although it did not completely end the Creek War, did reduce the scale of Indian hostilities in the South. With a slowdown of the Indian War, the emphasis of the conflict in that region shifted from fighting the Indians to fighting the British. The spring of 1814 saw the United States forces better trained and with better officers than ever before. In the South, American forces were now well led by an able and proven new general, Andrew Jackson.

On the Canadian border the American army was commanded by the young generals Jacob Brown and George Izard. The navy on the Great Lakes was also well led and had managed to destroy or stalemate British naval actions in the area. This notable improvement in American forces facing Canada came at a most opportune time. Napoleon was finally defeated during the spring of 1814, releasing Wellington's veterans for service in America. In spite of this new advantage, the Marquis of Wellington himself was not confident of victory in America, suggesting that there was no single spot in the United States whose capture would bring about an end to the war.

Perhaps in keeping with this view, the British tried several attacks. Sir George Prevost was given massive reinforcements in Canada, and Major General Robert Ross was sent with a small army as a mobile force to raid the coastal areas of the United States. Ross' troops were supported by the Royal Navy, which instituted a much tighter blockade. It was Ross' army around which Vice Admiral Alexander Inglis Cochrane developed his plan for an attack on the Gulf Coast. The British offensive against the South was already under way when Prevost's failure at Plattsburg and George

Downie's defeat on Lake Champlain in September 1814 left the great Canadian offensive in a stalemate. In late August, General Ross had captured Washington, giving the British a needed victory, one which was celebrated by doubling the number of men assigned to the southern campaign.[1]

A look at the British records will show their plans for the Gulf region. The long-time interest in such a venture by Charles Cameron, governor of Nassau, and numerous Nassau traders has been noted. When he became aware of the existence of large numbers of hostile Indians who were potential allies of Great Britain, he acted at once to notify his superiors of the situation and to gain more knowledge of Indian hostilities.[2*] Much of his information came through merchants who traded at Pensacola and other spots on the Gulf Coast. His best single informant was the trader J. A. Gordon, who supplied Cameron with detailed information concerning Mobile and Pensacola.[3]

Cameron informed his superior in England, Earl Bathurst, that many inhabitants of the Gulf Coast were sympathetic to the British cause. The reports that Bathurst received were fairly complete and included detailed accounts of both the Gulf Coast area and the Creek Indians, written by persons obviously familiar with each subject. This information was undoubtedly used by the higher authorities in London and probably formed a frame of reference for the whole British plan for the Gulf Coast. If the British could arouse these Indians, they would serve as a major diversion for the Americans. The British were for several reasons optimistic about their chances for support from the southern Indians. Most of the tribes had grievances against the Americans and had been allied with the British during the American Revolution. Since that time much of the trade with these Indians in the south had been carried on by the British house Forbes and Company, as noted earlier; and the Indians were partial to English manufacturers. At the time of this report to Bathurst, the Creeks were already at war with the Americans and had successfully tied down the most effective part of the American military establishment in the Gulf area.

The Creeks had attacked prematurely, and as a result the American military had moved into the Gulf area in force. This turn of events dealt a blow to British plans, since it would now be impossible to make a surprise attack on the Gulf. The Indians were potential allies in dire need of aid. The report

*Robin Reilly considers that the plan to capture New Orleans was originated by Admiral Sir John Borlase Warren in November 1812. Undoubtedly Admiral Cochrane was familiar with Warren's proposal, but it is not unlikely that the action was first conceived by Governor Cameron, who persuaded both admirals to consider the plan.

suggested that the best way to help the hostile Creeks would be to send large amounts of supplies to the Perrymans, near Apalachicola.

A second report reminded Bathurst that the Indians could be reached only by a passage through Spanish Florida. Spain was presumed to be neutral in this conflict, and use of her ports might be difficult. The only alternative was to use the unguarded inlets on the Florida coast. British merchants, trading illegally with the Indians, had been using these inlets for years, and pilots were doubtless available for them at Nassau. The report suggested that since Spain was on very good terms with the English, the Spanish might be willing to cooperate if they could do so without appearing nonneutral. This informant was probably aware that the Spanish had already given munitions and supplies to the hostile Creeks. In any case, it was suggested that the captain general of Cuba might be persuaded to evacuate the fort of St. Marks near Apalachicola. If the Spaniards were willing to do that, the British would be able to use the Apalachicola River and Spain could insist to the Americans that they had no knowledge of it. The river mouth was not a good port, but it was navigable to small schooners and would be entirely adequate to serve the Indians, especially if two or more store ships were placed near the entrance to the river. The proposal also suggested that if the British could send young noncommissioned officers to train the Indians, they would become a very effective force.[4]

Bathurst was much impressed by the information. He immediately ordered that every assistance be given to the Indians. His comment on the dispatch indicated that he agreed with Cameron's conclusions and that was the first knowledge he had had of Indian hostilities: "In transmitting the petition of the Creeks and other Indian nations, you have omitted to state whether you were enabled to take any measures for their assistance or relief. I fear, however, from the means at your disposal, that it will not have been in your power to do so, and that the length of time which has elapsed since the transmission of those Petitions to you, may have increased considerably their distress, at the same time it may have diminished their means of resistance to the Americans. You will however take the earliest opportunity of assuring them, that the Prince Regent feels for their situation and has given directions to the Admiral commanding on the station to furnish them with such supplies of arms and ammunition as may satisfy their more immediate necessities, and that no time will be lost by him in endeavoring to open a communication with them. If also it should be in your power to afford them any temporary assistance in the interim, I am sure you will not omit to avail yourself of an opportunity of engaging the attention of the Americans in that quarter and diverting some part of their force from the Frontier of Canada."[5]

There was nothing new in the idea of using the Indians against the Americans. Admiral Sir John Borlase Warren proposed very early in the war that Britain make coastal raids on the United States, especially on the Gulf states. He also believed that slaves in revolt could be used against the enemy. One of Warren's suggestions was to capture New Orleans and garrison the city with black troops. He believed that this tactic would create so much fear of a slave insurrection in the southern states that the South would fall without a fight.[6] The Indians, both northern and southern, had been used in every significant war fought in North America. The use of slaves against their masters was another thing. Bathurst was hesitant to start a servile war, but the idea of coastal raids as a diversion from Canada was uppermost in his mind. Aware that the slaves might support these raids and yet not wishing this activity to be considered a servile war, Bathurst tried to avoid such an allegation by ordering that all blacks who wished to fight the Americans be enlisted in regular units of the British forces.[7]

In some of his earlier correspondence, Bathurst also indicated reluctance to use the Indians as allies, but he soon modified his stand. He probably justified his orders supporting the Creeks by claiming that they were already at war with the Americans. He most likely further reasoned that, while he would have preferred that the Indians remain neutral, the Americans would have armed and used them if the British had not.[8] The order to send arms to the Indians was based on their petitions and on Cameron's first dispatch requesting aid for them.

At Bathurst's order, the British commander in North America, Admiral Alexander Cochrane, first sent Captain Hugh Pigot and later Major Edward Nicolls to Apalachicola to make contact with the Indians. Both men were instructed to confer with Governor Cameron, an expert on the Gulf Coast situation, and their ultimate plans followed closely the recommendations that the governor had sent Bathurst. In preparation for this expedition, Cameron supplied Pigot with an interpreter.[9] The young man in question was probably George Woodbine, a white Jamaican, described by Pigot as "an intelligent young man that had traded with the Indians and is known to many of the chiefs."[10] Pigot appointed him a second lieutenant of the Royal Marines, but he was so impressed with Woodbine that five days later he advanced him to the rank of brevet captain.[11] In addition to Woodbine, Cameron was able to provide Pigot with the services of pilots for the Florida coast, as well as an assortment of goods, which included ornamented cavalry helmets for the chiefs. Alexander Gordon, a Nassau merchant, furnished the expedition with a map of the Apalachicola River and the surrounding country.[12]

Pigot arrived at a point near the Apalachicola River on May 10, 1814, and promptly sent some of his officers ashore to assemble the chiefs. This effort eventually resulted in the gathering of ten Creek and Seminole chiefs and their interpreter, Alexander Durant, the same individuals who had requested English aid in September 1813. Thus eight months later in May 1814, when Pigot brought Captain Woodbine, two noncommissioned officers, and supplies, it was to answer this request.

Soon after his arrival at Apalachicola, Pigot learned that the Indians had suffered a severe defeat at Horseshoe Bend and that almost 1,000 warriors, largely unarmed and starving, had been driven from their homes by the Americans to take refuge in the swamps near Pensacola. Pigot immediately ordered Woodbine to purchase beef from Forbes and Company and send it to these Indians. In addition, Woodbine was ordered to arm them with the 2,000 muskets and ammunition that had been shipped on H.M.S. *Orpheus* for that purpose. Had this aid arrived four or five months sooner, the whole course of the Creek war, and possibly the War of 1812, might have been altered. If the weapons on *Orpheus* had been distributed at that time, the Creeks would have been better armed than their American enemies.

Pigot's report to Admiral Cochrane showed clearly that his estimate of the number of Indians was a guess, and there are significant numerical differences within the report. According to a list enclosed in Pigot's message, there were about 3,250 Creek and Seminole warriors friendly to the British and ready to take up arms against the Americans, but in the body of his letter he claimed there were 3,800 warriors in all. Part of the Indians were at Pensacola and part at Apalachicola. His account enumerated many tribes, but a substantial part of them were Seminoles.[13]

On shore Woodbine established himself at the Forbes' store at Prospect Bluff, several miles up the Apalachicola River. This was considered a good location, since it was a common Indian meeting place, but the harbor was poor. The river was too shallow for the ships, necessitating the use of small boats and Indian canoes for unloading supplies. Unfortunately for the success of the English effort, the shortage of food around Apalachicola was as severe as in the Pensacola area. This shortage proved to be the most serious problem at the Bluff. Until the British were able to send in supply ships with food, it was impossible for them to keep a very large force there. No offensive action could be taken until the Indians were assembled. So critical was the shortage of food in the entire Creek Nation that Woodbine claimed a number of Creek chiefs considered friendly to the Americans had offered to join the British for food, and the Choctaws would abandon the Americans if the British took Mobile.[14]

Captain Pigot was impressed with the Indians he saw, and he liked their enthusiasm. He thought they would make good cavalry men and that good horses were available in the Gulf region. Based on this assumption, Pigot requested 1,000 sets of cavalry accoutrements to be sent to the Creeks. He also believed that the young boys aged ten to fourteen would fight as well as the warriors but were too small to use a musket. Therefore, he requested that a stock of carbines be sent to arm these boys.[15] In due time all of these supplies were sent as part of the massive arms support eventually given to the Indians.[16]

The report, which was to have considerable influence on British plans in the Gulf region, proved, on the whole, to be fairly accurate. Pigot advised that there were only about 3,000 American regulars stationed in wooden forts scattered in various parts of the Creek country, Mississippi Territory, and Louisiana. The local militia and the friendly Indians were the only other available American forces near the Gulf Coast, and the latter would probably join the British as soon as Mobile fell.[17]

The number of American troops estimated by Pigot was accurate. In fact, Jackson did have under his command in the Seventh Military District 3,022 regulars.[18] In addition to an alliance with the Indians, the British captain envisioned the support of Negro slaves from the Georgia frontier. Intelligence furnished by Nassau merchants indicated to Pigot that the defenses of New Orleans were weak, that the French Creoles of Louisiana were generally disaffected toward the Americans, and that the Creoles would either ally themselves with the British or remain neutral. Likewise, he expected that Jean Laffite and the Baratarians, who had no love for the United States, might join the British cause. Encouraged by this information, Pigot passed on to Cochrane a strong recommendation that the British attack New Orleans.[19]

Pigot departed from the mouth of the Apalachicola River around the first of June 1814, leaving Woodbine in charge of the establishment at Prospect Bluff. Pigot immediately sailed for Nassau, where he made his report to Cochrane and prepared to ship additional supplies and arms to the Indians.[20]

The plan to invade the southern coasts and New Orleans must have occurred to a number of British leaders at about the same time. All of them were probably influenced by the proposals of Governor Cameron of Nassau, who sent his reports to Bathurst and also corresponded with Cochrane and Captain Pigot. There was supporting information from British ships which had been using Pensacola, Mobile, and New Orleans for years. One such account of West Florida and the attitude of the Creek Indians, already mentioned, was made by Lieutenant James Stirling of H.M.S. *Brazen*, who spent a month in Pensacola in September and October 1812.[21]

Cochrane's plan to invade the Gulf Coast, with the support of Indian allies, was first mentioned in a letter dated June 20, 1814, to John Wilson Croker, secretary of the Admiralty. This letter and other documents on the subject were later combined into a memorandum entitled "Expedition against New Orleans," a summary detailing the evolution of the entire operation and suggesting its value. The basic plan was to take advantage of the American weakness previously described by Captain Pigot. Cochrane wanted to arm the Indians and use them as a major ally for the proposed attack. They, along with units of runaway slaves, could be organized to assault the Georgia frontier and the land side of Mobile, thus preventing American troops from reaching the Gulf Coast, except by way of the Mississippi River.

The admiral then proposed that a main British force of about 3,000 men would capture Mobile by an amphibious landing. To assist in his assault, Cochrane wanted to charter a large number of light draft vessels which could carry about 100 men each. These vessels, equipped with naval guns and supported by flatboats, which the navy was to bring out from England, were expected to push up the Alabama River after the fall of Mobile and reduce the American forts there. Almost certainly Cochrane also planned to use these boats in the Mississippi Sound, Lake Pontchartrain, and the other approaches to New Orleans, his ultimate objective. A base at Mobile could be used by the British against the Americans, just as Lisbon had been used against Napoleon. Despite the fact that Mobile was on the American continent, it would be impossible to support any army from Georgia or Tennessee strong enough to defeat the British if the latter were supplied from the sea.[22] Proof of this was demonstrated by the fact that it had taken months for Andrew Jackson to stockpile enough food and keep enough troops together to reach the heartland of the relatively weak Creek Nation at Horseshoe Bend. Other American armies had failed altogether in this effort.[23]

Once Mobile had fallen, most of the Choctaws and Chickasaws would join the British cause, thereby eliminating the Americans from the entire Alabama River system. This accomplishment would give the British control of all land between the Georgia frontier and the Mississippi River.

Cochrane believed that it would be feasible, with the assistance of the Creeks, to advance overland to Baton Rouge. Once Baton Rouge was captured, a small force of gunboats in the Mississippi River could easily stop all communication with New Orleans. The Crescent City, completely cut off from the United States, would fall quickly. The operation would of course be made much easier if the French Creoles and men of Barataria joined the British. Later modifications changed this plan several times.

Cochrane's suggestion was answered by Secretary of the Admiralty Croker. He wrote that the government had planned to send Lord Rowland Hill with a large army on just such a mission as Cochrane was now proposing but that the project had been abandoned because of its size and cost. The plan was revived when Cochrane proposed the use of fewer men, requesting only about 3,000 troops. The British command was so impressed with the modest request that, to assure success, they provided a force of 6,000 men under General Ross for the service.[24]*

Sir John Fortescue in *History of the British Army* considered Cochrane's plan to capture New Orleans as a childish "piece of folly."[25] Unfortunately, Fortescue, whose opinions of the New Orleans campaign are often quoted by other historians, did not have a good understanding of the situation and he disliked Cochrane. Actually, at the time Cochrane made his proposal, New Orleans was commanded by the unpopular Thomas Flournoy, who had only a handful of troops. It is very probable that Louisianians would have been reluctant to support Flournoy and that Cochrane could have seized a virtually undefended city; and it is highly unlikely that, with the British Navy in the Mississippi River, the Americans could have taken it back.[26]

The original plan included making an attack in the Chesapeake Bay area against Washington and Baltimore. It is not entirely clear from the correspondence whether the attacks on Washington and Baltimore were originally designed as separate actions or were planned from the start as a diversion for the Gulf Coast attack. In any case, Cochrane quickly incorporated these operations into the overall southern plan. General Robert Ross' army and 900 marines under Admiral George Cockburn were allocated for the Washington-Baltimore campaign. Cochrane expected that the harassment of the Chesapeake area and the attack on the two cities would create a diversion not only for the Gulf Coast but also for the Cana-

*Robin Reilly argues that the plan to attack Louisiana had not been abandoned at the time Cochrane's proposal arrived in London. It had, however, been drastically reduced, and evidently Bathurst and Croker considered that it was being abandoned.

dian front and would keep the troops of Virginia, Maryland, and Pennsylvania occupied as well.[27]

The British admiral hoped to confuse the Americans as to his future actions by leaving Admiral Cockburn and his marines near the Chesapeake when he moved south with his main army and fleet. For all the American commander would know, the British might launch a new attack at any time. If everything operated as planned, after several weeks of harassing this region Admiral Cockburn would gradually move his raids down the coast to South Carolina and Georgia. Cockburn was instructed to recruit from runaway slaves as many black marines as he could induce to join the English cause. He was then expected to use these black troops along with his regular marines to seize islands and make raids which would terrorize the inhabitants in Georgia, North Carolina, and South Carolina. By this means he would force the troops in these areas to remain at home for the protection of their families and their property.

Having set up as many diversions as he could, Cochrane at first planned to land his main force at Mobile and at Pensacola, if the Spanish were cooperative.[28] His first move to implement his plans was to send Major Edward Nicolls of the Royal Marines with about 100 officers and enlisted men to train and support the Indians.[29] Cochrane regarded young Nicolls so highly that he wrote a special request to the Admiralty to have the young officer assigned to command the marines on board his own flagship, H.M.S. *Tonnant.* The admiral had good reason to consider Nicolls an outstanding officer. He had already distinguished himself by several feats of bravery, including taking the Island of Anholt with 120 marines.[30] Another 2,000 muskets, 2,000 swords, and 2 field pieces were sent along with Nicolls for the Indians.[31] Cochrane added to the prestige of Nicolls' marines by granting all of the officers a "local" or acting rank. Nicolls, for example, was given the local rank of lieutenant colonel and later of colonel. The practice of giving these ranks was later disallowed by the Admiralty.[32]

Nicolls would first raise a force of 500 blacks and Indians cadred with the officers and men under his command and organized as a regular military unit. He had authority to appoint as many as 8 additional officers to help with the command. Cochrane cautioned Nicolls not to offend the Indians nor to allow rivalry by assuming more power over them than their chiefs were willing to grant.[33] In an effort to prevent the Indians from scalping or mistreating prisoners, Nicolls and Woodbine were ordered to persuade them to treat prisoners humanely.[34]

As an additional duty, Cochrane ordered Nicolls to scout the country and locate all possible routes to New Orleans. Nicolls was cautioned to maintain a line of retreat into Indian or Spanish territory at all times and to avoid difficulties with the Spanish. In the event of war between Spain and the United States, the British officer was ordered to move immediately against Mobile and New Orleans.[35] To assure that communication with Nicolls was maintained, Cochrane ordered Captain Sir William Percy of H.M.S. *Hermes* to take command of the ships in the Gulf and to make certain that a British vessel was always available at Apalachicola.[36]

Governor Cameron of Nassau was well informed of Britain's long-term relationship with the Indians and was in the best position to assist Nicolls with interpreters, pilots, and advice. For this reason, Cochrane ordered Nicolls, just as he had Captain Pigot, to consult with Cameron before setting out for Apalachicola.[37] Nicolls not only received all he had requested from Governor Cameron, but he was also able with the governor's assistance to appoint four young men to commissions in his detachment.[38]

Cochrane wanted Cameron to smooth the way for Nicolls' anticipated violation of Spanish neutrality at Apalachicola. The admiral explained to Cameron the problem of British-Spanish relations in Florida about as clearly as possible in this statement: "It will be a matter of great importance to obtain the countenance of the Spaniards without their committing themselves to the United States. I fear their natural jealousy will induce them to consider our efforts in favor of the Indians, as pointed at obtaining possession of the country: should your Excellency have any communication with their governors, assure them that I have no motive whatever, but to preserve the Indians from being destroyed by the United States; the maintaining of them in their rights is the best barrier the Spanish Provinces in the Floridas, can have against their encroachments: You may also say that in the event of Spain being at war with America, I will assist them with all the force that can be spared from the Services."[39]

The advice of Cameron probably caused Nicolls to stop at Havana on his way to Apalachicola and seek an interview with the captain general of Cuba, Ruiz Apodaca. Cameron had supplied Nicolls with a letter to Ruiz Apodaca, assuring the latter of Britain's peaceful intentions in Florida and also offering British assistance to the Spaniards in the event of an attack by the United States.[40] Nicolls described Ruiz Apodaca's reaction to Cameron's letter and his own discussion with the Spaniard as being "extremely civil and extremely jealous." Under no circumstances did the captain general want British troops landed in the towns of Florida. In the ensuing conversations, Nicolls found that Spain considered only the towns of St. Augustine, St. Marks, and Pensacola to be Spanish territory, and that the British could do as they pleased in all other parts of Florida.[41] About the same time, the governor of West Florida, at Pensacola, stated to American officers exactly the same concept of Spanish territory as Ruiz Apodaca had described to the British.[42]

An examination of the correspondence between the captain general and González Manrique, the governor of West Florida, shows that the Spaniards fully realized their own weakness and had adopted a policy of holding small enclaves and avoiding any confrontation with either the British or the Americans.[43] The Spaniards did not protest the British operations at Apalachicola until after peace with the Americans and after the British had taken or damaged large amounts of Spanish property in Florida.[44]

Nicolls proceeded with his forces to Apalachicola after his conference with Ruiz Apodaca, arriving there August 10, 1814.[45] When he reached Prospect Bluff, he discovered that Captain Woodbine, due to the supply shortage, had gone to Pensacola and had left only a small part of his forces at the bluff. The food shortage was crucial.[46] Shortly after his arrival at the bluff, Woodbine had received a message from the refugee Creeks who had assembled near Pensacola. They said that they were determined to fight on against the United States if they could have food, clothing, and arms. They explained that the Spanish commander lacked enough supplies for his own garrison, and as a result they were starving. American cavalry was raiding into the area around Pensacola and killing the Indians like cattle, and they had no arms with which to defend themselves.[47]

This appeal for aid had caused Woodbine to leave Prospect Bluff and visit Pensacola to see for himself the conditions that existed.[48] At Pensacola he found even more hungry Indians than he had encountered at the bluff. He also found that the Spanish governor was expecting an immediate attack by the Americans and had requested British aid. Woodbine decided to remain at Pensacola. He sent Captain Lockyer back to Apalachicola with orders to return with all the remaining arms and a request for all British forces arriving there to join him at Pensacola.[49] When Lockyer reached Prospect Bluff, he was met by Major Nicolls, who had just arrived at that port.[50]

Nicolls landed part of his men and as many provisions as he could spare at Apalachicola and immediately sailed for Pensacola. He arrived there August 14, 1814, and received a request from the Spanish governor to help him repel the expected American attack. In answer to the request, Nicolls landed his troops at the Spanish town; he was given command of Fort Michael and allowed to fly both English and Spanish flags.[51] Well pleased with his reception by the Spaniards, Nicolls ordered Captain W. H. Percy to bring all of the marine detachment from Apalachicola. The entire British force took up residence in the fort with the full approval of the governor of West Florida.[52]

10

Fort Bowyer and Pensacola

CAPTAIN GENERAL Ruiz Apodaca was less than enthusiastic regarding the offer of British troop support brought to him at Havana by Major Nicolls. The Spaniards, who were aware of the designs of the British, had reason to fear the Americans and perhaps even the Indians. The seizure of Mobile and the constant pressure of American encroachment on their Florida possessions had greatly alarmed the Spaniards. As a result of their concern, they had provided some aid to their would-be Indian allies and had tried to strengthen their defenses.[1]

Nonetheless, rivalry between Britain and Spain in Florida, dating from colonial times, made it difficult for the two countries to cooperate against the United States.[2] Some Spanish officials believed that the destruction of Fort Mims by Spanish-supplied Indians would provide the Americans with an excuse to seize Pensacola, but Ruiz Apodaca felt that the Americans planned to attack anyway. He thought it was necessary to take all measures possible for the defense of the town, including arming the Indians.[3]

It was this well-grounded fear of the Americans that had led the Spaniards to overlook deliberately the violation of their neutrality at Apalachicola and to permit British agents to use Pensacola. However, when it came to allowing the British to land at Pensacola and establish a base there, Spanish officialdom was divided and obviously somewhat reluctant. The captain general refused Nicolls' offer of aid; but once the American forces were threatening Pensacola, Governor González Manrique requested their assistance in defending the town. Almost as soon as Nicolls arrived at Pensacola on August 14, 1814, he assumed virtual command of the town, established a strict passport system to control travel, and proceeded to recruit nearly all the local slaves for his black regiment.[4] The British action was high-handed, and their Indian and black troops were guilty of looting and terrorizing the local inhabitants. These moves alienated the population of Pensacola and probably caused John Innerarity of the Forbes Company, the largest local British merchant, to become actively engaged in furnishing information to the Americans.[5]

In asking the British to land at Pensacola, González Manrique was acting on his own initiative. He had already received threats of attack from General Jackson. He did not report to his superior, Ruiz Apodaca, that he had requested British aid; instead, he said that he could not prevent the British landing.[6] The captain general probably accepted González Manrique's explanation of the English action since he did not believe the British would honor their promise not to land at Pensacola. Ruiz Apodaca may have considered that the governor's action relieved him of any responsibility.[7]* Nicolls advised Admiral Cochrane that when Woodbine arrived at Pensacola, "he was received by the Spanish Governor in the greatest terms of friendship, and solicited by the Governor for his assistance in protecting the town of Pensacola from the immediate attack of the Americans. . . ."[8]

Nicolls, despite the warm reception by the governor, did not find conditions at Pensacola to his liking. He discovered that the Spaniards had not been able to give food or arms to the Indians and that many of the Spanish officers and the townspeople were planning to surrender to Andrew Jackson. Nicolls believed the leader of this surrender was John Innerarity, and thereafter he treated the Forbes Company as an enemy of the British. He believed that the Inneraritys were American agents. To support this belief, he captured a letter from John Innerarity ordering his agency at Bon Secour to stop sending supplies to Pensacola. It was probably this anti-British sentiment on the part of the citizens of Pensacola that caused Nicolls to take complete command of the town.[9]

The British forces available to Nicolls amounted to about 100 men, and thus he thought it necessary to continue Woodbine's recruiting of Indian and black troops. At Pensacola he eventually recruited and armed about 500 Indians and 100 blacks.[10]

In an effort to enlarge and strengthen his irregular forces, Nicolls tried unsuccessfully to recruit Jean Laffite and his Baratarians of Louisiana. These men, often referred to as pirates by American officials, including

*Some historians appear unaware that Gonzalez Manrique invited the British to land at Pensacola. Glenn Tucker says of the landing at Pensacola that the English "took the town from the docile Spanish Governor."

Andrew Jackson, were privateers operating under letters of marque from France, Cartagena, and several Latin American revolutionary governments. They used the island of Barataria and other isolated areas along the Gulf Coast as their headquarters, and they were more or less under the command of Jean Laffite. As far as the United States was concerned, the main crimes of the Baratarians were their engagement in an extensive smuggling trade and their illegal use of American territory as a base of operations.[11] The first suggestion by the British that the Baratarians might join forces with them and allow use of the base at Barataria as a point of attack against New Orleans is found in Hugh Pigot's report to Admiral Cochrane dated June 8, 1814.[12] The admiral was impressed by this suggestion. Though he did not direct Nicolls to contact Laffite in his written orders, there is little doubt that he told him to do so, a fact borne out by Cochrane's mention of the possibility of support by the Baratarians in his report to Earl Bathurst.[13]

Nicolls and his counterpart, Captain William H. Percy, needed no prompting. Soon after their arrival in Pensacola they sent Captain John McWilliams on the *Sophie* with a letter to Laffite. The messengers received a most unfriendly reception at Barataria: McWilliams, the ship's commander, Nicholas Lockyer, and the crew of the landing boat were placed in confinement. The boat and crew were eventually allowed to return to *Sophie*, but Lockyer and McWilliams were held overnight.[14]

Laffite's account of this meeting agrees on most points with that of Nicolls, except that he received the British letters and told Lockyer that he wanted fifteen days to decide whether or not to accept the proposal.[15] Nicolls offered Laffite a captaincy in the British Naval service and lands if he would join them. Lands and service rank were also promised to Laffite's men, according to their positions, if they would join the British cause.[16] Instead of accepting the offer, Laffite forwarded the communication to Louisiana Governor W. C. C. Claiborne. He appealed to Governor Claiborne to pardon the Baratarians and to allow them to join in the defense of the United States against the British. In support of his statements, Laffite provided the governor with an anonymous letter from Havana which reported the British plan to attack Louisiana after capturing Mobile.[17] The accuracy of the material contained in the Havana letter is apparent when it is compared with the correspondence of Nicolls and Cochrane.* Another

*Jane de Grummond believed that this letter was written by Renato Beluche, one of Laffite's Baratarians; but, as explained later, the letter has been traced to Vincent Gray in Havana. Since one copy of the letter must have been brought to Barataria, Beluche may have been the messenger.

copy of this letter was received by Andrew Jackson, and it almost certainly helped to convince him that an attack on Mobile was likely.

The reason for Laffite's refusal to accept the British offer, even when a bounty of $30,000 was added by Captain Lockyer, was really not hard to understand. Laffite's men were privateers and had gained much wealth raiding Spanish commerce. Some of the Baratarians were undoubtedly tempted by the British offer, but they would have lost too much as allies of the British because Nicolls had insisted that they should give up their raids on the Spaniards.[18] Whether or not the Baratarians were as pro-American as they claimed is a moot question, but it is certain that they had no love or trust for either Britain or Spain. Support of the United States in this critical time would present them with an excellent chance to receive a full pardon for their past offenses.

Although the stated purpose of Nicolls' mission was to aid the Indians and lay the groundwork for a large British landing, he considered it highly desirable for his force to make a successful attack on the Americans. An American defeat would give confidence to his Indian allies, causing more of them to join the British. Captain W. H. Percy, the naval commander of the expedition, wished to attack Fort Bowyer on Mobile Point.[19] Having doubts that the British were strong enough to accomplish the objective, Nicolls was reluctant to make the assault. Ultimately, the aggressive nature of this British officer prevailed over his doubts, and he decided to undertake the expedition.

Percy stated that according to the British plan it was necessary to take possession of Mobile in order to hold communication with the tribe of friendly Choctaws. Fort Bowyer on Mobile Point was chosen for the attack. It was a low, wood battery of little strength, mounting at the most fourteen guns of small caliber. Captain Percy described the depth of the water at Fort Bowyer as "sufficient for the squadron to anchor within pistol shot of their guns. The capture or destruction" of the fort, he claimed, would enable the British "effectually to stop the trade of Louisiana and to starve Mobile." The captain's plan called for 100 Indians to be sent "to divest the fort on the land side."[20]

Nicolls reported that he actually sent a detachment of 60 marines and 180 Indians. Some other accounts give slightly different numbers, but evidently the land force consisted of about 200 or 250 men, including both marines and Indians. In order to keep control of his forces, the British officer placed the Indians on ships, and the marines were sent overland. Illness prevented Nicolls from leading the detachment himself, and he was forced to turn over his command to Captain Robert Henry of the marines.[21]

The march continued until the afternoon of September 14. At this time Henry's forces had reached a point 800 yards from Fort Bowyer. Believing his men to be undiscovered by the enemy, Henry ordered his howitzer to commence firing at the American position. After a short time, he determined that the fort was entirely too strong for the force he had brought with him. He decided to wait and attack in concert with the fleet, using his troops to block any American retreat. During the afternoon, the ships arrived and began firing. At that time Henry's forces made an assault on the fort, but they were repelled, with the loss of one man killed. The detachment remained in position without further action until the end of the battle, at which time the men marched back to Pensacola.[22]

Of far more importance was the assault made by Percy and his ships. The naval force reached the bar off Mobile Bay on the morning of September 12, but because of the wind they could not cross over until the next afternoon. The squadron passed the bar in line at 3:00 P.M. and began firing about 4:30 P.M. with the battery of *Hermes*. *Sophie* managed to get into position a short time later and also commenced firing. In the meantime the wind died, and the ebb tide prevented the remaining two ships from reaching a position from which they could join the action. Loss of the wind was not the only complication faced by the fleet attacking Fort Bowyer; as soon as the bombardment started it was discovered that the ships had to elevate their guns to the maximum in order to hit the fort. At 5:30 P.M. the bow spring of *Hermes* was shot away, and the ship drifted into a position where she could be raked by the guns of the fort. Eventually Percy maneuvered his ship back into position, but after another hour of firing he discovered that the bombardment had not affected the fort and that *Hermes* was so severely damaged as to be ineffective. At this point, Percy cut loose his anchors and attempted to withdraw the ship. The sails and rigging had been so badly mauled that the vessel was unmanageable. She soon grounded with her stern toward the fort.

After consulting with the other captains, Percy conceded that he could not capture the fort and that *Hermes* was too disabled to be of any use. Removing the wounded and most of the crew, Percy and a small group set fire to *Hermes* and abandoned her. The next day the squadron returned to Pensacola. The British lost 24 dead, 44 wounded and the frigate *Hermes*, the strongest vessel in the squadron.[23] Despite Nicolls' illness, which had already forced his return to the ship, he took part in the battle from aboard *Hermes*. He was wounded twice, losing the sight of his right eye.[24]

The American defense of Fort Bowyer was made by a force of only 158 men.[25] The fort was located on the extreme end of a long sandspit, which extended many miles out across the entrance to Mobile Bay. It was on approximately the present site of Fort Morgan. This spit, in many places only a few hundred yards wide, was full of sand dunes and ditches and offered considerable cover to an attacking force, especially one which controlled the sea. Fort Bowyer was described by Latour as "a redoubt formed on the seaside, by a semi-circular battery for four hundred feet in development, flanked with two curtains sixty feet in length." The interior front of the parapet was made of pine, a resinous wood which could easily be set on fire by a single shell. The fort was "destitute of casemates (the only shelter from bombs) even for the sick, the ammunition or provisions." In addition to these inconveniences the fort was "commanded by several mounds of sand . . . at the distance of from two to three hundred yards. On the summit of those mounds it would be very easy to mount pieces of artillery, whose slanting fire would command the inside of the fort." There were "twenty pieces of cannon in the fort, distributed in the following manner: two twenty-fours, six twelves, eight nines, and four fours; the twenty-fours and twelves being alone mounted on coast carriages, and all the others on Spanish carriages little fit for service. The men serving as crews for these guns were exposed to enemy fire from their knees upward."[26]

At the time of the first British attack, Fort Bowyer was not as strong as Latour described it. Many of the guns were not mounted. Major Howell Tatum, writing at the time of the earlier action, stated that there were only eleven guns mounted and ready for use at Fort Bowyer. The American position was not undamaged by the bombardment. Several of the heavy guns, including the two twenty-four-pounders, were destroyed during the engagement.[27] Although the British fire was very heavy, only four Americans were killed and five wounded.

An examination of the records of both the British and Americans show clearly the reason for the failure of the attack on Fort Bowyer. First of all, Major William Lawrence, the American commander, had a detachment of regulars who were well disciplined and expert in the use of their guns. This skill of the fort's defenders was doubtless a surprise to the British officers, who expected all Americans to run at the sight of red coats, especially when the redcoats were accompanied by Indians. The idea of simultaneous land and sea attack was sound, but the British land force was far too small and too much composed of untrained Indians to have any chance against the entrenched regulars. Second, as the British learned, the waters of Mobile Bay were entirely too shallow for them to make use of large ships. The British needed their shallow-draft vessels for such an attack.

The loss of this battle was a major British blunder: it caused many of their leaders to exaggerate the strength of the American defense of Mobile. As the British were soon to learn, Fort Bowyer was no match for a real siege and could easily be taken by an adequate force. In the last analysis, it can be said that the British plan to take Mobile was an excellent one, but in their failure to commit an adequate force they showed their usual underestimation of the Americans.

The American reaction to this attack was strong. As soon as Jackson, who had already planned to strengthen the fort, learned of the encounter, he dispatched a large reinforcement. These men, however, did not reach their destination in time to be of any use in the defense.[28] Of a more long-range nature, Jackson ordered the fort repaired and increased the garrison.[29]

The defeat probably gained one important advantage for the British: this engagement convinced Andrew Jackson more than ever that Mobile was the main point of attack. Had he not received later information, he might have been strengthening Mobile's defenses while the British walked into New Orleans unopposed. Jackson used this attack as an excuse to call all available militia into service. He already had evidence and rumors that the British planned to launch a major offensive somewhere along the Gulf and probably planned to use Mobile and Pensacola as their bases of operation. He resolved to raise a force and drive them from Pensacola once and for all.[30] Always the aggressor, Jackson ordered J. P. Kennedy to take all the Choctaw Indians in pursuit of the retreating British.[31] This maneuver failed, and the British reached Pensacola safely.

Jackson immediately demanded that Governor González Manrique drive out the hostile Indians using Spanish territory and prevent the English from using Pensacola as a base. Receiving no satisfactory assurance from the Spanish governor, Jackson determined to attack the city itself to drive out the British.[32] Acting without orders, Jackson stated his reasons for taking Pensacola in a letter to Secretary of War James Monroe: "As I act without any orders from the Government, I deem it proper to state my reasons for it. . . . The hostility of the Governor of Pensacola resigning his post to the British Commander . . . his permitting them to remain there [and] to fit out one expedition against the United States . . . added to his having acknowledged that he had armed the Indians [and] sent them into our territory."[33]

Jackson assembled his forces near Fort Montgomery on the Alabama River.[34] This army was composed of militia and volunteers, and it was strengthened by 520 regulars and 750 Choctaw and Chickasaw Indians, in all about 4,100 men. Upon reaching the area of Pensacola on November 6, Jackson immediately dispatched a messenger under a flag of truce to communicate with Governor González Manrique. The first messenger was fired upon near Fort St. Michael and forced to retire; the second messenger, a captured Spanish corporal, reached González Manrique with Jackson's demand for capitulation. The message insisted that the British must completely evacuate Pensacola and that Fort St. Michael and Fort Santa Rosa were to be garrisoned by United States troops.

The Spaniards rejected the demand, and Jackson prepared to assault the town.[35] In reality, the rejection was more bluster than fact, since the Spanish garrison was small and extremely weak in equipment and discipline. An American who visited Pensacola in 1814 reported that the "whole Spanish regular force including invalids here and at the Barrancas, black and white, does not exceed 500 at most, and they are without subordination or discipline; a most spiritless corps, commanded by an old set of lazy pot-gutted officers. The effective militia are about 500, a mere calico generation without principle or love of country. . . ."[36]

I. J. Cox believed that in 1814 there were only 288 men in the Spanish garrison at Pensacola. The estimate of Alexander Campbell, quoted above, stated that there were about 500 Spanish regulars in the area of Pensacola. The governors of West Florida during this period reported having between 800 and 1,000 men available, including militia. For this reason, 500 men would appear to be a credible figure for the size of the Pensacola garrison.[37]*

The smallness of the force was not the main problem faced by the Spaniards. As stated earlier, the garrison was poorly armed and short of supplies and rations. All the Spanish officers agreed that while the town could, with difficulty, be held against the Indians, there was no chance, without supplies and heavy reinforcements, of defending it against the Americans.[38] There is no evidence that this situation had become better to any appreciable extent by the time of Jackson's attack. The only improvement noted by the Spaniards was the obtainment of some powder from private sources.[39]

Although Pensacola's fortifications were somewhat more formidable, the Spaniards could not have offered serious resistance to either the Brit-

*I. J. Cox believed that the garrison of all of West Florida, which was mainly at Pensacola, was only 288 men, much smaller than the 500 soldiers described in other accounts. The discrepancy probably resulted from Cox's failure to count the troops of Colonel José de Soto, numbering 272, which had been sent from Cuba after the fall of Mobile.

ish or the Americans. The town, which had two streets leading to a square, was defended by several forts and a number of blockhouses, but its outer roads ran through swamps and were poorly protected. Properly manned these fortifications might have made a reasonably good defense.[40] It was the danger of attack in the face of the critical weakness which caused González Manrique to decide to allow the British to land troops and to use Pensacola as a base of operations.[41]

Nicolls was critical of the manner in which the Spaniards treated the Indians, saying that the Spaniards had allowed them to starve. By the British officer's own admission, however, there was little they could do.[42] The supply situation, always bad, had been made much worse by an American internal blockade, and food was extremely scarce. Most of Pensacola's provisions came from Louisiana, an area now cut off by the blockade. When Jackson arrived at Mobile and discovered Spanish ships were buying corn and other rations, he immediately ordered an embargo on the shipment of all goods to Pensacola. This action not only worsened the city's already critical food shortage but also disrupted the British squadron which was being supplied from Pensacola.[43] When the defeated Creeks took refuge in Florida, they found that there was no food available. To avoid starving, they were faced with the necessity of surrendering to the United States in order to get food. The timely arrival of the British changed the situation completely, and the Indians prepared to resume hostilities.[44]

González Manrique's decision to accept British aid for the defense of West Florida received at least the tacit approval of the captain general. The Inneraritys, along with many Spanish officials, did not agree that defense was possible and considered González Manrique foolish to accept British aid.[45] One of his severest critics was Don Juan Ventura Morales, a former Spanish intendant at New Orleans. Morales regarded González Manrique as incompetent and believed him to be entirely responsible for the losses that later occurred at Pensacola. Perhaps if neither the British nor the Indians had been allowed to use the city, the American invasion would not have occurred.[46]

In defense of the Spanish governor, it is almost certain that he thought the British planned a massive invasion of the Gulf region, and the forces of Nicolls and Woodbine were only a preliminary. He was led to believe that Pensacola would be a major base for this operation. All evidence indicates that this was exactly what Nicolls promised the governor. The rumors of the proposed expedition were well known in Pensacola.[47] González Manrique and certainly Ruiz Apodaca, who was also well informed of the plan, probably believed that the safest course under the circumstances was to cooperate with the British while maintaining as much independence as possible.[48]

As long as the British seemed able to defend Pensacola against the Americans, González Manrique was perfectly willing to aid them without question. When the overconfident Nicolls was defeated at Mobile Point, the Spanish governor began to have grave doubts concerning the ability of the British to defend his town. This feeling was quickly manifested in a far less friendly attitude toward the British, and an examination of all accounts from this time forward shows clearly that González Manrique had less and less interest in having them in Pensacola.[49] On their part, the English also adopted a more hostile attitude toward their Spanish allies.[50] Runaway slaves and Indians had been enlisted by the British at Pensacola, and there had been some looting by these recruits from the outset. It was not, however, until after the defeat at Fort Bowyer that the English and their black and Indian allies committed most of their depredations.

On the retreat from Mobile the Innerarity-Forbes Company holdings at Bon Secour were looted by the marines and Indians under Captain Robert Henry. Several slaves were carried off as enlistments for Nicolls' black regiment.[51]* In describing the recruiting for this regiment, John Innerarity stated that as soon as the British returned from Fort Bowyer they began to set traps and "to put their tools to work, to catch negro slaves. Their Serjeants Dogherty, Caldwell, Wallace, and Perdu with another American Renegade named McGill were actively employed in this laudable occupation, under the immediate orders of Captain Woodbine." These British soldiers, according to Innerarity's statement, "assiduously visited the negro cabins in this town, attended their meetings and by every means that the genius of seduction could invent endeavoured to entice the slaves of the Spanish citizens to join them—whenever they succeeded, the evasion of the slave was easy he had but to walk to the fort, at noon day or at night, he was sure of reception—did the owner complain? He was answered with scurrility—did the weak government interfere? Its request, its orders, or its menaces were alike treated with insulting contempt."[52]

The result of this process, which was carried out all over Florida, caused the loss of over 100 blacks in Pensacola, and doubtless many times more

*To protect their property, the Inneraritys obtained Spanish citizenship in October 1812. In taking Spanish citizenship, they did not lose their British citizenship because they had permission from the British government "to reside, and uniformly receive the necessary facilities from His Majesty's government, to enable them to carry on under any flag best suited for the purpose" (Potts to Bathurst, Nov. 22, 1815, PRO WO 1/143).

than that in the other areas of Florida.[53] These losses were protested, but the slaves were not returned. Some damages were paid in the years after the war.[54] For example, the Forbes Company was able to collect $20,000 for the damages done to their property, but there is doubt as to whether the other citizens were as fortunate.[55]

In the face of this increased hostility between the British and Spaniards, it is not surprising that González Manrique showed considerable indecision when Jackson's army advanced on Pensacola. The governor could not decide whether to seek British aid or to surrender the town. Eventually he did request help from Captain W. H. Percy and his British naval force, which had been anchored off the Apalachicola River since the Mobile Point incident. This detachment, in addition to Major Nicolls and some marines, was hastily brought back to reinforce Captain Woodbine, who had remained in Pensacola. By the time help arrived, however, González Manrique had changed his mind and refused the assistance. Later, when Jackson's army was actually approaching Pensacola, Percy's replacement, Captain James Gordon of H.M.S. *Sea Horse* and Major Nicolls again offered all the British forces in defense of the town. Instead of accepting the offer, the governor reverted to his original orders, which were that the English troops were not to violate American territory or compromise Spanish neutrality, a remarkable shift from his previous position.[56]

On November 2, a few days before Jackson's attack, Gordon and Nicolls issued a final demand. They promised to defend Pensacola with all forces available, including the Indians, if the governor would place the Spanish garrison and all the fortifications under English command.[57] The Spanish officials not only refused, but they also made no preparations for the American attack. When the assault finally came, not a single fort in the area had as much as one day's supply of provisions or water. Even Fort Barrancas was without supplies, although the Spanish had provisions enough to support 500 men for a month stored only a few hundred yards away.

At the very last minute González Manrique changed his mind once more and demanded full assistance from the British. At this point Gordon refused to have any more to do with the defense, but Nicolls remained in the city and fought a rearguard action.[58] The final remarks made by the British before the evacuation were harsh. Gordon reportedly threatened to level the town with naval gunfire as soon as it was in the hands of the Americans. While this threat was a bluff, the harbor forts were "leveled" by the British as promised.[59]

The actual attack on November 7, 1814, was a surprise to the Spaniards. Jackson's camp lay to the west of the town, and it seemed logical that the attack would be made from that side. In this belief, the main Spanish forces were manning the defenses on the west, where their artillery and blockhouses were strongest. Also, the British ships in the harbor were in position to fire easily on the Americans advancing from the west. Disgusted as he was, Gordon was willing to use his guns to fire on the Americans.[60] As a part of his deception, Jackson left 500 men in his camp for a diversion and moved his main force through the woods before daylight, to the east side of the town. The deception worked well, and he was not discovered by the enemy until sunrise, when the attack from the east got under way.[61]

The assault was made by four columns, three composed of the white troops and the fourth of Choctaw Indians. According to Jackson's second in command, General John Coffee, the eastern approach was less heavily defended and would have been safer, even if the element of surprise had been lacking. The columns, nevertheless, had to pass close to the bay where, if discovered, they would come under the fire of the British fleet. But the British were so surprised by the sudden appearance of Jackson's forces on the east that their fire was ineffective. Once the Americans had entered Pensacola, the British stopped discharging their guns.[62]

When Jackson's army reached the town, it was found that the Spaniards had moved two cannon into the street and were producing a heavy fire on the advance columns.* Jackson had assumed that he would face field batteries in the streets and had ordered one company of his regulars to form the lead element in each of his columns, thus giving each one a well-disciplined point. The regular companies were ordered to storm any batteries encountered.

So successful was the assault that resistance in the town ended within minutes. Governor González Manrique, after running about with a white flag, finally located an American officer of rank and surrendered. He agreed to surrender the town as well as the forts, but the fort commanders delayed for several hours. This procrastination prevented Jackson from launching an attack on the harbor forts until the following morning.[63]

Concerning his early surrender, González Manrique reported that his total force in the town at the time amounted to 268 men, including cannoneers. This detachment did not include the garrison of Fort Barrancas under

*These cannon were apparently of British manufacture and were, according to some accounts, manned by Nicholls' men; since Jackson listed no English prisoners, it is possible that Nicolls' men had already withdrawn and that these were his cannon manned by Spanish troops.

the command of Manuel Ordóñez, which was not taken by Jackson until the next day.[64] The delay allowed British naval forces to retreat to the Barrancas, embark the troops there, and sail away. Before they left, the British blew up Fort Barrancas and Fort Santa Rosa, leaving the entire harbor defenseless.[65] They also forcibly embarked 200 Spanish troops, along with Ordóñez. According to Captain Gordon, the British naval force remained in the area until November 10 so as to protect the Indians who were retreating overland. On that day Gordon sailed to Apalachicola, where he unloaded Nicolls and his men along with the Spanish troops.[66]

This attack was carried out with few losses. Only five Americans were killed and ten wounded. Spanish losses were also very light, fourteen killed and six wounded. There is no record of British or Indian casualties.

General Coffee believed that Jackson would have tried to hold Pensacola if the forts had not been destroyed and the town rendered defenseless against future British attack.[67] Coffee's view may have been partially correct. If Pensacola had been defensible, Jackson might have decided to garrison the town. It was while Jackson was in Pensacola that he received definite information that the British had a large force of men and ships at Jamaica and their plan was to make a direct assault on New Orleans, probably through Lake Pontchartrain.[68] Acting upon this information, Jackson immediately marched most of his army back to Mobile.

Despite all criticism of his action, Jackson considered that he had accomplished much by the attack. He claimed that it had disrupted and scattered a large part of the hostile Indians. The incident had the additional advantage of completely alienating the British from the Spaniards.[69]

This claim of success needs no stronger substantiation than the enemy's reports. Regarding the invasion of West Florida, Admiral Cochrane reported, "The attack made by the Americans upon Pensacola has in a great measure retarded this service [the British Gulf offensive]."[70]

One noticeable benefit gained was González Manrique's more amiable attitude toward the United States. This change resulted from a combination of several factors. Not only did the Americans refrain from looting or mistreating the people of Pensacola, but their assault proved conclusively to the Spanish that the British would not and could not protect them.[71] More important was the arrogant British disregard of Spanish rights, so vividly illustrated when the British carried off almost all the slaves in Pensacola and much other property. A large number of blacks, including 25 from the Pensacola area, were taken from the influential John Forbes Company. This blunder cost the British whatever friendship they might have enjoyed with the people of West Florida.[72] The British also took away 200

Spanish black troops who were kept at Apalachicola as a labor force. Upon the restoration of peace they were returned to Pensacola in wretched condition.[73] It would thus seem that Jackson's decision to attack Pensacola was entirely correct, and the invasion may have had considerable significance in the defense of the country.

11

The Defense of New Orleans

JACKSON'S ARRIVAL in Mobile on August 27, 1814, placed him in a much better position to watch the activities of the British and to be prepared to meet any attack. Upon reaching his new headquarters, he found a mass of information. There were two letters from Havana, significant because of their remarkable accuracy. Both related in considerable detail to the expedition of Edward Nicolls, which had landed at Havana in July. The letters, which later sources revealed were written by Vincent Gray, an American merchant in business in Havana, described the various officers of the expedition and gave some information regarding the background of these men, including the outstanding military record of Nicolls in Europe. The documents also sketched the plan of the British to arouse the people of Louisiana and the Gulf region to join their standard as part of a proposed invasion of the area by a much larger expedition. One item which must have impressed Jackson was Nicolls' expressed interest in capturing Mobile and Fort Bowyer.

The letters described an interview between Nicolls and the captain general of Cuba, during which Ruiz Apodaca refused to allow the British to use Pensacola as a base. Nicolls made bold statements at a public house and was reported to have said, after the interview with the captain general, that he planned to land at Pensacola with or without the permission of the Spaniards.[1]* He was also quoted as saying that "he expected to make an easy conquest of the whole of that country [the United States] as he should

*From subjects covered, the unusual style, and other internal evidence, both of these letters appear to have been written by the same person. According to Latour, the letter dated August 8, 1814, was delivered to Governor Claiborne by Jean Laffite. The other, dated August 13, 1814, was obviously sent by another route to Andrew Jackson. Both letters contain the same material, except that some addi-

have to contend with a cowardly and dastardly set who knew nothing of warfare and when their own slaves were turned upon them would soon fly the country." The colonel, it was reported, stated "that a large portion of Louisiana was ready to join them as that state was to be given back to Spain and by satisfying the Louisianians on this head little or no opposition would be made to them."[2] These unsigned letters, probably sent on two different vessels with the hope that at least one of them would reach the Americans, contained an almost perfect account of the British plans as they existed in August 1814.[3]

The intelligence concerning a preliminary attack on Mobile Point coincided with Jackson's own ideas concerning the importance of that place. As early as July 26 he wrote the secretary of war that Mobile Point must be reinforced.[4] Citing information from Antoine Collin of Pensacola, Jackson later justified the importance of the position by explaining that "Mobile Point . . . will be able to protect the pass from New Orleans, and prevent the enemy from cutting off our supplies. Should this fail our only dependence will be Tennessee."[5]

Concern for Mobile Point and the Mississippi Sound was demonstrated by Jackson's urgent request to Commander Daniel T. Patterson, the naval commander at New Orleans, to send some gunboats to protect the area. The general first requested Patterson to send his gunboats to defend Mobile Bay itself and to support Fort Bowyer. Patterson replied that because the bay could be entered by large British warships, his gunboats could do little to guard it. He suggested that instead his force would be far more valuable if it was stationed in the Mississippi Sound and Lake Borgne.[6] Later, with a better understanding of the limitations of the American naval forces, Jackson asked the commander to use his boats to secure communications between Mobile and New Orleans. He believed that if the link between Mobile and New Orleans were permanently cut, the supply situation of the army at Mobile would be precarious.[7] The possible loss of provisions also worried Jackson for he would then be unable to feed the Indians. He believed that both the friendly and the formerly hostile Creeks

---

tional information was added to the later letter. Two letters, found in the Jackson Papers at the Library of Congress, dated Havana, December 30, 1826, and February 14, 1827, are signed by Vincent Gray. Gray wrote in the letter of December 30, 1826, that the time had arrived when he could divulge the secret of his identity. He wrote that he was an American engaged in business in Havana and that he had served for several years as United States vice-consul at that port. He also stated that in order to serve his country better it had been necessary for his identity to be concealed.

would be driven to join the British if they were allowed to go hungry.

Wilburt Brown believed that Jackson's request of Patterson that the gunboat fleet be used to protect Mobile Bay against the large British ships was a good demonstration of the general's complete ignorance of naval matters. Brown was undoubtedly correct in assuming that Jackson, who had probably never seen a gunboat, did not at that time understand the limitations of the available naval forces.[8] However, in spite of Jackson's reputation for stubbornness, he learned rapidly and readily followed Patterson's advice to use the gunboats in the Mississippi Sound. Jackson continued to listen to Patterson's recommendations, and the two men cooperated well throughout the campaign. It should also be noted that, while Jackson did not know the limitations of the naval vessels of the day, he developed the best possible defense against the unlimited mobility of the British amphibious campaign, an operation that denied victory to the superior British forces.

In early summer the secretary of war had not believed that the British had any interest in the Gulf Coast. By the middle of July, having received information about British landings, the government was becoming concerned. Because of the well-known British fear of the tropical Gulf Coast climate, Washington still believed these landings to be a diversion.[9] In August the secretary of war had confirmed that the British were planning a major expedition against Louisiana. Washington then authorized Jackson to call 5,000 troops from Tennessee and 2,500 from Georgia, thus giving authority for what he had already done.[10]

By the late fall of 1814, the secretary of war was increasingly alarmed by Jackson's seeming neglect of the defense of New Orleans itself. When faced with some rather strong suggestions that he should move his headquarters to New Orleans, Jackson showed a lack of interest and reported in answer to prods by the secretary that he would go to New Orleans as soon as the Mobile sector of his district was made secure. In the meantime, he wrote the secretary that he had "directed that the forts be put in the best state of defence"; also the militia of Louisiana was in the field, and "should an attempt be made to approach that quarter, mounted men could by forced marches soon reach any point of attack."[11]

Jackson's view of the importance of Mobile, supported by the mass of information from his intelligence network, was that Fort Bowyer would be the first point of attack; if they carried it, the British would penetrate the Indian country and "excite the Indians to war, the negroes to insurrection, and then proceed to the Mississippi and cut off the communications between the upper and lower country." If this should happen, the general

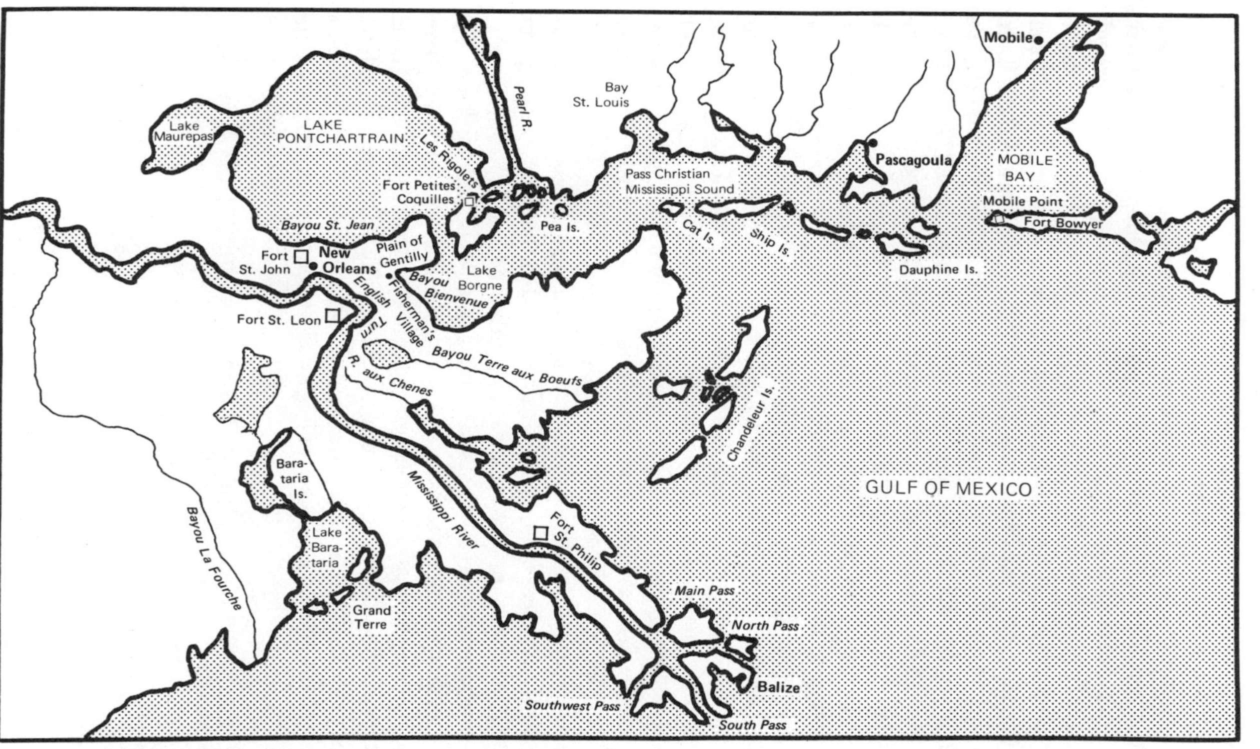

Battle of New Orleans

believed, that section of the country would fall as a matter of course.* Perhaps Willie Blount's statement that New Orleans could easily be defended best expressed Jackson's view. He gave a more detailed account of what he believed the British had in mind regarding New Orleans in a letter to the secretary, dated February 18, 1815: "It is true Mobile, in point of wealth, is a trifling object with the British compared with this city. But in point of harassing us, and stirring up the Indians Hostility against us, it is all important and if once possessed by the [British] and by Spain, it will cost much blood to regain it—tho regained, it must be, or the enemy menaces the country constantly, and in fact a real military man with a full knowledge of the geography of this country, would first possess himself of it, drive to his standard the Indians, advance by way of fort St. Stephens, and march directly to the walnut hills [Vicksburg] and by a strong establishment there being able to forrage on the country he could support himself, cut off all supplies from above and make this country an easy conquest."[12]

The English, or at least Admiral Cochrane, had studied the advantages of capturing Mobile and, like Jackson, believed it was a vital base; but Cochrane envisioned a small action conducted by the Indians and a few thousand British troops. Later, as the expedition was enlarged, the admiral became interested in a more direct operation against New Orleans. He wanted Mobile and Pensacola as bases for his attack on the Crescent City. But when Jackson captured the West Florida town and seemed firm in his intention to remain in Mobile, Cochrane decided that a direct assault on New Orleans was feasible even without a mainland base in North America. Nonetheless he continued with his earlier plans to mislead Jackson. The final decision to make a direct attack on New Orleans may not have come until the admiral reached Jamaica and discovered that his plans had been compromised and that Jackson was marching to New Orleans.[13]

General Jackson never abandoned the idea of the importance of Mobile.[14]** His best course of action might have been to post a small garrison

*Virgil Davis in *History of the Mobile District of the United States Army Corps of Engineers,* pp. 1-5, confirms that the records of the corps indicate that there were good road connections with the Mississippi River through either Baton Rouge or Natchez.

**Henry Adams considered Jackson's defense of Mobile foolish in the extreme and thought that, if anything, Nicolls' Indian attack was a diversion. In his own citations, Adams refers to Cochrane's letter of June 20, 1814, which proposed an attack on Mobile. Adams was of course aware of Nicolls' activities at Pensacola and Apalachicola, but he was apparently unwilling to believe that the British proposal was ever taken seriously.

at Mobile with perhaps a slightly larger force at New Orleans, and station the main part of his army up the river at Baton Rouge; from there he could quickly have advanced to meet a British attack on either city. Certainly if a direct British assault against New Orleans had been successful, it would have been far easier for the Americans to pull back up the river than to have retreated into the wilderness above Mobile.[15]

The American general was well aware of the criticism of his efforts to hold Mobile, as is shown by a note which he wrote on the back of the letter from Vincent Gray dated February 14, 1827, twelve years after the War of 1812 had ended. Jackson wrote that the letter was to be filed with others from Vincent Gray, "being important for the historian to shew that AJ had earlier information of the intended attack on the lower country thro' Mobile, than the Govt, & the propriety & necessity of his march & expulsion of the British & Indians from Pensacola." The note contains the reasons for Jackson's continued occupation of Mobile against the orders of the War Department to advance for the defense of New Orleans.[16]

The dilemma which no American commander could easily solve was how to cope effectively with the great mobility of an amphibious attack. So long as the British knew the location of American ground forces, they could easily shift their landing to a point which was not well defended. If Jackson moved all of his strength to Mobile, they would occupy New Orleans. If he moved it to New Orleans, they would take Mobile. An overwhelming superiority of troops would have been the only possible way that the Gulf Coast could have been completely defended by land forces alone. The Americans did not have any such strength, and Jackson's one alternative was to outguess the enemy. These problems show clearly that naval power was absolutely essential for a proper defense of the coast.

Although Jackson committed too much of his strength eastward trying to hold Mobile, he conducted the best possible defense of the Gulf region, given his limited land and sea forces. Throughout the campaign, he maintained movement and conducted spoiling operations which disrupted British plans to a considerable degree and may have made the defense of New Orleans possible. The November attack on Pensacola, already described, was such an operation, and he was convinced that there he had disrupted British plans. The capture of Pensacola and the British defeat at Mobile Point helped influence the undecided Indians. Such maneuvers prevented the English from establishing bases and thus did much to protect the American rear. In another effort to eliminate a threat to his flank, Jackson detached Major Uriah Blue with men to kill or capture the Indians retreating from Pensacola and to destroy the British base at Apalachicola.[17] This expedition was unsuccessful but it was also one of Jackson's spoiling operations, by which he hoped to obstruct the British attack.

While in Pensacola, about the middle of November 1814, Jackson received positive information from his intelligence network that the British were planning an immediate assault on New Orleans. Therefore, he made plans to move his troops there.[18]* Having done all he could at Mobile, the general left James Winchester in command of the city with a substantial army. On November 22, 1814, Jackson himself set out overland for New Orleans. Considering the poor conditions of the trails and the bad weather, Jackson and his small staff made exceptional time, arriving at New Orleans on December 1.[19]

New Orleans, located about 150 miles above the mouths of the Mississippi, would have been difficult for any army to attack. It is located on dry land but is largely surrounded by marshes, swamps, shallow lakes, and the river itself. Except for a few trails and boat channels, the marshes and swamps were impassable. It would have been easy to defend these routes provided they could be located, but few of the passages were shown on the maps.

Students of the New Orleans campaign generally consider that there were at least seven possible routes the British might have used to attack New Orleans from the Gulf of Mexico. A cartographic study of the area indicates that there may have been even more approaches to the city, but none was a good route over which an army could easily be moved. There were seven promising ways to reach New Orleans.

The first of these was Bayou La Fourche, a narrow deep stream running from a point on the Gulf of Mexico well west of the delta and joining the Mississippi River at a location between Baton Rouge and New Orleans. It was really a mouth of the river, but because of its length and narrowness it could easily be obstructed.

The second route was Barataria Bay, opening on the Gulf of Mexico, 70 miles west of the main mouth of the Mississippi at a point almost directly south of the city of New Orleans. Above the bay were located a number of narrow channels leading to the Mississippi across from New Orleans. Laffite's Baratarians, who inhabited that area, were familiar with this route, and had they joined the British this would probably have been the best way to attack the city. Without pilots, however, the passage was difficult, and the channels could easily be closed and defended.

*Jane de Grummond mentioned that this intelligence leaked out in Jamaica because of the death of the admiral on that station. However, she was concerned with the Baratarians and failed to relate its significance to Jackson's movements.

The third of the routes was the main channel of the Mississippi itself, which was certainly the best approach to the city and was the only way that permitted naval vessels of any size to be used in the attack. The river was guarded by forts and batteries. Fort St. Philip was situated about 30 miles from the mouth, and about 40 miles farther up was Fort St. Leon, located at the English Turn. This particular spot was a strong point where the river made an *S*-shaped turn, and sailing ships normally had to wait for a change in the wind to advance up the river.

The fourth route was River Aux Chenes and Bayou Terre Aux Boeufs. These were small streams emptying into the Gulf just east of the mouth of the Mississippi and extending inland almost to the English Turn on the Mississippi. They were navigable by small boats but were also easily defended.

Three approaches were possible by way of Lake Borgne. The English could have ascended the Chef Menteur road to the Plain of Gentilly, a segment of dry land over which they could have marched to the city itself. Another route from Lake Borgne ran through one of the small bayous that came within a mile of the Mississippi River. The final, and possibly the best, choice was through Lake Borgne and the narrow strait known as the Rigolets across Lake Pontchartrain and up Bayou St. Jean. This course would take a landing party within two miles of the city and was in fact a well-known route of commerce. It was the one which the British had originally planned to take, but the shortage of light vessels chartered in Jamaica forced the abandonment of the plan.[20]

While still in Mobile, Jackson had sent Colonel Arthur P. Hayne, one of his aides, to New Orleans for an examination of the defenses of the city. Armed with Hayne's reports, the general on his arrival immediately began planning his defenses by a study of the various approaches that could be used by the British. His first concern was the defense of the river. He ordered Hayne to examine the Balize, the main mouth of the river, to see if it were possible to establish batteries there and prevent an enemy force from crossing the bar. Hayne advised that this point was indefensible and that Fort St. Philip was the key to the river. St. Philip was a well-developed fort, and in case extra guns were available, Hayne suggested that they should be used to support that fort rather than downriver.[21]

Jackson apparently agreed with Hayne and selected Fort St. Philip as the first line of defense. To provide a second line of defense, he ordered the fortification at the English Turn to be strengthened. Having made these preparations, he believed the river would be secure against the British fleet. Jackson was accompanied on his inspection of the forts by Commander Daniel Patterson, who no doubt furthered the general's education on naval matters.[22]

After a careful study of maps and reports on the topography of the area, the general sent detachments of Louisiana militia, commanded by Major General Gabriel Villeré, to fell trees and to act as scouts and guards for the numerous small streams that could be used to enter the city. Having provided troops to guard these easily defended routes, he turned his attention to Lakes Borgne and Pontchartrain. For the protection of the lakes, Jackson counted heavily on the gunboats belonging to the navy.[23]

Closer to the city, Jackson used Major Pierre Jugeat with a command of Choctaw Indians and Major Pierre La Coste's battalion of free men of color to guard the Chef Menteur road; and he sent Major Jean Plauche's uniformed New Orleans militia companies to Fort St. John and Fort Petites Coquilles north of the city there to keep watch upon the Lake Pontchartrain approach.[24]

Probably the most alarming factor that Jackson discovered at New Orleans was apathy. The Louisianians had not been willing to provide the funds that were needed for protection, and the credit of the United States was in bad repute in New Orleans. There were several groups, ranging from the governor to special citizens' committees, charged with guarding the city. This division of authority and duplication of effort caused great confusion and a waste of the available materials.[25]

Not only were the British threatening invasion but ill will and distrust between Anglo-Americans and citizens of French origin had been intensifying in recent months. General Thomas Flournoy, Jackson's predecessor in command of the Seventh Military District, had held the citizens of New Orleans in contempt, and he had made no secret of his feelings. His attitude was especially appalling to the sensitive Creoles of the city, whom he considered disloyal. Flournoy wrote Secretary of War Armstrong that the people would have commerce even if it meant trading with the enemy, and "they have no respect for the laws—& are ready at all times to oppose those who do." Finally, Flournoy concluded, "I do believe that there is not one person in twenty throughout this State, that is friendly to the United States, or who would take up arms in its defence."[26] He substantiated this belief in later communications in which he reported that 100 men of the Louisiana militia deserted when called to active service.[27] This fight between Flournoy and the Louisiana officials, though probably Flournoy's fault, was real enough and was well demonstrated when the state legislature in January 1814 refused to call out the militia when he requested it.[28]

The militia was eventually activated and paid by the state; but friction existed between various authorities, and there were many unpaid government accounts.[29]

The disaffection of the people of Louisiana was well known to the British, who believed that these citizens would never bear arms for the United States. The spirited defense of New Orleans by the French inhabitants came as a complete surprise to the British and was a severe blow to their morale. Bernard Marigny, the Creole leader, best described this change of heart on the part of the French in the following manner:

> When General Jackson arrived in New Orleans, all the inhabitants wished to fight. We know moreover that one cannot be French, or of French origin, without detesting the English domination. Our fathers had risen up in a body under M. de Galvez, to conquer, at the time of the war of American Independence, the two Floridas. We were then under the Spanish domination and all the world knows that men cannot degenerate under a republic like that of the United States. In 1812 the territory of Orleans was erected into a State and henceforth its inhabitants were in the enjoyment of all their rights. But the desire to fight was not sufficient. There was among them a sense of uneasiness, arising from a defect of organization. Governor Claiborne was a very honest man of personal bravery, but he had not the energy necessary to give a great impulse to the population of Louisiana. Besides the Government of the United States had not sent us any means of providing for our defense. In the magazines of the United States there were not 500 guns to distribute.
>
> Such was the state of affairs when General Andrew Jackson launched the Proclamation in which he announced that he was hastening to the defense of our State. Unfortunately in that Proclamation he declared that he would not make use of the Pirates who inhabited the Islands of Barataria.
>
> Never was a general received with more enthusiasm. His military reputation, his well-known firmness of character contributed to call forth a spontaneous movement. From all quarters, the cry was "to arms!" The whole population arose in a body. It would be impossible for our detractors to cite a single Louisianan, a single Creole, or a single naturalized Frenchman, who in the moment of danger, abandoned the country or refused to fight.[30]

Obviously what had been needed at New Orleans was a strong, energetic leader, and Jackson was just such a man. Perhaps some degree of the confidence inspired in the people of New Orleans by Jackson is best expressed in the words of Mrs. Edward Livingston: "Erect, composed, perfectly self possessed, with martial bearing, the soldier stood before them. One whom nature had stamped a gentleman."[31] If there had been apathy before he arrived, as one observer noted, it vanished overnight: "General Jackson arrived here yesterday and has already begun to put us in motion." While it was true that this frontiersman from Tennessee sometimes ran roughshod over the sensibilities of the inhabitants and had his battles with the local government, he commanded enough respect that the leaders of all factions smoothed each others' ruffled feelings in his behalf. In the last analysis, he was given all the support New Orleans had to offer, every gun and every able-bodied man, including the "free men of color."[32]

It would be appropriate to ask why New Orleans and Louisiana chose to support the United States, to which they had been attached for so few years. Marigny has undoubtedly supplied part of the answer, but there was more. Regardless of the attitude of the people toward the United States, they all disliked the British; worse, they feared what the English would do to their city. Everyone had seen the proclamation of the British requesting the Indians and slaves to rise up and join their standard. This manifesto did not call directly for a servile insurrection, but it did invite blacks to join His Majesty's forces. To the people of Louisiana, the real intent of the decree was to incite a slave revolt. Thoughts of a slave uprising especially terrified the people of Louisiana, many of whom had come to the area as refugees from Haiti.

An examination of the correspondence between Edward Nicolls and Admiral Cochrane confirms the worst fears of these citizens.[33] In addition to the British proclamations urging slaves to join the English cause, there were constant reports of black units being sent from Barbados, Jamaica, and the Bahamas. News of this kind gave additional substance to the idea of a British-supported slave insurrection.[34] Another factor which might have influenced the Louisianians was the report of English mistreatment of the Spaniards at Pensacola. These citizens, like those of Louisiana, had been promised British protection but had in fact been robbed and abused.

At New Orleans the American army grew daily with the arrival of troops from Tennessee and Kentucky. Had time permitted, Jackson would have had a very large army in the area.[35] The most immediate problem was the procurement of arms to equip these forces. In August, Jackson had ordered a large supply of muskets from Pittsburgh to be sent for the defense of New Orleans. These weapons, dispatched by slow flatboats, had not arrived, and a serious shortage resulted.[36] It was reported that there were only 500 muskets in the government arsenals of the city. Many American troops were without arms altogether. Some had arms but no flints, and all guns were in poor condition from hard use. Jackson is said to have obtained 7,500 flintlock pistols from Jean Laffite and his Baratarians. However, there is no record of Jackson's ever arming any of his men with pistols, even though many of them had no arms whatsoever. For this reason, one must suspect that Laffite supplied 7,500 pistol flints rather than 7,500 flintlock pistols.

There are many accounts of Jackson's change of heart in permitting the Baratarians (whom he had once described as "hellish banditti") to join his force. According to Marigny, the New Orleans Committee of Defense spent hours trying to persuade him to accept Laffite, with little apparent success. Edward Livingston, who was both Laffite's attorney and a good friend of Jackson, also attempted to persuade the general to accept Laffite's help. It was only after Laffite himself visited Jackson that the general finally accepted his services.

There were probably many factors involved in this change of mind. Jackson was much impressed with the man who showed considerable bravery in coming in person to talk to him. He respected this type of confrontation, as was demonstrated in his pardon of William Weatherford; and this respect, added to the persuasions of so many of his advisers, might well have been sufficient to change the general's mind. In any case, Laffite offered Jackson flints, powder, shot, possibly the above-mentioned pistols, and about 1,000 fighting men. To a general trying to defend a city against a superior force, such an offer was irresistible. The services of Laffite were accepted, and very quickly the two men appeared to have gained considerable respect for each other—so much so that the chief of the "banditti" almost immediately became one of Jackson's trusted lieutenants. Laffite furnished seamen to man the guns of *Carolina* and *Louisiana*, and their services proved invaluable during the battle. Since a large number of the Baratarians were well-trained cannoneers, they were used to man many of the batteries as well as to add strength to the all-important forts guarding the river and other approaches to the city.[37]

There was much discussion of Jackson's shortage of all kinds of arms and equipment before the battle of New Orleans. Yet once the action started, he appears to have been well supplied with most items. There is no doubt that Laffite supplied much matériel for the defense of New Orleans, although the exact quantities are not known. It is probable that both the Baratarians and the navy provided Jackson's troops with additional muskets. It is not clear whether the navy muskets were included in the 500 previously reported in government arsenals, or if the navy's contribution amounted to a large number of weapons; but some muskets were loaned to Jackson's militia units by Commander Daniel Patterson of the navy.[38]

Far more important, the navy depot at New Orleans contained a large amount of artillery of all types, from fieldpieces to large naval guns. Many of these cannon had been sent to New Orleans to be mounted on the gunboats that were to be built there. These vessels were never constructed, and the cannon had been placed in storage. Some of these guns were thirty-two-pounders, the largest available at that time. This artillery was to play an enormous role in the defense of New Orleans. Along with the rifles of the frontiersmen, they were Jackson's secret weapon.[39]

Before the battle with the British, there were constant hints that Jackson was short of cannon powder and balls, but the record shows that his batteries fired constantly at the British positions.[40] With this kind of fire from the American guns, it is evident that the defenders of New Orleans had accumulated a good supply of powder and balls from some source. While some of this material came from Barataria, there is no doubt that the navy also supplied much of it. An explanation of the good supply of the navy may be found in a letter of Paul Hamilton, then secretary of the navy, written in July 1812. Hamilton ordered the New Orleans station to be supplied with 100 tons of assorted shot and 200 barrels of cannon powder. The powder and shot were to be delivered in six months.[41] There was no reason to believe that these munitions were moved or expended, and certainly the contractors had delivered it by the end of 1814. This supply may explain why Jackson was able to keep up such a heavy bombardment of the British positions.

With the troops, arms, and defense in readiness, Jackson could only wait for the British to land and hope that his plans were complete.

12

The British Advance on New Orleans

THE PLAN for a British attack on the Gulf Coast evolved (in the beginning) from two separate but similar ideas: Cochrane's small-scale Indian operation, and the revived British plan to send a large force of men to be used directly against New Orleans. Some historians have not been aware of the plan for an Indian operation, and most of those who were cognizant of it have not recognized that these two plans of attack, the Indian and the direct assault, developed as different proposals and have therefore tended to treat them as one and the same.

Since both designs had New Orleans as their objective, ultimate or direct, and since the contemporary American commanders were themselves not aware that two plans existed, nearly all American records are inaccurate. During the late months of 1814, Cochrane and the British shifted their main emphasis to the direct attack on New Orleans. The Indian plan was retained as a diversion and an alternative action in case of failure of the direct attack.[1]*

*Marquis James apparently had no knowledge of Captain Pigot or the Indians at Apalachicola. Harry L. Coles was aware that Captain Pigot was sent to the mouth of the Apalachicola River to help the Creek Indians, but Coles was more concerned with the fact that Pigot proposed an attack on New Orleans. Because of his emphasis, Coles made little effort to understand the proposed new Indian campaign or to relate it to the Creek war. Reginald Horsman, John K. Mahon, and Robin Reilly's works are better in this regard and show a fairly good understanding of the operations; but because their main concern is with the New Orleans attack, the Apalachicola account is brief and it is not clear that either Reilly or Horsman is aware of the extent of the British operations with the Indians. Mahon's is the only work which develops the West Indian background of the movement at Apalachicola

Orders issued to General Ross and Admiral Cochrane gave the two men a maximum amount of freedom as to place and method of attack.[2] General Ross was killed during the assault on Baltimore, leaving the planning phase of the expedition in the hands of Cochrane and Colonel Arthur Brooks. The latter was an able officer but much junior to the admiral. Even the arrival of Major General Keane did not alter the situation. The newly appointed general was very young and inexperienced and was probably overawed by the admiral. The expedition was, therefore, planned almost entirely by Cochrane.[3]

With this great option in the instructions given to the expedition, there would have been no violation of orders or intent had Cochrane, and any general London sent out, decided to continue with the Indian plan which included first an attack on Mobile. It was apparently the wish of the government to cut off American communication through New Orleans and to capture the city, if possible. Also the British wished to occupy some valuable possession of the United States in order to improve the terms for peace.[4]

All indications are that well into August, or perhaps into September, Cochrane's plan was to use the Indians and the Mobile route. In fact, it is probable that the decision to strike New Orleans itself was made as a direct result of the knowledge that Andrew Jackson was in Mobile with a large army and that the city of New Orleans was almost entirely unprotected. Such indeed was the case in the fall of 1814.[5] Cochrane may have made his final decision to strike New Orleans without attempting to secure a mainland base after reaching Jamaica and discovering that his plans were known by the Americans.[6] The great increase in the number of troops assigned to the expedition may also have influenced Cochrane to dispense with the preliminary operations and to strike New Orleans directly.

The Atlantic diversion under Admiral Cockburn and the renewed Indian war and slave uprising under Nicolls would have been useful in an attack on any part of the Gulf Coast. Consequently, there was no reason to change the orders of either of these men.[7] Although Nicolls was ordered to bring his Indians aboard ship and to join forces with Cochrane at New Orleans, there is little doubt that the admiral intended for him to bring only a few chiefs who would be impressed by the great British victory.[8]

The theory that Cochrane intended using the Indian operations not only as a diversion but also as a secondary offensive is supported by the excessively large amount of arms sent to them. These included 3,000 muskets,

---

and tries to relate the events to the Creek war. None of these is a detailed study, and little is done to explain the British relations with the lower Creeks or the Spanish role in this conflict.

1,000 pistols, 1,000 carbines, 500 rifles, more than 1,000,000 rounds of ammunition, and 1,000 sabers. This was more than enough to arm all the surviving Creek and Seminole warriors.[9]

Nicolls' forces were expected to perform several important functions, one of which was to divert as many American troops as possible from the defense of New Orleans. Since Nicolls' Indians and blacks were never able to make significant raids on the Georgia frontier, they cannot be said to have inflicted any serious damage. The diversionary value of Nicolls' forces, however, was considerable. His little army was directly responsible for distracting from other duties 2,500 Georgia militia and friendly Indians, along with Major Uriah Blue's force of about 1,000 men, which included a substantial part of John Coffee's brigade. The Georgia militia and friendly Indians might not have been used in another area, but 1,000 selected men from Jackson's own army would certainly have been useful at New Orleans. Another fairly successful part of Nicolls' plan was to disrupt communications between the Georgia frontier and Mobile, thus delaying and reducing the size of General McIntosh's army of Georgia militia, which was intended for the reinforcement of Mobile and New Orleans.[10]

The other diversion was intended for the area of coastal Georgia and South Carolina. This expedition was to be composed of Cockburn's fleet and a force of almost 2,000 marines. It was planned that Cockburn would harass the Atlantic coast, starting in the Chesapeake area and gradually working southward, seizing the offshore islands and making raids inland. In addition, the group was reinforced by enlisting runaway slaves into special regiments of "colonial" marines. Some units of West Indian black troops were assigned to Cockburn's expedition to serve as cadres for these recruits.[11] Cochrane intended to excite fear with his black troops, not unlike the terror engendered by a slave revolt. He wrote Lord Bathurst, "The blacks are all good horsemen thousands will join upon their masters horses—and they will only require to be clothed and accoutred. They will with the assistance of officers, to bring them a little regularity, be as good Cossacks as any in the Russian army—and I believe more terrific to the Americans than any troops that could be brought forward."[12] Not all officers agreed with Cochrane's idea of the value of black troops. Admiral Cockburn considered that most of the slaves simply wished to accompany the British to freedom, and in fact had no desire to fight anyone. Nonetheless, he was well pleased with the blacks who were willing to serve.[13]

Cockburn's raids were delayed for lack of ships and men. Once this difficulty was overcome, he began making attacks on the coastal islands of Georgia. Early in January, 1815, he occupied Cumberland Island and a short time later captured St. Marys, Georgia. These operations netted considerable plunder, and numbers of blacks joined the British forces. Cockburn was planning an attack on Savannah when the end of the war was announced.[14]

Wilburt Brown believed that the Atlantic coastal operation came too late to have any diversionary value in the Louisiana campaign. The actual attacks took place after the English defeat at New Orleans. The Americans were aware of the probability of Cockburn's raids well before this time, and great efforts were made to defend the Atlantic Coast. These preparations undoubtedly diverted or delayed the reinforcement of Jackson's army from Georgia and South Carolina. Several thousand troops were reassigned to the Atlantic coastal defense.[15] General John Floyd was stationed near Savannah with about 2,100 Georgia militia; General Thomas Pinckney had several regiments of Georgia and South Carolina militia and about two regiments of regulars at Charleston and other points along the coast; and General David Blackshear's unit of 900 men was diverted from its march to New Orleans, first to fight the Indians, and later to reinforce Floyd. In all, Cockburn must have diverted at least 6,000 American troops from other duties. The operation could hardly be called a waste of time.[16]

The main expedition against the Gulf Coast was to be formed at Negril Bay, Jamaica, around November 20, at which time Ross' army and Cochrane were to rendezvous with the army units arriving from Europe.[17] As soon as Ross' death was known in London, Lieutenant General Sir Edward Pakenham was appointed in his place as commander of army forces in the New Orleans expedition. The general was given the same orders as Ross and sent out to meet Cochrane at Negril Bay. Pakenham, a trusted subordinate and brother-in-law of the Duke of Wellington, was doubtless one of the best generals available.[18]

One problem faced by Cochrane that disrupted the attack on both New Orleans and Mobile was a shortage of flatboats and light-draft vessels. Such craft were needed for an attack on either city and were absolutely essential for moving British forces into Lake Pontchartrain. Cochrane complained bitterly that the orders to send out flatboats with the troop transports had not been obeyed and that he had been unable to hire enough light-draft schooners. Considering the stress he had laid on shallow-draft boats, it seems certain that his plan at this time was to attack New Orleans through Lake Pontchartrain and that the lack of landing craft was a major factor in changing his mind.[19] This breakdown in Cochrane's plan was largely due to the death of the admiral on the Jamaica station and the subsequent confusion caused by the change of command. This emergency also led to serious intelligence leaks, described by Admiral Cochrane in his letter to Croker, December 7, 1814.

> I conceive it highly encumbent upon me to state to their Lordships that on my arrival at Jamaica, I found to my very great astonishment, the intention of sending an expedition against New Orleans and Louisiana which I had taken the utmost precautions to keep profoundly secret, publickly known throughout Port Royal and Kingston a very few hours after the arrival there of their Lordships instructions, and my secret and confidential letters to the Late Rear Admiral Brown relative to this service, which I forwarded to him from the Chesapeake in September last.
>
> It appears that these were opened by Captain Thorgill, who at the time of their arrival was senior officer in Port Royal, and upon them he issued to Captain Bremer, the agent of transportation an order of which I send here with a copy. Submitting for their lordships consideration, whether, under the strict secrecy enjoined Captain Bremer was not furnished with more particulars than there was any necessity of detailing to him for his performance of that part of the service which Captain Thorgill thought proper to entrust him.
>
> To one or the other of these officers must be attributed the publicity of the intended operations, of which correspondence of the enemy have not failed to avail themselves, four days after the arrival of these letters, a Mr. Hudson who is connected with a mercantile house in New Orleans sailed from Jamaica in a small schooner that cleared out for Pensacola, and I have to consider that through him, about three weeks since the information was brought (via Orleans) to General Jackson at Pensacola, where he had entered a few days before with an army of three thousand men, and had made his dispositions for remaining during the winter months; this information however caused him to relinquish his intentions and proceed immediately for New Orleans.[20]

Not wishing to make major changes in the expedition at this late date, the admiral decided to waste no more time at Jamaica and to make the assault at once. As a result, he left Negril Bay on November 26 and immediately headed for New Orleans. The fact that Cochrane remained in Jamaica only eight days leaves little doubt that he intended to reach New Orleans ahead of Jackson's army. Considering his implied plan of getting to New Orleans first, it seems probable that, contrary to the view of some historians, Cochrane was not trying to make the attack before General Edward Pakenham arrived but was using good sense in trying to salvage what he could from a bad situation. Faced with the same circumstances, Pakenham and most other commanders would have followed an identical course.[21]

In an effort to charter or buy additional small schooners, Cochrane dispatched Captain Robert Spencer to Pensacola. Spencer's mission was only partly successful, and Cochrane was not able to obtain enough of the needed landing craft.[22] The fleet arrived off Chandler Island, the new rendezvous point, on December 8 and began to scout the area. Captain James Gordon of H.M.S. *Seahorse* reported sighting five American gunboats.

By this time Cochrane had decided to land his force at a place he called Bayou Catalone at the head of Lake Borgne. His description of Bayou Catalone indicated that he was referring to Bayou Bienvenu, which was the point where the expedition finally landed. He had determined that it would be necessary to capture or destroy the gunboats before he could land the army. This step was essential because the troops had to be transported over 60 miles of shallow water in small boats where they would be vulnerable to attack by these American vessels. Cochrane sent Captain Lockyer of H.M.S. *Sophie* with all the launches and barges of the squadron to board and capture the enemy squadron.[23] The gunboats' commander, Thomas ap Catesby Jones, first sighted the British fleet on December 12. When Jones first observed the large British flotilla of barges, he thought they were unloading troops. However, when the English proceeded through Pass Christian and continued westward, Jones realized that they intended to attack his gunboats. Outnumbered as he was, he decided that the best place to make a defense was near the Petites Coquilles, a pass from which he could retreat into Lake Pontchartrain if necessary.

The British barges first pursued and cut off the American schooner *Seahorse,* which was in Bay St. Louis attempting to remove supplies. Thus separated from the gunboats, *Seahorse* fought off a force of seven English vessels for about thirty minutes before being blown up.[24] Jones continued to retreat before the fleet of barges and boats until the morning of December 14, when the wind died completely. Unable to continue his retreat, Jones drew his five gunboats into a line across the channel at the west end of Malheureux Island and prepared to fight. The American tender *Alligator,* separated from Jones' main fleet, was captured by the British about 9:30 A.M. Subsequently, the British carefully formed their boats for the main assault, which was launched at 10:30 A.M. Jones' position was weakened slightly by the current, which caused two of his boats to drift about a hundred yards out of line, making them more vulnerable to boarding. After repelling the boarders several times, Jones' boats were all finally captured a little before 1:00 P.M. The British used the first two captured gunboats to assault the others.[25]

This battle was not an easy victory for the British. They had to row for

36 hours to catch the Americans, and the resistance was spirited.[26] Jones' fleet gave an exceptionally good account of itself, exacting a very large number of casualties from a much greater British force. The English flotilla consisted of 45 barges and boats carrying 1,200 men and 43 guns ranging in caliber from twelve-pounders to twenty-four-pounders. The American squadron carried 183 men and 23 guns, ranging in caliber from six-pounders to thirty-two-pounders. Most of the American guns were small, but each gunboat carried at least one long gun of large caliber. This gave the Americans a range advantage over the British guns, all of which were carronades of short range. The advantage was, however, offset by the tiny targets. In spite of their small size, Jones did sink several British boats; their destruction was a real tribute to his marksmanship. He described his loss in killed and wounded as slight.[27] The British casualties of 17 killed and 77 wounded were much heavier and included a high proportion of officers.[28]

One interesting feature of this battle was that Commander Patterson had been ordered by the secretary of the navy to replace all his sailing gunboats with vessels of the type which could also be rowed.[29] Had Jones' gunboats been equipped with oars, as ordered, the British barge fleet would probably have been unable to catch them, and the outcome of the battle would have been quite different. The British captured the five gunboats and the tender *Alligator.* Cochrane found them to be in good condition, and he immediately ordered them manned by British crews.[30] It has been rightly suggested that Jones should have blown up his gunboats to prevent their capture when escape became impossible, but this would have been a very difficult thing for the young naval commander to do. Jones and his men wanted to fight the British and would have probably considered it dishonorable to have done less.

Jackson rightly considered the loss of the gunboats as extremely serious. He reported that all possibility of sea communication with Mobile was cut off, and that city was effectively blockaded. The only contact with Mobile was now on interior roads, a system which was not satisfactory.[31] Even more serious, the loss of Jones' squadron gave the British command of Lake Borgne, enabling them to use any of the numerous bayous and canals which were the approaches to New Orleans. Although reports of this loss caused Jackson to redouble his efforts to obstruct and guard these routes, the gunboats had been the general's scouts. Without them he could not tell where the enemy would land.[32]

In spite of the great amount of criticism of the American gunboat fleet, these vessels were very useful in the shallow water off the Gulf Coast. C. S. Forester, in *The Age of Fighting Sail,* declared that the Americans had badly neglected the defenses of New Orleans. There were about twenty-five gunboats and a blockship authorized for the defense of New Orleans, but only six were actually in use. Forrester estimated that "an energetic construction program on Lake Borgne . . . might have foiled Cochrane altogether." The naval engagement postponed the landing of the British army for several days. Forrester contended that the gunboat action gave Jackson six extra days to prepare his defenses.[33] Probably the most significant feature of this delay was that it allowed many additional American troops to reach New Orleans.[34]

Wilburt Brown believed that Patterson was in error in trying to use his gunboats to scout the British fleet. Brown thought that the gunboats should have been used to reinforce the guns of the forts at the Rigolets and smaller, faster vessels used to scout the English.[35] Brown is undoubtedly correct in recommending the use of smaller scouting vessels; but the mission was assigned to the gunboats, and their loss made it impossible for Jackson to know in advance the location of the British landing.

There was a significant difference of opinion concerning the naval defense of New Orleans between William Jones, the secretary of the navy, and the officers commanding the naval station at that place. Patterson's predecessor had started the construction of a blockship, and Patterson had continued its building to a point where it was fairly close to completion. Jones considered the blockship entirely worthless, and in March 1814 he ordered Patterson to suspend all work on the vessel at once.[36] The decision to abandon the blockship was probably one of the worst mistakes of Secretary Jones' career. This vessel was designed to carry as much armament as a small frigate and had a draft of only six and one-half feet.[37] Had it been completed, the British landing would probably have been impossible.

American strategists had usually thought of the gunboat as a defensive weapon, but Cochrane considered gunboats an extremely useful offensive weapon. He rightly considered a light-draft vessel carrying a heavy gun to be especially helpful in support of troop landings.[38]

Having cleared Lake Borgne of all enemy vessels, Cochrane was now in position to go forward with his landing operations. The route in question, Bayou Bienvenu, was a stream or ditch which drained the area east of New Orleans into Lake Borgne. It was supposedly discovered by the British through interviews with fishermen and American deserters, and it was scouted by Lieutenant John Peddie and Captain Robert Spencer on the night of December 18.[39] As indicated in Cochrane's correspondence, he and General Keane had already jointly decided to use this route before Peddie and Spencer scouted it.[40] Harry Coles and others have suggested

Cochrane probably was the dominant figure in determining the landing site, although there is no positive evidence in the records to indicate that Keane disagreed with the decision.[41]

A much better approach to New Orleans, the route which Cochrane had first planned to use, would have been to pass through Lake Borgne and the Rigolets into Lake Pontchartrain and land behind New Orleans. The admiral, however, was deceived into believing that Fort Petites Coquilles was defended by 40 guns and 500 men.[42] While this alleged defense may have been a factor in Cochrane's decision, the lack of the necessary light-draft vessels was probably more significant because his men would have had to row even farther. In any case, the hardest task facing the British was that, even without opposition, their troopships could not come within 60 miles of the landing point on Lake Borgne. This situation made it necessary to row all troops and supplies that distance in open boats.[43]

As soon as the news of the capture of the gunboats reached the British fleet, General Keane assembled the advanced elements of the army and ferried them to Pea Island at the mouth of the Pearl River. This island, not much more than a swampy sandbar, was not a good base of operations. It did, however, allow the force to be advanced 30 miles into Lake Borgne, about half the distance. The ferrying operation started on December 17 and lasted until December 22. After a cold, wet stay on the island, the light brigade composed of the Eighty-fifth, Ninety-fifth, and Fourth regiments, under the personal command of General Keane, was again loaded into boats on the morning of December 22 and started toward Bayou Bienvenu. Keane's division reached the bayou at daylight the next day and went ashore without any opposition.

The British seized the Villeré plantation and made it their headquarters. When Keane arrived at this point, a few miles below New Orleans, he was faced with the choice of advancing immediately to the city or waiting there for the rest of the army. The fishermen who had guided the army and served as pilots stated that Jackson had only about 2,000 men in New Orleans. If this were true, a fast advance might make possible the immediate capture of the city by surprise. On the other hand, Keane had received information from several sources, including the doctors who had been sent by the Americans to treat the wounded prisoners taken in the gunboat battle, that Jackson's army at New Orleans had about 20,000 men. After consideration, Keane chose the course of caution and decided to wait, thus losing what may have been the best chance to capture the city. Estimates of Jackson's strength at this time vary, but he probably had around 4,000 men.

Keane's decision was to remain on the Villeré plantation in a defensive position until the boats could land the rest of his troops. In the meantime, his men, wet, tired, and many of them ill from the days in the cold, open boats or on Pea Island, established a bivouac.[44] The British had expected Louisiana to be a warm area. Instead, there was much rain and frost every night. The 1,000 Jamaican black troops, without proper clothing, suffered the most and were demoralized by illness.[45]

The advanced party of Keane's army, commanded by Colonel William Thornton of the Eighty-fifth Regiment, arrived at the Villeré plantation, at the head of Bayou Bienvenu, around 4:00 A.M. At about 11:00 A.M., they surrounded General Jacques Villeré's house and captured the general himself with a company of militia. While this incident does not speak well for the militia guards, at least the general's son, Major Gabriel Villeré, was able to escape and warn Jackson of the English landing. The first news of the invasion was reported by men of the militia under Colonel Denis de Laronde. Since this information was sketchy, Jackson sent Major A. L. Latour and Major Howell Tatum to ascertain whether the British had actually landed in force. Major Villeré, whose escape from the British had forced him to take a roundabout route across the river, reached New Orleans with his warning a short time later. About 2:00 P.M. Latour returned and presented a detailed report that the British had landed in force and were already establishing themselves.[46] Jackson immediately began getting his troops ready for action. Latour's information indicated that the British had landed from 1,600 to 1,800 men. Jackson realized that this was only the advance guard of the British army, and he resolved to attack immediately, hoping to defeat or weaken the enemy piecemeal.[47]

The Americans had between 3,500 and 5,000 men in the immediate vicinity of New Orleans. Probably the situation was so fluid that the exact number of American troops who were able to reach New Orleans was not known even to the commanding general. In any case, Jackson attacked the British with about 1,600 to 2,000 men. Accounts vary as to the exact number of men in the striking force. This group was composed of General Coffee's detachment of 800 men, about 400 militia, and about 600 regulars of the Seventh and Forty-fourth regiments. The remainder of his army, including all of General Carroll's men and the New Orleans' city militia, was dispatched to guard the Gentilly Road.

Another very important asset for this attack was the naval support. On the afternoon of December 23 Jackson had requested Commander Patterson to bring as many vessels as he could downriver to the Villeré plantation and to fire on the British encampment. Patterson had two armed vessels available to him, the *Carolina* and the *Louisiana*.[48] The latter was not ready for action at this time, leaving only *Carolina* to participate in the attack. She was a new ship, built in Charleston, South Carolina, and normally carried a crew of 95 men and twelve-pounders or eighteen-pounders for her battery.[49]* In this engagement she carried only one long twelve-pounder and a number of light twelve-pounder carronades.[50] With these preparations Jackson planned to meet the British in the first day's battle for New Orleans.

*One of the reasons the *Louisiana*, and perhaps some other naval vessels, were not available for the battle of December 23 was the extreme shortage at New Orleans of experienced seamen. The problem was solved when the Baratarians were pardoned and allowed to serve; but because this action was taken only a day or two before the attack, some available guns and vessels, such as the *Louisiana*, were not ready for action. According to Jane de Grummond, a large part of the *Carolina*'s crew during the fight for New Orleans were in fact Baratarians.

13

The Battle of New Orleans (I)

WITH PART of the British army ashore and planning its assault, Jackson, always aggressive, decided to attack immediately. The general realized that only a small part of the British army had debarked and that by a surprise attack he might be able to destroy it. In any event, whether the attack resulted in a total victory or not, it would throw the British off balance and disrupt their operations.

Jackson's intelligence had informed him that the British planned to make their main attack through Lake Pontchartrain. Believing that the landing below New Orleans was a diversion, he posted General Carroll's brigade and the Louisiana militia on the Gentilly Road, located between New Orleans and Lake Pontchartrain. On the evening of December 23 he marched his remaining force of 1,600 to 2,000 men to meet the enemy.* The Americans reached a point near the enemy encampment by 7:00 P.M.[1] This movement was made after dark, but a full moon gave enough light for the army to march with little difficulty.[2]

The right wing of the army, composed of most of the regulars, was placed on a line perpendicular to the river stretching from the levee well into the Laronde plantation. The artillery was stationed on the road and guarded by a company of marines.[3] General Coffee's brigade, along with Colonel Thomas Hinds' Mississippi dragoons, largely armed with rifles, were sent to the extreme left in order to attack the British flank.[4] The schooner *Carolina* was to open fire on the British camp from the river. This bombardment, the signal for Jackson's army to attack, began about

*Wilburt Brown believes that had the British made a move toward the Plain of Gentilly, Jackson would have probably pulled his entire army to the east of the city.

7:30 P.M.[5] In her passage down the river, *Carolina* was frequently hailed by the enemy sentries, but they apparently mistook her for a merchant ship and no alarm was given.

The British had built large campfires, and probably for the first time in a week they were trying to get rested and warm. The earliest warning came when *Carolina* shot into their campfires. They were completely confused by this bombardment, but quickly took cover. Colonel Thornton's Eighty-fifth Regiment was immediately placed along the levee and opened a heavy musket fire on the ship. Although caught by surprise, the British claimed that they suffered only one casualty during the initial bombardment.

The only cannon the British had on shore were three-pounders, which were considered useless against a ship. Congreve rockets were fired at *Carolina*, but these inaccurate weapons were entirely unsuccessful. After some forty-five minutes, the British ceased firing on the ship. The American vessel continued to bombard the British flank until about nine o'clock. Commander Patterson reported that after the campfires were extinguished it was too dark to see the enemy, and the ship shot at flashes of the British muskets. Once these were silent, *Carolina* ceased fire.[6]

The land action began as soon as *Carolina* started her bombardment with Coffee's men rushing the enemy's right. These forces continued to push the enemy's flank until they had reached a position near the levee. A ground fog had arisen and Coffee withdrew, realizing that he would be unable to dislodge the British from their cover. Part of the British Eighty-fifth Regiment, moving forward to reinforce the advance guard fighting Jackson, ran directly into Coffee's men. There was heavy hand-to-hand action in which both sides took a number of prisoners and casualties.[7]

Concurrent with Coffee's attack, the right wing of the American army engaged the British advance guard and drove it back to a defense line along a fence and ditch. This British position held; and when the ground fog became too thick for the American units to hold together, Jackson called off the assault.

During the course of the battle, the Americans' main force advanced about three hundred yards, but because of the fog and darkness the units became separated. The British counterattacked between the Seventh and Forty-fourth regiments and nearly captured the American artillery. Jackson took direct command and saved his guns by pushing a company of the Seventh Infantry with bayonets into the fight. The firing ceased about 9:00 P.M., after which Coffee's troops rejoined the main army. About five o'clock in the morning, the Americans withdrew two miles and took up a defensive position behind the old, partly filled Rodriguez Canal.

Around 11:30 A.M. the Louisiana militia under General David Morgan moved up the river and attacked the rear of the English position. Morgan's men were stationed at the English Turn below the British forces, and learning of the landing they had marched north to engage the enemy. Although Morgan's attack did not succeed in driving the invader back, it served as a diversionary action.

The heaviest loss during the fight was to Beale's rifle company, which had been part of Coffee's command. This detachment, composed largely of New Orleans merchants and lawyers, became separated in the darkness and advanced directly into the center of the British camp area where 38 of the unit's 64 men were captured.[8] The cost of this engagement was high, each side losing over 10 percent of its men. British losses were 46 killed, 167 wounded, and 64 captured, a total of 277 casualties.[9] Jackson's army lost 24 killed, 115 wounded, and 74 captured, for 213 casualties.[10]

The American general was disappointed that he had not succeeded in destroying the British, but the attack was clearly an American victory. It had a disruptive and demoralizing effect on the British and convinced the British general that the Americans must have at least 15,000 men in New Orleans. As a result, Keane did not consider any advance until his entire army had landed. Jackson thus gained a few more days to increase the fortifications without any sign of enemy movement.[11] During the night following the battle, both armies on the line were reinforced.

Jackson realized that as soon as the British discovered that there were only 350 Louisiana militia at the English Turn, they would attack and capture the Americans. He therefore ordered Colonel Reuben Kemper, the old filibusterer, to take 100 of the men and Morgan's artillery and reinforce Fort St. Leon on the west bank. Morgan with the rest of his command was to cross the river and establish a defense line opposite Jackson's position on the Rodriguez Canal.[12]

After breaking contact with the English, Jackson left Hinds' Mississippi dragoons and the Feliciana (Louisiana Militia) dragoons at the Laronde plantation to observe the enemy's actions. The British had placed their camp between two parallel levees, which it was thought would offer them some protection against a land attack and from constant fire by *Carolina* and the newly arrived *Louisiana*. These two ships poured a steady fire day and night into the British camp. While the British suffered few casualties, the effect on their morale was disastrous.[13]*

*Wilburt Brown considers that this breakdown of British morale was the major factor in the British defeat. While Brown's view may be an exaggeration, the morale factor certainly hurt the British.

The arrival of Lieutenant General Pakenham on Christmas Day with a sizable reinforcement animated the army once more. Pakenham, the new British commander, was not pleased with the position in which he found his army. According to some accounts, he wanted to withdraw and attack at another point; but he was dissuaded by Admiral Cochrane, whose contempt for the American troops had convinced him that they would break and run before a frontal attack.* Cochrane agreed that it would be desirable to be rid of *Carolina* and *Louisiana* before making any assault; with this in mind, he brought ashore heavy ships' guns and built a furnace for making hot shot. On December 27 the new British batteries opened fire with hot shot and soon *Carolina* was on fire.[14] If the captains of *Louisiana* and *Carolina* had realized the danger, they could have dropped downstream out of range of the British batteries. Instead they tried to move upstream, and in doing so they subjected the ships to British fire for a much longer time. *Carolina* burned, forcing the crew to abandon her; shortly thereafter she exploded.[15]

In addition to the bombardment from the ships, the American riflemen, especially the Choctaw Indians, hurt British morale with their nightly raids on the English pickets. Although this action did not result in heavy losses, the British complained bitterly that such tactics were against the rules of civilized warfare.[16]

Jackson ordered that the levees above and below the British encampment be cut as another part of the planned harassment of the British. Since the river was high, he hoped to flood the area above and below their camp, completely isolating the enemy or at least causing them to become mired down. This tactic proved useless as the level of the river dropped.[17] The cutting of the levee actually helped the British: the breaks let in enough water to fill the canals and made it easier for them to move up their heavy guns by boat.[18]

In the meantime, Jackson, in his position at the Rodriquez Canal, continued to dig his ditch deeper and pile his mud bank higher. In order to eliminate any cover which might aid the attacking British, Jackson ordered all

*Fortescue argues that Pakenham wanted to withdraw but did not believe that he could evacuate his army without first disrupting Jackson's army by some sort of attack. According to Fortescue's reasoning, Pakenham was in such a bad position that an effort to withdraw without some weakening of the Americans might leave the British army open to destruction should Jackson attack during the withdrawal. Actually both Cochrane and a number of the army commanders did not have any great respect for the American fighting qualities, and it is doubtful that Pakenham could have withdrawn without widespread accusations of cowardice (Fortescue, *British Army*, 10:161–62).

brush in the area in front of his lines removed and the buildings on the Chalmette and Bienvenu plantations burned. The American forces destroyed the Chalmette buildings but were prevented from burning the structures on the Bienvenu plantation by a British advance. At first, Jackson's line was to extend only to the cypress woods, leaving a substantial amount of undefended dry land on the left end of the American position. This flaw in his defense was called to the general's attention by Jean Laffite, and Jackson immediately ordered the line extended to the swamp.[19]*

The batteries in Jackson's line were placed on wooden platforms laid on top of cotton bales, which prevented them from sinking into the muddy soil. The covering breastwork was made of mounds of earth with openings formed of cotton bales. These bales caught fire when hit and had to be replaced after the first action. It is difficult to determine the exact amount of artillery Jackson had in place during the first engagements. Throughout the series of battles he continued to add more and more guns to his line. According to one account he had established four batteries by December 28 and increased the number to eight by January 8. The first four American batteries emplaced were composed of two six-pounder field guns, a six-pound howitzer and two naval twenty-four-pounders. The naval guns were manned by Laffite's Baratarians. In the river *Louisiana* was in position to cover Jackson's right.[20] The American line, when it reached the swamp, was about three-fourths of a mile long, one-third of it in the cypress forest.[21]

At daylight on December 28 Pakenham attacked, moving forward in two columns toward the American lines. The formation nearest the river, under General Keane, advanced to within 800 yards of Jackson's right and opened fire with two field guns. Keane's men took cover and waited for their bombardment to disrupt the defenses. His hope for a successful assault, however, was quickly dashed when the guns of *Louisiana* and the artillery on Jackson's lines caught his troops in a crossfire, forcing them to remain under cover.

The second British column moved close to the woods out of range of the ship's guns. It had more success. This unit under General Samuel Gibbs and Colonel Robert Rennie succeeded in driving back Carroll's skirmishers, who had taken a position in advance of the line. Although Rennie took some heavy rifle fire from the Choctaw Indians hidden in the woods,

*Apparently by December 25 Jackson had become so enamoured of this Baratarian bandit that he had made him an aide. His choice was excellent. There was probably no man in New Orleans who knew the unusual means of getting to the city better than Jean Laffite.

he had very nearly reached Jackson's line at its weakest point when he received an order from Pakenham to retreat. Had Sir Edward been able to see Rennie's near success, he would undoubtedly have continued the attack; but observing Keane's failure, he believed that his second column was doing no better.[22]*

While there is no list of British casualties for this battle alone, army records show 16 killed, 38 wounded, and 2 missing, a total of 56 casualties between December 25 and December 31.[23] American casualties on December 28 were 17, 9 killed, 8 wounded, and none missing.[24]

The effectiveness of American fire persuaded Pakenham that the only way to defeat Jackson's army was to bring up more artillery and silence the enemy guns. Some had already been brought to sink *Carolina,* but Sir Edward believed he now needed more. Because of the serious transportation problem, Pakenham was unable to get his batteries until December 31.

Another part of Pakenham's plan was to have Admiral Cochrane make a diversion. Sir Edward probably knew from prisoners that Jackson had first expected an attack through Lake Pontchartrain, and he believed that Cochrane could give him effective support by making a diversion toward either the lake or the mouth of the river.[25] The admiral made both of these distracting operations as requested and did in fact draw off some of Jackson's troops.[26]**

Following the attack of the twenty-eighth, the American general continued to improve the breastworks. He also made a considerable addition to his artillery. He mounted a thirty-two-pound naval gun at the center of his line and to the left of this he added another six-pounder, a twelve-pounder, an eighteen-pounder and an old brass carronade. All his guns except the carronade were manned by regular army gunners, naval gunners, Baratarians, and former French artillerists.[27] In addition to the artillery on Jackson's line, Commander Patterson established a battery of two twelve-pounders and a twenty-four-pounder on the west bank of the river, so positioned as to fire on the flank of any attack on Jackson's line.[28]

During the last four days of December, Pakenham, with incredible effort, landed ten eighteen-pounders and four twenty-four-pound carronades. These guns and their ammunition were brought from the ships by

*Major C. R. Forrest, Pakenham's quartermaster, reported that this action took place on December 27, but since all other accounts give the date as December 28, it seems probable that Forrest's date was in error.

**It must be remembered that Jackson had expected the main British landing in the area of Chef Menteur, an expectation which he had probably passed on to the officers who commanded the position. Since a landing had been the original British plan, which to Cochrane's knowledge had leaked to Jackson, one cannot help wondering if Cochrane were not trying to take advantage of an intelligence leak.

boat across Lake Borgne and up the canal to within a quarter of a mile of the main road. At this point they were unloaded from the boats and placed on carts or the limbers of the field guns and dragged in place by large parties of seamen. Four eighteen-pounders were placed on the main road in a battery protected by dirt-filled hogsheads. This battery was designed to fire upon *Louisiana* if she came within range. Another battery of six eighteen-pounders was placed in position to breach the center of Jackson's line. Still another of the four twenty-four-pound carronades, with the field guns and howitzer, were established to keep up a fire while the British troops advanced to storm the breastworks. The batteries were completed and the guns put in place during the night of December 31.

The British opened fire on the morning of January 1, 1815, as the fog cleared at nine o'clock.[29] When the bombardment started, great confusion appeared for a time, in the American line, but soon Jackson's guns returned the fire and a heavy cannonade took place. The British barrage did not breach Jackson's mud wall, and it soon became apparent to Pakenham that the artillery was ineffective. The British general therefore ordered the guns withdrawn to a safe position.[30]

When one considers the advantages enjoyed by the British, it is surprising that they did so poorly in this bombardment. The English batteries were mounted low, whereas Jackson's were on high platforms. Presumably this made them easier targets. Also, the British had between twenty-six and thirty guns, allowing them to throw a heavier weight of metal than the Americans. Some historians report that Jackson had planned a parade of his army for the morning of January 1. However, the first British shots were fired at the Macarté house, Jackson's headquarters. The general and his staff were in the house at the time, and it is unlikely that any parade was actually underway. The fact remains that the American troops were not in position nor ready for an encounter, and there was apparently some confusion.[31]* Under these circumstances, it is not surprising that the Americans were slow to return the fire. In spite of the confusion, the professional coolness of the American gunners was well demonstrated when they shot a number of single guns in order to get the British range. The British had not taken the time to find the proper range, perhaps because they wanted maximum surprise. The result of this haste was that by the time they realized that their shots were landing in the fields well behind Jackson's lines,

*Robin Reilly shows clearly that, though Jane de Grummond and Charles Brooks both give accounts of a parade, neither lists a good source. Reilly also shows that the only contemporary reference to a parade is by George Gleig, who was entirely too far from the action to have seen anything.

they had wasted a good part of their ammunition, already in short supply.[32]

The Americans clearly won this engagement. Some British guns were smashed or dismounted, and many others were partly damaged by the extremely accurate fire of the Americans. The dirt-filled sugar barrels used by the British in their efforts to speed the construction of breastworks proved utterly useless and were quickly shattered by the American bombardment. The British failure to place any flooring in some batteries and inadequate flooring in others caused the emplacements to become quagmires and, when some of the barrels still containing sugar burst it became almost impossible to operate the guns.[33] Patterson's naval batteries succeeded in disabling the British artillery mounted on the levee and may have helped in the destruction of the other positions. The balls that hit Jackson's mud breastworks simply sank into the mud, leaving hardly a mark.[34] The British fire was not completely without effect. Three American guns were damaged, including the thirty-two-pounder. Sir Edward did not realize that his guns had done any damage.

Rear Admiral Sir Edward Codrington considered the defeat a blot on the artillery service, and he was correct in his criticism that they had wasted far too much ammunition before finding the range of the American lines.[35] British artillery commander Colonel Alexander Dickson noted in his private journal that the English guns were forced to cease fire for "want of ammunition." He also complained that the navy-type gun carriages did not work well in the poorly floored positions. Dickson denied that any of his heavy ordnance was damaged but admitted damage to its traveling carriages and numerous casualties among the gun crews. Reilly rightly describes Dickson's statement that the artillery was inadequate as an admission that Pakenham's army was already defeated.[36] Pakenham had planned to make a general attack when and if the artillery succeeded in breaking the American line, but this penetration failed. An infantry attack was made by the British through the woods on Coffee's line, but it was turned back by a determined fire.[37]

The American losses in the battle were 11 killed and 23 wounded; none was reported missing.[38] British casualties in this engagement were not listed for the day, but it was the only action of significance between January 1 and January 7, and the report for that period lists 32 killed, 44 wounded, and 2 missing, for total British casualties of 78.[39]

After the artillery battle of January 1, there was a lull in the fighting. Jackson did not risk an attack on the main British army because his effective force was still numerically inferior. The American army remained smaller than the British even after the arrival of 500 Louisiana militia on

January 1, and 2,250 Kentucky troops the next day. Unfortunately, the latter troops, commanded by General John Thomas and General John Adair, were largely unarmed. Only 500 of these men had weapons; the rest expected to be armed by Jackson. The general had no muskets to spare. Even after a search of the city he was able to supply only about 400 of the Kentuckians.[40]

Jackson was well aware that his line might be flanked or breached, and he thus prepared a defense in depth. After he considered his first line to be fairly secure, he built a second line on the canal on the Dupré plantation and a third was started on the Montrevil plantation. The second emplacement on the Dupré plantation may have been stronger than his front line. The canal in front of this position had five or six feet of water in it, and the mud breastworks were at least as high. The second emplacement was supported by three batteries, well arranged to have overlapping fields of fire. Jackson posted his unarmed Kentucky militia on the second line, as a holding force already in place. His strategy was that in the event the British assault succeeded, he would have two rallying points before the enemy could reach New Orleans.[41]*

During this period there was considerable uneasiness in the city of New Orleans. The construction of the extra lines and the inability of Jackson to drive off the British army were interpreted by some as an indication that the general did not believe he could hold the city. Rumors were spread that he planned to burn New Orleans rather than allow the British to capture it, an idea which may have been correct; certainly Jackson never denied it.

The anxiety of the local people reached its high point prior to the engagement of December 28. Abner Duncan, an aide to Governor Claiborne, informed Jackson that the state legislature wanted to surrender the city to the British to save their property. Jackson was reported to have told Duncan to recommend to Governor Claiborne that he should "blow up" the legislature, if he was assured that their wishes were to surrender the city in order to save their property.

*Since Jackson used the Kentucky troops as a reserve, even though they were not armed with muskets, one must wonder why Jackson did not issue them the 7,500 flintlock pistols he was supposed to have received from Laffite, or, if he did issue them, why there is no mention of them in the record. Probably there were no such weapons, because if they had existed, they would have been useful at close range, as, for example, when the enemy reached and attempted to scale the breastworks. Privateers and naval personnel used this kind of weapon when boarding an enemy ship or repelling boarders from their own ship. Repelling an enemy scaling breastworks was the same kind of action.

Claiborne did not blow up the legislature, but he did lock the doors, post guards, and prevent it from meeting until he had more orders. Greatly enraged by this action, Bernard Marigny went to Jackson and persuaded him that the legislature had no intention of surrendering. His explanation satisfied the general to the extent that he ordered that there should be no more interference with the governing body. Although some carping continued, there was no further serious trouble with the legislature.[42]

Between January 1 and the attack on January 8, the British may have appeared inactive. This was not the case. After the unsuccessful artillery engagement on January 1, Pakenham decided to wait for the arrival of Major General John Lambert with a substantial reinforcement of the Seventh and Forty-third regiments. He would then have almost 2,000 more men.

After the failure of the artillery to breach Jackson's line, Cochrane proposed a plan to land a part of Pakenham's army on the west bank of the river. There he would be able to silence Patterson's batteries and perhaps use them to fire on Jackson's flank. The general approved the plan but apparently left its execution entirely to the navy. It was necessary for the navy to move boats from Lake Borgne into the Mississippi River. As a first step, work parties cleared and widened the Villeré Canal so that the boats of the fleet could be brought to the river. On the evening of January 6 the work on the canal was finished, and the next day 47 boats were brought up the canal from the bayou. As soon as it was nearly dark on the evening of January 7, Cochrane's seamen started moving the boats from the end of the canal into the river. The labor of dragging the boats a distance of 250 yards proved to be an extremely arduous task, and it was not completed until nearly daybreak on January 8.

The detachment designated for the west bank was under the command of Colonel William Thornton. It consisted of the Eighty-fifth Regiment, about 300 strong, 200 marines, 200 sailors, and a part of the Fifth West Indian Regiment. There were not enough boats to carry the entire force on one trip, and the first part of Thornton's unit, about 600 men, landed on the west bank just at daylight.[43] Thornton was a full eight hours behind schedule, and his men were not ashore when Pakenham's attack began on the east bank. Thornton's mission was to silence Patterson's batteries and, if possible, to use them against Jackson's flank in support of Pakenham's advance.

The British were first discovered by an American picket who resisted briefly and then retreated. An orange grove obstructed Thornton's view of the main American defense line until his troops had advanced within 700 yards of it. The American line was secured on the river by a redoubt and then extended back to a thick woods. Thornton realized that the weakest point in the line was near where it reached the woods, and he deployed his forces in three columns to attack there. The main part of the Eighty-fifth assaulted the weak end of the line and carried the position, capturing 30 prisoners and 16 guns in the redoubt. The American forces retreated in disorder.[44]

Among the guns captured in this attack, including Patterson's batteries of heavy naval artillery, were three twenty-four-pounders and three twelve-pounders. Perhaps the most interesting piece of ordnance seized in the assault was a ten-inch brass howitzer inscribed "taken at the surrender of York town 1781."[45] There was no separate breakdown of the casualties suffered by Thornton's forces on January 8, but in the Eighty-fifth Regiment there were 2 killed, 41 wounded, and 1 missing. In the naval and marine forces, which appear to have seen action only on the west bank, there were 4 killed and 35 wounded for a total of 83 British casualties in the battle west of the Mississippi.[46]

The attack on the west bank was a British victory, but it did not, because of the delayed landings, come soon enough to have the desired effect. *Louisiana* was not sunk; the batteries were not overrun until after they had helped defeat Pakenham's attack. Thornton's victory was useless.[47]

The battle on the west bank did not come as a surprise to Jackson. General Morgan, after the battle on December 23, had crossed the river and eventually established a position opposite Jackson with about 260 men of the Louisiana militia. Morgan was reinforced by additional Louisiana militia, raising his strength by January 6 to 546 men and several cannon.[48] On January 1 Jackson became aware of the weakness of his position on the west bank and sent Latour with a force of blacks across to Morgan to help in constructing a line. In a spot where the woods came within 900 yards of the river, Latour proposed building an emplacement which would have been defensible. In an effort to protect the naval batteries, Morgan took his position at a point where the open area was nearly 2,000 yards long. Only about 200 yards of this line had been fortified by the time of the attack. The defense for the remainder was a shallow ditch which the British had no trouble in crossing.[49]

Jackson has been criticized because he did not strengthen his defenses on the west bank. With his limited resources, this reproof is not entirely justified. The general realized that in order to make a major attack on the west bank, the British would need boats in the river. That would give him advanced warning of their intentions. As he expected, Commander Patterson reported that the British were moving boats into the river on January

7.[50] This movement could have been a diversion, but, taking no chances, Jackson dispatched Colonel Davis with 400 Kentucky militia to reinforce Morgan. Of these 400 men, arms were available for only 170. The remaining 230 returned to camp, without Jackson's knowledge, rather than go to the west bank unarmed.[51]

The general had not misjudged the British intent to use the west bank, but Morgan had a smaller force than Jackson himself and had a more difficult line to defend. No boats had been brought down from New Orleans to send reinforcements directly across the river. Morgan distributed the troops under his command poorly. Instead of attacking the British as they landed or concentrating his entire defense along a single line, as Jackson had done, he committed his army piecemeal. When the Kentuckians who had been sent out as skirmishers fled back into the line, they screened the British from Morgan's artillery, making his guns useless. Their flight probably panicked his entire line.[52]

Morgan's report of the battle was obviously a defense of his own command. It placed most of the blame for the defeat on the Kentuckians. Commander Patterson, who had nothing to hide, gave an account of the battle which agreed in almost every detail with Morgan's, except that Patterson did not attempt to defend the Louisiana militia. Patterson was supported in his view of the Louisiana troops by at least one of their own officers, who described Morgan as "an old woman."[53]

These reports, when contrasted with Thornton's account, agree on the general areas of the action and their results. Considering the number and extremely poor armament of the Kentucky troops, it is probable that they did about as well as they could. There were several notable errors in this defense for which both Jackson and Morgan must share the blame. First of all, Jackson should have sent more effective troops to defend the west bank, especially once he knew that an attack was planned there. The second misjudgment was Morgan's failure to make his stand in a more defensible position, as suggested by Latour, or to attack the British while they were landing. The third error, and the one which cannot be excused, was the fact that Morgan divided his inferior forces into scattered units, which the British defeated piecemeal.[54]

Fortunately for Jackson the British attack on the east bank was already blunted before Morgan was overrun and what was otherwise a good British plan was, as stated before, foiled by poor timing. Whether the capture of Patterson's guns could have turned the tide of battle against Jackson remains a moot point, but there is no question that Jackson's position would have been far weaker without their support.

14

The Battle of New Orleans (II)

THE BATTLE on the west bank of the Mississippi was a disaster for the Americans, but the battle for New Orleans itself was a different story. After the arrival of Lambert's army on January 6, Pakenham held a council of war at which it was decided to make a massive assault on Jackson's main works.[1]

During the night and the pre-dawn hours of January 7–8 Pakenham's army made its final preparations for the great assault. In addition to moving up boats for Thornton's crossing, the British built an advance battery of six eighteen-pounders. Another enterprise that was essential to the charge was the preparation of a large number of ladders and fascines, necessary for crossing the ditch and scaling the mud wall. The fascines, very heavy bundles of sugarcane, were to fill the ditch so the advancing men could place their ladders and climb over the embankment. The complexity of this operation under fire indicates the great problem faced by Pakenham in his effort to break Jackson's line. The bank thrown up by the Americans was by this time at least eight feet high, except in the swamp area.[2]

All accounts of the British army during the period before the attack on January 8 mention the hardships it faced in its landing and exposure to the cold, wet weather. The morale of both officers and men was low. A number of the British officers were outspoken in their doubts about the success of the mission, and it appears that this sentiment was widely felt among the men. Colonel Thomas Mullens of the Forty-fourth Regiment, which was appointed to lead the attack and to carry the sugarcane fascines and ladders, stated publicly and perhaps before his men that his regiment had been ordered to its execution and that the dead bodies of his men were to be used to fill the ditch.[3]

The army never had adequate shelter during its entire stay in Louisiana, and food supplies had to be brought ashore in small boats just as the arms, ammunition, and the men themselves. The result was that the British had poor rations of salt pork and usually not enough of that. A large part of the army was sick, including nearly all of the men of the West Indian regiments.[4] With this state of morale, it is a real tribute to the discipline of the British army that the attack lasted as well as it did.

Pakenham divided his army into four groups for the assault. A force of about 2,200 under Major General Sir Samuel Gibbs was to attack the left part of Jackson's line. This position was held by General Carroll and was considered weak in artillery. It was thought that by attacking this sector Gibbs would be able to advance his men under the cover of the woods until he was about 200 yards in front of the American line. The first West Indian Regiment was ordered to attack Coffee's troops from the cover of the woods to create a diversion, preventing their use as a reinforcement for Carroll. This formation was supposed to have 500 men, but it was much reduced by sickness.

A third group of about 1,200 men commanded by Major General John Keane was to advance in column between the river and the levee. This narrow front would be in range of Patterson's batteries, but it was expected that Thornton would already have captured them by this time. Keane's section was intended primarily as a diversion for Gibbs' attack, but there was every chance that, with the support of Patterson's captured guns, it would be Keane's troops who broke the line. The remaining forces of about 1,400 men under General Lambert were held as a reserve. Including the reserves, the troops committed to this attack were approximately 5,300 men. If seamen, engineers, artillerists, and the 1,400 men assigned to Thornton were counted, there were between 8,000 and 9,000 British troops below New Orleans.[5]

From the outset the British attack was disorganized. The original plan had been to charge before daylight in order to reduce the effectiveness of the American fire, but the delay in launching Thornton's troops to the west bank caused the postponement of the general attack. More time was lost when it was discovered that Colonel Mullens of the Forty-fourth Regiment had allowed his men to advance 500 yards beyond the redoubt in which the fascines and ladders were stored. When this error was discovered, Mullens' troops were ordered to double-time to the rear to get this essential equipment. Before the Forty-fourth could get back into position, the rocket was fired ordering the general assault.[6] Pakenham, who was waiting to hear Thornton's attack before ordering his own troops into action, was running out of darkness. Probably, in his extreme anxiety, he ordered the attack as soon as Thornton fired on the first American outpost. The assault started with all the British troops in front of the Forty-fourth Regiment, which should have been in the lead. When the firing started, the men of this regiment threw down their heavy fascines and joined the shooting, leaving the British troops who first reached the American lines with no means of scaling the rampart. All advance was stopped, and the battle was probably lost at this point.

Jackson faced this attack with a line about 1,650 yards, 950 yards of which ran through the swamp and woods. This swampy emplacement did not need to be heavily manned because the British could not mass a large attack against it. The entire section was held by Coffee's troops and Captain Pierre Jugeat's Choctaws, in all between 800 and 1,200 men.[7]* The remaining 700 yards of the line faced an open area. Realizing that this was the obvious point of attack, Jackson concentrated thirteen guns to cover this section. In addition to the artillery in his line, Jackson was also supported by three twenty-four-pounders and a number of smaller guns in Patterson's battery on the west bank of the river. The line was manned by Carroll's brigade of Tennessee militia, amounting to about 1,400 men, the marines, the regular regiments, the New Orleans uniformed companies, and the battalions of free men of color. Estimates differ as to the strength of these units, but most accounts consider that their combined strength was somewhere between 1,300 and 1,600 men.[8]**

In addition to the troops listed above, Jackson had about 520 Kentucky militiamen who were armed. They were stationed behind Carroll's men as a reserve, and many of them moved up into the line during the battle. As an additional reserve, Jackson had Hinds' Mississippi dragoons and a force of Louisiana militia, making a combined strength of about 675 men. Altogether Jackson had an army of 4,000 or 5,000 men in his line and in ready reserve. This force gave the Americans a strength of 3 or 4 men per yard over the entire length of the 700 yards of exposed line. Had Jackson put any more men into this position they would have been in each other's way. The remaining 950 yards of the line in the woods and swamp was manned

*Accounts differ considerably as to the number of men in Coffee's command. The range of from 800 to 1,200 is common, the larger figure usually given for the number present on January 8. It is probable that some of Coffee's troops were used in other points around New Orleans before this. Also it is likely that some of his troops continued to straggle in.

**It is probable that the high figure given in these estimates was actually the number of men enrolled in the units, the low number the number fit and present for duty. The latter, therefore, is very likely the correct number.

at the rate of about one man per yard, which he considered ample to hold the woods.

Behind the line Jackson posted Major Hinds' mounted dragoons and several other small mounted forces of Louisiana militia which could reinforce any part of the front. Jackson had at least another 3,000 men in the general New Orleans area, but many of them were unarmed. The general ordered his men on the line into four ranks; one was to shoot, step back, and reload, while the next stepped forward and fired. In this way, when the fourth rank had discharged their weapons, the first would have been able to reload and the American line could keep up a steady fire. This plan was used at the beginning of the battle, but in many units it quickly broke down. The men were soon firing as quickly as they could reload, as individuals rather than as ranks.

As Jackson had predicted, the main British assault force under Gibbs attacked Carroll's troops, who were closest to the woods. This sector was out of range of Patterson's river batteries, and the advancing enemy would be screened by the woods until he was close to the American lines. Gibbs undoubtedly expected to find a weak spot between two separate units at this point of attack. It is standard military practice to strike between units, and in anticipation of such a maneuver Jackson had placed Brigadier General John Adair and his Kentucky men behind this part of the line. Gibbs, without knowing it, attacked the heaviest concentration of men and rifles in the entire line. All the rifle companies, except Beale's, were stationed in this sector. While Gibbs managed to avoid the bombardment of Patterson's batteries, his men were exposed to heavy fire from at least six of the thirteen guns Jackson had in his line, several of which were heavy naval guns.[9] In describing this portion of the attack, Major Tatum reported that the British lost a fearful number of men to ball and grapeshot fired with great accuracy, especially from the large naval guns. These units, already weakened and demoralized, could not stand up to the fierce small-arms fire of the Americans.[10]

When the British attacked, the battleground was covered with patches of fog, which Pakenham probably hoped would give him the same advantage as the darkness he had lost. Unfortunately for the British, a quickly rising wind dissipated the fog when their columns were about 650 yards from the American lines. The American artillery opened fire when the British reached a range of about 500 yards. With excellent discipline, the British columns continued to advance in spite of the losses. Jackson ordered his rifle companies to open fire when the enemy reached about 300 yards. They were instructed to shoot the British just above the crossbelt, a vital spot about the center of the chest. When Gibbs' column reached a point about 150 yards from the American line, the general ordered it to oblique to the left so that it would not be directly in front of American battery number seven. He gave this order without knowing that Jackson had directed that battery to cease fire when Gibbs' men had reached a range of about 150 yards, as its smoke was spoiling the aim of the riflemen. When the British reached musket range, the entire American line began shooting. This proved to be too much for the redcoats, and they broke ranks and returned the fire.

It was at this time that Mullens' men of the Forty-fourth threw down their fascines and started shooting at the Americans, catching a large part of their own troops in the cross fire. Some platoons advanced to the ditch, only to break when they found no fascines or ladders. Many of these men actually sought cover in the ditch, where some of them remained all day, finally crawling off that evening or surrendering. In order to justify their defeat, British reports of this action could be expected to inflate the power of the enemy. Even allowing for exaggeration, their accounts of the battle indicated that the American fire was the heaviest and most accurate they had ever encountered.

When both Gibbs and Pakenham were killed in an attempt to get the stalled attack moving again, most of the column fell back. Keane then sent the Ninety-third Highlanders, an elite unit, to lead a second assault. This regiment was literally shot to pieces with grapeshot and rifle fire; when the commander, Colonel Samuel Dale, was killed, the advance of the Highlanders failed and they began retreating. The Highlanders never got closer than 150 yards to the American lines, which was about the limit of the musket range. Their retreat threw the whole army into confusion and succeeded in breaking their morale completely. Though the officers used the flats of their swords, kicking and cursing, the British soldiers would advance no more. A last futile effort was made by Major Thomas Wilkinson of the Twenty-first North Britain Fusiliers, who took about 100 men and charged. Wilkinson reached the top of the bank where he fell, mortally wounded.

The remainder of Keane's command, advancing up the riverbank under Colonel Robert Rennie, had been better covered by the fog and had been able to reach the American line almost undetected. Rennie and Wilkinson and perhaps a few men with them were the only British who managed to get into the American lines, and both these men were killed almost immediately, as were most of the men with them. After this last attack, General John Lambert, who now commanded the army, concluded that the battle was lost and ordered a withdrawal. At almost exactly the time that Lambert decided to end the battle on the east bank, Thornton carried Morgan's lines on the west bank. The assault of January 8 lasted two hours, with the main attack only thirty minutes, but the British had no stomach for any more frontal assaults.[11]

A graphic account by an unidentified Kentucky militiaman serving under General Adair described the field after the battle:

> When the smoke had cleared away and we could obtain a fair view of the field, it looked, at the first glance, like a sea of blood. It was not blood itself which gave it this appearance but the red coats in which the British soldiers were dressed. Straight out before our position, for about the width of space which we supposed had been occupied by the British column, the field was entirely covered [by] prostrate bodies. In some places they were laying in piles of several, one on top of the other. On either side, there was an interval more thinly sprinkled with the slain: and then two other dense rows, one near the levee and the other towards the swamp. About two hundred yards off, directly in front of our position, lay a large dapple gray horse, which we understood to have been Pakenham's.
>
> Something about half way between the body of the horse and our breastwork there was a very large pile of dead, and at this spot, as I was afterward told, Pakenham had been killed, his horse having staggered off to a considerable distance before he fell. I have no doubt that I could . . . have walked on the bodies from the edge of the ditch to where the horse was laying, without touching the ground. I did not notice anyother horse on the field.
>
> When we first got a fair view of the field in our front, individuals could be seen in every possible attitude. Some laying quite dead, others mortally wounded, pitching and tumbling about in the agonies of death . . . some had their heads shot off, some their legs, some their arms. Some were laughing, some crying, some groaning, and some screaming. There was every variety of sight and sound. Among those that were on the ground, however, there were some that were neither dead nor wounded. A great many had thrown themselves down behind piles of slain, for protection. As the firing ceased, these men every now and then jumping up and either running off or coming in and giving themselves up.[12]

The casualties, as bad as they were, were not as numerous as at first thought. There were a number of British soldiers who played dead rather than advance any farther. Some of these men crawled back to the British lines and were never counted as casualties; after firing ceased others arose from the piles of dead and wounded and surrendered. Jackson had the following comment to make concerning the battlefield: "I never had . . . so grand and awful an idea of resurrection as on that day. After the smoke of the battle had cleared off somewhat, I saw in the distance more than five hundred Britons emerging from the heaps of their dead comrades, all over the plain, rising up . . . coming forward and surrendering as prisoners of war. . . ."[13]

The British casualties in this battle were extremely heavy, with a large proportion of officers, two out of four generals being killed and another wounded. The British landed between 11,000 and 14,450 men at New Orleans, including 2,000 sailors. Out of this force they suffered 2,037 casualties on January 8, of which 291 were killed, 1,262 wounded, and 484 captured. This loss was not proportionately much greater than the battle of December 23, but that night the Americans had been driven off and had suffered casualties equally as heavy as the British. The American casualties in the engagement of January 8 on the east bank were only 6 killed and 7 wounded. The total American casualties for the four-day battles on both the east and west banks were only 333 men, of which 55 were killed, 185 wounded, and 93 missing. Including the British victory in the west, the American casualties were far less for the entire four days than the English. Several British regiments were hardly in combat and lost little; on the other hand, many of their best units, such as the Ninety-third Regiment of Highlanders, lost as much as 50 percent of their total strength.[14]

On the surface this battle seems to be the slaughter of well-trained British regulars by raw militia. But Jackson's army in New Orleans was not typical of the militia. These forces were well practiced in the use of firearms and were in fact far better marksmen than the British regulars, whose claims to invincibility rested on discipline and the bayonet rather than on marksmanship. Many of Coffee's men and probably part of Carroll's troops had been in the field with Jackson for a long time. They were well disciplined, comparatively speaking, and had some combat experience. Although Jackson's army at New Orleans was not the same one he had commanded during the Creek campaign, most of his officers and probably a number of his men had served with him in at least one campaign. He had commanded three different armies in fighting the Creeks, which must ultimately have included most of the able-bodied Tennessee militia. Marquis James noted that Jackson knew an astonishing number of the rank and file of the Tennessee troops by name, a further indication that they had been with him for some time.[15]

Less is known concerning the Kentucky militia, although some of these had probably served in campaigns in the north. Jackson's regulars were new but were in the charge of experienced officers. The unknown factor in Jackson's army was the Louisianians. A large part of these people had had some previous military experience. Jane de Grummond names a large number of Louisianians who had previously served in the armies of France and other European powers. Major Louis Daquin's battalion of free blacks had served France in the Haitian War and had been evacuated as a unit. New Orleans had long been a center of filibustering and Latin American revolutionaries, and many of these men, including Colonel Reuben Kemper, General José Alvarez de Toledo, and General Jean Humbert, an old Napoleonic officer, were serving in Jackson's army.[16]

Among the most significant additions to the American forces were Jean Laffite and his Baratarians, who provided Jackson with supplies and a large number of expert artillerists. Other help came from the navy, which provided additional gun crews, artillery, and munitions. The American artillery, which was probably superior to the British, was manned by French-trained United States regular army artillerists, United States naval artillerists, and the Baratarians, all well disciplined and experienced in their work. According to Chevalier Anne Louis de Tousard, the French consul in New Orleans and an old artillery officer in both the French and American armies, it was the fire from Jackson's artillery that broke the British ranks. Tousard reported that the artillery "was nearly all handled by Frenchmen, especially too, by the amnestied rebels of Barataria, who, in truth, performed miracles."[17]*

Although the long rifle has been credited with much of the damage done to the British ranks during the Battle of New Orleans, there is evidence to indicate that the British suffered at least as many casualties from ordinary musket fire as from rifles. All of the rifles used were individually owned; none in this battle was furnished by the federal government. For this reason, only Beale's Rifle Company, part of Coffee's men, and a small number of Carroll's and Adair's units were armed with rifles. Most of Jackson's army were equipped with the standard musket of the day. No record has been found of the number of rifles in use at New Orleans but it is reasonable to suppose that there were between 800 and 1,200.[18]** Lambert reported

*Tousard was especially interested in Jackson's artillery and delighted with its good record in this battle, because the Frenchman had written the artillery manual then used by the United States Army.

**Probably not more than half of Coffee's men had these weapons, but since

January 29 that the wounded were recovering fast and that the ammunition used by the Americans was for the most part composed of buckshot, which was the ammunition of muskets. This statement supports the belief that muskets were the basic weapons used by Jackson's army.[19] Also, since the main British attack was on Carroll's part of the line, his statement that before the battle his men had made "fifty thousand cartridges in the best manner, each containing a musket ball and three buckshot" is significant in confirming the conjecture that the major portion of his unit was armed with muskets.[20]

On the west bank the Americans had not fared as well. Thornton had carried Morgan's lines and had forced Patterson to spike his guns. The British chased the American troops about three miles before Morgan was finally able to establish a line of sorts on an old sawmill canal.[21]

Upon learning of the defeat on the west bank, Jackson was enraged, and he promptly sent General Jean Humbert with another 1,000 men as a reinforcement and Jean Laffite as a guide and adviser to Morgan.[22] Unfortunately, immediate action was not possible. Morgan refused to relinquish his command to Humbert, who was not an American citizen and who did not have written orders from Jackson.[23]

Morgan finally advanced with great caution, and on January 9 he reoccupied his old position. Thornton's forces had been withdrawn. Patterson was able to reestablish his batteries and to remount his guns. He had two twenty-four-pounders ready for service by January 10.[24]

Lambert had already put a stop to the useless slaughter on the east bank when he learned of Thornton's success across the river. In an effort to decide on the feasibility of following up the victory on the west bank, Lambert dispatched Colonel Sir Alexander Dickson, his artillery chief, to determine what force would be necessary to hold the batteries which had been captured from Patterson. Dickson reported that it would take at least 2,000 men to hold the position. Lambert's army was already weakened and he did not think that he could safely spare that many troops. Considering the reinforcements which Jackson had sent to the west bank, Dickson's estimate of the number of men needed to hold this position was not unrea-

most of his command was in the woods and swamps they did not receive the main attack. At best, only a part of Coffee's rifle companies were in this engagement. Carroll had a force of 1,414 men in the line, of which 1,100 were furnished with muskets. Of the remaining 314, probably not all had rifles. Adair's armed Kentuckians, amounting to 520 men, were also placed in Carroll's section, but certainly not all, perhaps no more than half of these men, had rifles.

sonable. Lambert therefore ordered the force on the west bank to withdraw, after destroying Patterson's guns.[25]

Colonel Burgoyne, Admiral Codrington, Admiral Cochrane, and other officers believed that Lambert should have held the west bank and renewed his attack with the captured batteries.[26] There may have been some merit to the idea of renewing the attack on the west bank, but such a movement involved extreme difficulties and risks to the entire British army.

While Jackson's forces would have been in a much weaker position had they been flanked by fire from the captured battery, there is no certainty that a bombardment by these guns could have forced the Americans out of the Rodriguez line. Even if that line had been so weakened as to fall, Jackson had a good second line completed and a third started.

The value of guns on the west bank is best demonstrated by the damage that Patterson's ships and batteries did to the British camp. They caused a few casualties and undoubtedly hurt British morale, but there was never any suggestion that the British thought of evacuation or believed that this damage was too great to withstand. Lambert described the fire of Patterson's batteries as "unremitting day and night since the first of January when the position in advance was taken up."[27]

If this bombardment could not dislodge the British from their camp or cause too many casualties, certainly the same fire could not have forced Jackson to withdraw his line. The difficulty of supply made it unlikely the British could have maintained anything like the heavy continuous fire described by Lambert. Had Pakenham made his main attack on the west bank and succeeded in capturing it, he would not have been in possession of New Orleans. When one considers that Jackson probably planned to burn the city rather than allow its capture, it is extremely unlikely that he would have surrendered the town as a result of an artillery barrage. The enormous difficulties of moving men and supplies from the fleet to the British position on the east bank would have been compounded had it been necessary to move part of their meager supply of boats to the Mississippi and extend their supply line west of the river.[28]

Transportation was not the only consideration of the British commander in deciding whether or not to extend his efforts in the west. Dividing an army is dangerous in any situation, and it would be an extreme risk to divide a demoralized and recently defeated army, even though reinforcements were arriving. If Jackson had succeeded in defeating the British rear guard in the east or if Patterson had destroyed their boats on the river, the entire British army would have been cut off and lost. These were the risks of an offensive in the west, and they were too great for any British commander to take.

Although their attack had been repulsed, the British were still a powerful enemy. The American army held a strong position on the Rodriguez Canal, and Jackson declined to risk his polyglot army in a dangerous counterattack.[29]*

While Lambert had decided against more frontal assaults after the disaster of January 8, he did not show any great haste to withdraw his troops. He delayed the withdrawal for several days, but he was faced with a critical food shortage, having provisions for only six more days. The pressure of this shortage was relieved when it was learned on January 12 that a fleet of victualers had arrived from England. Perhaps under the prodding of Cochrane, Lambert waited until the British admiral could try another scheme to turn defeat into victory. This last plan was to make an attempt to reduce Fort St. Philip and to bring the navy up the river. Exactly what Lambert himself thought of this plan is unknown, but he probably had little confidence in it. The proposal was never mentioned in his correspondence. He left himself an open course of action, since he requested Admiral Cochrane to make preparations to evacuate the army on January 9; but he seemed in no hurry to implement the plan.[30]

In his report Cochrane described the attack on Fort St. Philip as a diversion and implied that it was to protect the withdrawal of the army. There is, however, every reason to believe that he had placed high hopes in the success of the maneuver. When it failed, he could by calling it a diversion escape an admission of defeat. This conclusion is strongly supported by the fact that Cochrane's vessels reached the fort on the morning of January 8 before there was any thought of evacuation and entirely too late to affect the disposition of troops before the big attack.[31]

Latour maintained that Fort St. Philip was the key to Louisiana, and Jackson agreed with this interpretation. It was the first point he reinforced

*Reginald Horsman agrees that Lambert did not have enough men to hold both sides of the Mississippi and that his supply line across the river was inadequate. Therefore, Horsman believes that Lambert had no choice but to withdraw. Carson Ritchie and, to a considerable extent, Robin Reilly seem to think that Thornton's brigade could have secured the west bank and that this would have given the English a good opportunity for a renewed attack. Reilly believes that Thornton could have easily cleared Morgan's troops from their new line and could have advanced all the way to the area across from New Orleans. This view fails to consider the effect of the heavy reinforcements which Jackson sent to Morgan or the risk that Jackson might have landed even more troops in Thornton's rear, had the latter tried to advance up the river.

upon his arrival at New Orleans. The improvements made included the removal of all flammable material, such as barracks and other wooden structures. They were to be replaced by bombproof buildings to protect all magazines and troops in the fort. Fortunately for the Americans, Fort St. Philip was strongly fortified. Latour believed that a land attack on the fort would be impossible because of the swampy land surrounding it. The importance of this fort to the British would make it seem that an amphibious assault, though costly, would have been worthwhile. The fort could not be taken by bombardment alone.[32]

The significance of Fort St. Philip lies in the fact that, if this position had been taken, only the relatively weak American fort at the English Turn would have remained to prevent the British fleet from advancing up the river. The English Turn batteries were dangerous to shipping but were vulnerable to land assault. If the British had been able to get a large number of ships up the river, New Orleans would have faced bombardment not by four or five guns, but by a hundred or more; and, worse, English troops could have been landed in the rear of the American army.

Once Cochrane decided to reduce the fort by bombardment, he sent two bomb vessels, a sloop, a brig, and a schooner, five vessels of all types. The small fleet reached the vicinity of the fort on January 8 and immediately began to take soundings and measurements. Eventually, after considerable preparation, the British opened fire on January 10 with six ten- and thirteen-inch mortars, from a range of 3,960 yards. At this distance, the bomb vessels were beyond the range of the guns of the fort, and ammunition for the American mortar proved to be faulty. As a result, the 400-man garrison had to keep under cover and take the bombardment in silence. This attack lasted from January 10 until January 18, at times reaching the intensity of a shell every two minutes, day and night. Although the Americans were unable to return the fire, the bombardment failed to damage the fort in any significant way. On January 15 several boats brought supplies from New Orleans and delivered serviceable ammunition for the fort's thirteen-inch mortar. Finally, on the evening of January 17 the Americans were able to fire the mortar against the British vessels. It is not known whether or not this fire was effective, but the British did withdraw the next day. During the bombardment, the British fired more than a thousand heavy shells from their mortars and a number of lighter shells from boats which approached the fort during the night. The total effect of this bombardment was that two men of the garrison were killed and seven wounded.[33]

By January 15 preparations for the evacuation of Lambert's army were well under way, and it was evident to the Americans that a withdrawal was in progress.[34] Lambert made his decision to withdraw on January 9, but the final evacuation of the camp did not take place until the evening of January 18. Lambert covered his evacuation by placing part of his army in position along the bayou, while the remainder was sent out to the fleet. The last of the troops were withdrawn across Lake Borgne on January 27 without serious incident, the navy performing a flawless evacuation.[35] Jackson made no effort to attack the British during this time.[36]

The only effort to harass the evacuation was made by a small group of four American armed boats under the command of Thomas Shields. On the nights of January 20, 21, and 22 these boats went into Lake Borgne, where they captured a schooner and a number of British boats, including one loaded with 14 seamen and 40 officers and men of the Fourteenth Light Dragoons. Some of Shields' prisoners were probably the civil administrators appointed by the British for Louisiana. Shields decided that these people could not be treated as prisoners of war, so he released them.[37]

The reasons for the British failure were legion, but their single most important error was the belief of many English officers that the Americans would not fight. Another serious misjudgment was the British belief that the people of Louisiana would not be loyal to the United States.

In reflection, concerning this battle, at least one British newspaper exhibited a reasonable but revealing attitude. This paper reported that the losses at New Orleans might "run as high as 2,000 men in all classes, and that the enemy was surprisingly strong, and that because of his strength it is surprising that the British losses were not greater," and "considering the strength of his position the British are to be congratulated for doing as well as they did." It was, according to this paper, "a real surprise . . . that they ran into such strength." The British had expected the population in Louisiana would be friendly to them, but "they were with the Americans to a man."[38]

15

The Last Campaign

THE DEFEAT on January 8 was serious, but the British army remained so strong that Jackson believed it might try another attack. With this possibility, he continued to increase the strength of his lines and to hold his troops in readiness. Even after the scouts reported that General Lambert was abandoning his positions, Jackson was not convinced that the movement was final. Fort St. Philip was still under siege, and he judged that the enemy planned more action at another point. When at length the British camp was abandoned and most of the army had embarked, Jackson withdrew the greatest portion of his forces to New Orleans. On January 23 he held a victory parade, and the people of New Orleans provided a tremendous celebration.[1]

Jackson was unwilling to begin demobilizing his army or to end martial law as long as another attack was expected. The last land fighting below New Orleans came on January 25, when Major Hinds fought a brief skirmish with the British rear guard at the mouth of Bayou Bienvenu.[2]

The citizens of Louisiana were most unhappy over the continuation of martial law after the defeat of the English, but Jackson was justified in keeping his army on the alert. The British were receiving numerous reinforcements on or near Lake Borgne. While Jackson's informant did not know the extent of these reinforcements, they were believed to be sizable. Later reports gave the additions as 5 new regiments, 5,600 men.[3] With a British force of such numbers so near New Orleans, a new attack seemed probable. After learning of the reinforcements, Jackson also received the disturbing news that the British were building many flat-bottomed boats. This information was definite proof that they planned other operations, but the location was a mystery. He hoped, however, that the disastrous British defeat at New Orleans would discourage the Indians, especially since Josiah Francis and other chiefs had been brought to New Orleans expecting to witness the great British victory.

Although Jackson still considered Mobile the best route by which to attack New Orleans, he thought that the British had given up the idea of making their main assault on Mobile. Even so, he did believe that they would try to reestablish themselves at Apalachicola and that Mobile could expect hostilities with British-supported Indians. Jackson was under the impression that Blue or McIntosh had destroyed the position at Apalachicola, and it would be necessary for the British to reestablish themselves. His assessment of British plans must have been colored by this assumption.[4] Since Jackson expected another British attack on New Orleans, he no longer considered Mobile to be in danger. Consequently he ordered General James Winchester to send the Third Regiment to New Orleans.[5]

Jackson was correct in his assumption that the British planned a new offensive and that they expected to make good use of their Indian allies. However, he misjudged their intentions concerning Mobile. Large reinforcements having reached Lambert's army, the British leaders held a council of war. Once again Admiral Cochrane convinced the army command that an offensive against Mobile was not only possible but desirable. Cochrane's idea this time was to revert to the original British plan and capture Mobile. Once the town was taken, an overland attack on New Orleans would be possible.[6]

Before deciding on this operation, Cochrane had already sent Nicolls and the Indian chiefs back to the British-constructed fort at Prospect Bluff with orders to take about 1,500 men and attack the Georgia frontier. A second part of Nicolls' orders was to dispatch men across Florida so they could act in concert with Admiral Cockburn on the Georgia coast. It was expected that by means of this two-pronged attack the state of Georgia would be completely neutralized. The third part of Nicolls' orders was to take the remainder of his men and cross overland toward Fort Stoddert, cutting all land communication with Mobile while attacking the land side of the city. This last operation was to be made in conjunction with General Lambert, who was to attack the city from the bay. Cochrane proposed to support Lambert with the small ships of the fleet, which he believed could land the army within a few miles of the city. As an economy of effort, Cochrane suggested that his light-draft vessels could be used to go around Dauphin Island and bypass Fort Bowyer. He also suggested that the main base of the army be established on Dauphin Island, which would be safe and accessible. Cochrane's only concern was that Lambert must use dispatch in conducting the operations, since he expected Jackson to reinforce the city from New Orleans. In his reports the admiral noted that there was a good road between Baton Rouge and Mobile, and Jackson could easily move his cavalry from New Orleans to Mobile in 15 days or less. The knowledge of this road shows clearly that a serious study had been made of the interior routes to New Orleans, and considerable thought had been given to a British attack by that route if and when Mobile was taken.[7]

After the defeat at New Orleans, Lambert was naturally cautious. He believed that the capture of Mobile would be reasonably easy and agreed to follow Cochrane's plan, though with a noticeable lack of enthusiasm. His dispatch indicated that he and Cochrane had discussed future operations but that he was unwilling to make any plans until Mobile was secured. The general stated that the subjection of Mobile would, he thought, "enable us, according to Vice A. Cochrane to put ourselves in communications with our Indian allies."[8] Lambert, obviously not completely trusting Cochrane's judgment, reported that he could not determine the attitude of the Indians and seriously doubted if they would be of much help to the campaign.[9]

While the British general was willing to undertake the capture of Mobile, he had no intention of putting his men into the bay by means of the poor shallow route around Dauphin Island, as suggested by Cochrane. Instead, he was determined to capture Fort Bowyer and open the main ship channel. On February 8 Lambert made an unopposed landing with 600 men on the sandspit 3 miles east of Fort Bowyer. The British general then disembarked the rest of his army on Dauphin Island. The troops attacking Fort Bowyer advanced until they were within about 1,200 yards of the fort before meeting any Americans. The first Americans to be encountered were scouts, who fell back to the fort without firing on the British. The United States forces took no action until the English were within 300 yards of their lines. During the night of February 8 the British landed guns and advanced to within 100 yards of the American position. In the next three days they positioned sixteen guns around the fort and added the bomb vessel *Etna* as a supplementary battery.

With the guns in position, Lambert demanded surrender of Colonel William Lawrence, the American commander. After examining the British positions and his own, Lawrence realized that defense was impossible and agreed at 3:00 P.M. on February 11 to surrender the fort. The British suffered 31 casualties, including 13 killed in this attack. The garrison's 375 men and large store of heavy guns and ammunition immediately fell into British hands. In addition, they captured 20 women, 16 children, and 3 servants who were living at the fort.[10] The next day they succeeded in making prizes of two American schooners which were trying to supply the fort.[11]

The British account of the action and the surrender of Fort Bowyer differs little from the American reports, but the hopelessness of the situation was best explained by Colonel Lawrence. He reported that he was induced to surrender the fort because of the shortage of provisions and the fact that he was "completely surrounded by thousands—batteries erected on the sand—mounds which completely commanded the fort—and the enemy having advanced, by regular approaches, within thirty yards of the ditches, and the utter impossibility of getting any assistance or supplies." He stated that it was "the unanimous opinion of the officers" that the post could not be retained and "that the lives of many valuable officers and soldiers would have been uselessly sacrificed." For these reasons Colonel Lawrence thought that it was "most desirable to adopt this plan."[12]

The question might be raised as to how Fort St. Philip could be held against such bombardment and Fort Bowyer be forced to surrender. There were several differences in the forts. Fort St. Philip had plenty of bomb shelters. During the shelling the entire garrison and all ammunition were safe. No part of Fort Bowyer was bombproof, and a lucky shot into the magazines would have blown up the entire position.[13] St. Philip was attacked only by water, whereas Fort Bowyer was attacked by land and water. At Fort Bowyer the British heavy guns were moved within close range on the weak landside of the fort, where they could blast the unprotected garrison at will. Fort St. Philip was always able to maintain communication with New Orleans and receive supplies and reinforcements, but Fort Bowyer was completely cut off from all communication with Mobile.[14]

When Jackson left Mobile at the end of November 1814, he turned his command over to Brigadier General James Winchester, providing what he believed to be a good supply of food at Fort Jackson and other points. The American general expected these supplies to be used in the event water communications with New Orleans were cut. But the British navy entered the Mississippi Sound and cut the sea routes to New Orleans. Winchester then discovered that the contractors had not been able to stockpile the necessary provisions in the interior, and his army suffered severe shortages.[15]

Because Jackson believed that Mobile was the key to New Orleans, he had left Winchester what he thought was a large army. But Winchester did not have nearly as many troops available as was supposed. Jackson had thought that the British would make another attack on New Orleans and expected that General John McIntosh would reinforce Mobile with a large army from Georgia. Therefore, he had withdrawn the Third Regiment from Mobile. In spite of his orders, McIntosh had not arrived at the time of the British attack on Fort Bowyer. Without the Third Regiment, Winchester claimed that he had about 1,700 armed men in the city. His actual troop strength was about 2,900, but he was plagued by a serious shortage of arms. For example, Colonel Thomas Coulter's Tennessee militia was almost completely unarmed, and many of them were sick. The worst tactical error was made in planning the defense of Mobile. Jackson believed that Fort Bowyer could stand a long siege, which of course it could not. Winchester understood this situation and was completely demoralized by the prospect.[16]

The lack of naval support, as has been detailed, not only made Fort Bowyer indefensible against a major attack but also caused a serious communication problem. The distance from Mobile made it impossible for Winchester to stay informed of the conditions at Fort Bowyer or to know when the fort was under attack. When at length he found the fort under attack, Winchester sent a large part of his men under command of Major Uriah Blue to relieve the siege. Blue arrived too late to prevent surrender of the fort.[17]

Considering the strength he had and the special problems of his command, Winchester did as well as any general could. Small detachments which could observe the British movements were posted on a number of the islands, and on January 5 and January 27 he sent *Grinder*, a small naval craft under command of Lieutenant M. M. McKinzie, to scout and report on enemy activity. McKinzie scouted west all the way to Pascagoula and passed near the British position on Ship Island, returning to Mobile on January 13 and February 4, respectively. He reported that the British were actively collecting beef and preparing for some sort of action.[18]

Following the fall of Fort Bowyer and the report of a large number of British ships entering the bay, Winchester realized his extremely dangerous position and redoubled his efforts to improve the roads to the interior, especially those north of Fort Jackson. In his report to Jackson he explained that this effort was made in an attempt to get supplies moving, but in view of Winchester's despondent attitude it is probable that he was preparing a route for the evacuation of Mobile.[19] Bad roads were not the only problems Winchester faced in the interior. Because of the British activities the Indians had begun to show new hostility, and another major Indian war was considered probable. Such a conflict, if it spread on a large scale, would have disrupted communications in the rear of Mobile, and Winchester's army would have been completely surrounded.[20] This confusion was precisely what Admiral Cochrane had visualized when he had given orders to Nicolls to attack Fort Stoddert.

In addition to his other problems, Winchester had reason to fear the wrath of Jackson, who had expected Mobile and Fort Bowyer to be held.[21] Early in the war Winchester had been forced to surrender his army to the British in Canada; and although the blunders causing this surrender were not of his making, he had been accused of cowardly action. After he was exchanged, he had been given command at Mobile, but many of his superiors considered him unfit for command. Unwilling to face the prospect of another humiliating surrender, Winchester resigned when he learned of the capture of Fort Bowyer. He planned to relinquish his command to General McIntosh on the latter's arrival.[22] But before Winchester could act, news of the peace treaty reached Mobile.[23] This information brought an end to all British operations, and Mobile was saved from certain capture.[24]

News of the signing of the Treaty of Ghent ended all British action at Mobile, but what of the Indians who had retreated to Apalachicola? It will be remembered that after the capture of Pensacola, Jackson had dispatched Major Uriah Blue with 1,000 men to destroy the remaining hostiles.[25] In order to assure success, Jackson also ordered General McIntosh to send whatever part of his Georgia forces he believed necessary to destroy these Indians. The American general thought that this objective had been accomplished, and because of the poor communication he did not learn of the failure of the mission for some time.

The expeditions sent against the Creeks and Seminoles at Apalachicola experienced exactly the same impossible supply shortages that Jackson himself had faced during the first part of the Creek War. On several occasions these troops were diverted to other duties by the danger of a British attack. Because of the shortage of supplies at Mobile and the critical lack of forage for the horses, Major Blue's expedition was delayed for several weeks. Another factor that delayed the pursuit of the fleeing Indians was heavy rains, which made the roads and streams impassable. These complications resulted in Blue's remaining at Fort Montgomery until December 8. Even then he was forced to dismount half of his men so that their horses could be used for pack animals, since the roads were too wet for wagons. By doing this, he was able to carry twenty days' rations into the field.

Blue spent the next ten days searching the swamps of the Escambia River, and he found a camp of about 150 Red Sticks. These scattered when he attacked, but he was eventually able to round up 81 prisoners from this camp and from others along the river. Some of the camps were only a few miles from Pensacola. On December 26 he reached and destroyed the village of Choctawhatchee, but nearly all of the hostiles had already evacuated the place. With his supplies exhausted, Blue was forced to retreat to

Fort Montgomery, near Mobile.[26] Apprehensive that the British might attack in the area, Winchester ordered Blue to remain near Mobile.[27] Thus it was that the major and his men never reached Apalachicola.

The second force ordered into the field was made up of a large detachment of loyal Creek Indians recruited by Benjamin Hawkins and a detachment of troops from the army of Major General John McIntosh. Jackson ordered General McIntosh to make contact with Blue and the Creek detachment and to reinforce them with whatever number of men he believed necessary to capture Apalachicola.[28] On receipt of these orders, John McIntosh immediately consulted with Hawkins and Major William McIntosh, who was in active command of the Indians. Following this conference, the proposed expeditions were merged. For this campaign General McIntosh detached Brigadier General David Blackshear with a regiment of Georgia troops to join with Hawkins and his Indians.[29] But before Blackshear and Hawkins were able to reach their destination, Governor Early countermanded Blackshear's order and instructed him to march to Mobile immediately, rejoining McIntosh.[30]

In the meantime, the British captured St. Marys and Brunswick, Georgia. Early once again countermanded Blackshear's orders and directed him to march to the coast to defend the state against invasion.[31] Without the Georgia troops, Hawkins had only his 1,000 friendly Creeks to face the British and their Indian allies at Apalachicola. He maintained a position at the confluence of the Flint and Chattahoochee rivers, making a few attacks on hostiles and pushing them back toward Florida, but he did not have enough troops to defeat their main force. Hawkins and his Indians were at the confluence of the rivers when news of peace arrived.[32]

Following their evacuation of Pensacola in November, Nicolls and Woodbine, along with the Indians and Negroes they had collected, retreated to their base at Prospect Bluff near Apalachicola. There they were joined by 1,400 or 1,500 more Indians. Upon his arrival at the bluff on November 17, Nicolls found the base in good order. In addition to the Indians, a number of blacks had joined his army. The main difficulty that he faced in collecting a large number of men was the extreme shortage of provisions. The food shortage at Prospect Bluff was eased to some extent by supplies from the fleet, but this deficiency remained serious during most of the British occupation of that location.[33] In December 1814, Nicolls reported that the activities of American forces, presumably Major Blue and others, were restricting travel and preventing many of the Negroes and Indians from joining him. He believed that many of the friendly Lower Creeks were about ready to associate themselves with the British cause.[34]

When Nicolls was sent to serve at Apalachicola, he was given authority to commission men to assist him. One of those commissioned was William Hambly, an agent of the Forbes Company at Apalachicola. Although Nicolls considered the firm's senior partners, James and John Innerarity, to be traitors, he thought Hambly was entirely reliable. Nicolls' good opinion of Hambly was reflected in his report to Cochrane. He stated that Hambly had sacrificed "everything for his Majesty's service, his father was one of the old torys, and stuck to his country to the last. His son has followed him in his honorable track, and I am sure he will meet with a protection in you."[35] This view of Hambly is especially interesting since the latter never broke with the Inneraritys and furnished them with detailed information concerning all of the British activities at Apalachicola. The data collected by the Inneraritys were carefully recorded, along with other intelligence they received, and passed on to the Americans. The Forbes Company eventually became one of the best sources the Americans had for information on the Gulf Coast.

Admiral Cochrane had directed Nicolls to join the British expedition against New Orleans with whatever Indians he could muster. The young marine officer had brought only a handful of chiefs with him, but Cochrane was satisfied. Nicolls and his Indian observers departed from Apalachicola about December 7, leaving Captain Robert Henry, a marine, in command.[36]

The supply situation at Apalachicola did not improve. Twenty-two hundred men, women, and children were being fed.[37] By the middle of January it became necessary to turn away around 1,100 Indians after giving them a small ration and a few presents. The almost complete lack of food in the Creek nation was the result of the total war waged against them by various American forces. The American armies had systematically been destroying crops and cattle belonging to the Creeks for more than a year; and though the lower Flint and Chattahoochee rivers had not been raided extensively, there were so many refugee Indians in that area that the food supply had been exhausted.[38]

Upon receiving these urgent requests for provisions, Cochrane reacted in an energetic manner. He ordered Nicolls and his Indian chiefs to be placed on board the sloop *Erebus* and immediately returned to Apalachicola. Along with *Erebus* he sent *Mars* transport and *Florida*, carrying presents for the Indians and provisions.[39] This expedition arrived at St. Georges Island on January 23, and with much difficulty the supplies were landed in small boats. This convoy brought a marine reinforcement and a company of West Indian Negro troops. Because of the difficulties of transportation in boats, the ships were not completely unloaded until January 28.[40]

At this point Nicolls began to develop the next part of Cochrane's plan, an attack on the Georgia frontier and on the inland side of Mobile.[41] His initial action was to train the Indians in simple military tactics and to place them and their black allies in a defensive position. He claimed that he had 3,551 Creek, Seminole, and Negro fighting men ready to defend the fort at Prospect Bluff.[42] This appraisal was probably optimistic, but doubtless many Creeks supported a strong British attack.

Not all of the Indians of either side were loyal; there were a number of Indians thought to be friendly to Nicolls who were spying for the Americans. Some or all of Big Warrior's representatives who visited the British were also reporting to the Americans exactly what the British were trying to do. Coppichimico, the chief of the Mickasukies, who was said by Nicolls to be extremely friendly to the British, claimed loyalty to the Americans and reported on all the British activities at Apalachicola. Probably all of the Indians were hoping to join the winning side.

According to information Hawkins received from these Indians, the British were paying $40 each for all scalps brought to them by the Indians. They also offered a bounty of $100 for the capture of every Indian countryman, cow buyer, or trader. No substantiation of this report can be found in British records. As a matter of fact, this story may have been fabricated by the Indians, who thought they would receive more concessions from the Americans by such reports.[43]

Before Nicolls was able to take the offensive as Cochrane had ordered, the uppermost towns were threatened by a force of about 900 Indians and 50 American cavalry under the command of Benjamin Hawkins. The major reported that his troops and Indians forced Hawkins to withdraw to his original position.[44] According to Hawkins' report, Nicolls' Indians withdrew during this engagement. The accuracy of these accounts cannot be determined, but the action was in no way decisive. On February 25, before any more action was taken, Hawkins learned that the peace treaty had been signed; and there is every reason to believe that Nicolls received the information at about the same time.[45] There was no more fighting of consequence around Apalachicola at this time; but, unlike the British commanders at Mobile, Nicolls did not prepare to withdraw immediately. There followed a long wrangle between Nicolls and Hawkins. After Nicolls and his marines finally withdrew, there was renewed hostility between the Indian and Negro allies and the Americans.

16

War's End: Unfinished Business

ALTHOUGH THE Treaty of Ghent was signaled as the end of hostilities, the status of the Gulf Coast was not settled with the treaty's conclusion. Historians have suggested that the attack on New Orleans was not really significant because it took place after the signing of the treaty and the area would have been restored to the Americans, regardless of the victor. There is compelling reason to doubt that this would have been the case. The English commanders, especially Admiral Cochrane, had been led to believe that Britain did not recognize any of the Gulf Coast as American territory, and the English government considered the Louisiana Purchase illegal. Therefore, New Orleans was not covered by the Treaty of Ghent. The position taken by the British in their proposal to attack New Orleans was that the London government might either make the area independent or, more likely, restore it to Spain.[1]*

In its statement of policy to field commanders, the government suggested that in all probability Louisiana would be restored to Spain; similar indications were given to the Spanish representative. The reports of var-

*Until recently nearly all historians have contended that the Battle of New Orleans was useless and that its outcome made no difference since the Treaty of Ghent had already been signed. Wilburt Brown, however, reminds his readers that not only did the British consider Louisiana not to be American territory but also that since the Treaty of Ghent had not been ratified there was considerable evidence to support the view that the British planned to reopen the negotiations when they defeated Jackson. Robin Reilly contends, as do I, that Louisiana was not included in the Treaty of Ghent, since Britain did not recognize the legality of the Louisiana Purchase. An examination of the Spanish records that Reilly did not use adds weight to this conclusion.

ious Spanish officials who discussed the matter with the British indicate that, while they were given no promises, they were given encouragement and did not completely give up hope until after Jackson's victory at New Orleans.[2] Though of less importance, the status of Mobile was more doubtful than that of New Orleans. Mobile had been claimed by the United States before the war, but the Spanish were not expelled from the city until after hostilities began. For this reason, it was thought not to be covered by the Treaty of Ghent.

Another provision of the treaty concerned the status of the Creek Indian lands. According to Article Nine of the treaty, the United States agreed that all Indian allies of the British with whom the United States might still be at war at the time of the signing of the treaty would have all rights and lands restored to them as they had existed in 1811. According to the view of all of the British commanders on the Gulf Coast, this provision clearly meant that the Treaty of Fort Jackson was nullified and that all of the Creek lands would be restored. As noted earlier, only a few of the Creek chiefs had signed the Treaty of Fort Jackson, and for that reason the British believed that the Indians had not made peace with the Americans.[3]

When news of the treaty arrived, Admiral Cochrane decided to leave Nicolls and a body of marines and West Indian black troops at Apalachicola to protect the Indians until some final settlement was made.[4] He did not expect this interval to be long. Cochrane never thought that the United States might fail to carry out the provisions of Article Nine, unless it refused the entire treaty.[5] He instructed his successor, Admiral Pultney Malcolm, that before leaving the station he should "direct the *Cydmus* and two (or more if necessary) Sloops of War, to remain for the Protection of the Indian establishment at Apalachicola, until such time as they are restored to their possessions in terms of the treaty of peace." When this was done, the admiral affirmed, "there will be no farther occasion for the Marine Garrison; which with the field guns you will order to be embarked and sent to Bermuda, if not wanted at Apalachicola."[6]

In other instructions to Malcolm, Cochrane ordered his replacement to persuade the Indians to make peace with the United States and to inform them that the United States was "bound to restore to them all the territories of which they were in possession of in 1811."[7] Malcolm was told to leave the Indians all the cannon and other military supplies they might need to protect their fort from attack.[8] The number of arms and supplies to be given to the Indians was left to the discretion of Major Nicolls.[9] These orders were repeated to Nicolls later by Admiral Malcolm.[10]

Until the end of March, Nicolls' orders were clear. However, on

March 29 Malcolm, having been informed of the ratification of the Treaty of Ghent and, like Cochrane, assuming that Article Nine was being implemented, directed that Nicolls withdraw his troops and embark them for Bermuda. Thus Nicolls was faced with conflicting instructions, having first been ordered to stay until the lands were restored to the Indians and then ordered to embark his troops immediately.[11] Although Nicolls did not follow Malcolm's orders at once, he was unable to remain at his post beyond June.

The Americans eventually took the position that the Creeks were not covered under the provisions of the Treaty of Ghent. It was the American view, greatly influenced by Jackson, that the Creek nation had made peace with the United States according to the terms of the Treaty of Fort Jackson. This treaty was signed long before the end of the war, and the Creeks were not considered to be hostile at the time of the signing of the Treaty of Ghent. Their lands were therefore not covered by Article Nine. According to the American interpretation of the situation, the Indians represented by Nicolls were Seminoles and Creeks who lived below the line in Spanish Florida and were not legal spokesmen for the Creek Nation.

There were always some Americans, Hawkins, for example, who believed the Treaty of Fort Jackson was a fraud. Official correspondence at the end of the war seems to indicate that many of the higher officials in Washington had accepted the idea of returning the Creek land. In June 1815 the secretary of war reminded Jackson of the provisions of Article Nine and suggested that he should put them into effect and cooperate with the Indians.[12] In spite of these instructions, Jackson continued to enforce the provisions of the Treaty of Fort Jackson, and eventually the government recognized his action.

Probably what actually took place was that Jackson on his own authority expelled the Indians from their land and used the argument that the terms of the Treaty of Fort Jackson superseded those of the Treaty of Ghent, since the Creeks had made an early peace. Once Jackson had acted, his superiors in Washington decided to go along with his views, especially since they were very popular in the West and the British seemed unwilling to use force to prevent the land cession. In the entire debate and later conflict with these British-armed Indians, the United States insisted that they were Seminoles or Creeks living in Florida and had therefore lost no land to the Americans. Most American accounts admitted that some Red Sticks and other hostile elements of the Creek Nation had taken refuge at Apalachicola, but they insisted there were only a few such renegades.[13]

The crux of the dispute was whether or not the refugee Creeks were of large enough numbers to constitute a really significant part of the Creek Nation. Nicolls insisted that he had armed more than 4,000 hostiles altogether, and that at least 1,000 Upper Creeks, Red Stick warriors, had joined him late in the war. He even claimed that at the very last, many Tookaubatchee and Coweta Indians who had been fighting on the side of the United States had come to join him, along with several entire towns theretofore neutral.[14]

It was because of this impasse that Nicolls refused to evacuate his forces until June 1815, during which time he carried on a continuous argument with Benjamin Hawkins concerning terms for the Indians. When it became apparent to Nicolls that the Americans were not going to accept the British interpretation of the treaty, he organized a government for the Indians. In support of this government, Nicolls made a treaty which, if ratified, would have extended formal British recognition to the Creek Nation and established a regular Creek-British military alliance.[15] The Indians agreed to keep the peace and sent Josiah Francis to England to serve as their representative when Britain ratified the treaty. The Indian chief, his son, and another Indian arrived in London with Nicolls on August 14, 1815.[16]

A short time after their arrival, Nicolls presented Francis (or Hidlis Hadjo, as he was called by the British) to Earl Bathurst, requesting that he be given an interview with the Prince Regent. The purpose of this audience would be to allow Francis to present a communication, probably the treaty.[17] This request for an interview was not answered for some time. Apparently the British officials were embarrassed by the whole affair and really had no wish to see Hidlis Hadjo.[18] The main reason for the delay in meeting with the Indian representative was the fact that the War Office and the Foreign Office were not aware of the work that had been done by Nicolls among the Creeks. They had seemingly accepted the statement of the United States that the Creeks were not to be included under Article Nine of the Treaty of Ghent because they had previously made peace. For this reason, Nicolls' appearance in London with an Indian chief was a surprise to them. Faced with this situation, for which they were totally unprepared, the Foreign Office and Bathurst made an urgent request that the Admiralty furnish the government with information about the Creeks.[19]

Eventually Bathurst agreed to see Hidlis Hadjo and Nicolls, but there is no record of any meeting between the chief and the Prince Regent. At the time of this meeting it was certain that Britain had no intention of ratifying Nicolls' treaty or of making a new military move to support the Creeks.[20] Wishing to pacify the Indians and to salve a guilty conscience following their refusal to sign the treaty, the British government lavished a large number of presents, amounting to more than £325 in value, on Hidlis Hadjo and arranged for his passage back to the Creek Nation.[21] After more than a year in England, the chief finally sailed for Nassau on December 30, 1816. Upon reaching Nassau, the chief was paid another £100 by Governor Cameron as additional evidence of British friendship.[22] As a favor to the chief, Nicolls agreed to keep his son in England so the boy could be educated. Beyond this there is no record of the outcome of this arrangement, except that a request was made by Nicolls for funds from the government for the boy's keep.[23]

It would appear that when the British government finally got Hidlis Hadjo out of England, there was no further interest in the Creek Indians. Bathurst in September 1817 refused to accept any further communications with Nicolls on this matter.[24]*

Hidlis Hadjo, or Francis, returned to Florida by way of New Providence. There George Woodbine took custody of most of the gifts which Francis had received and plundered them.[25] The Indian reached Florida in June 1817. Immediately upon landing, he called a meeting of all chiefs and gave them a talk which he claimed to have received from the Prince Regent.[26] It was first reported of Francis that he was preaching new hostility. However, later information indicated that he had taken a more moderate approach and was now a supporter of peace and cooperation with the Americans.[27] This change may have come about as a result of the increased number of American troops in the area, but it is probable that the message from the Prince Regent had encouraged the Indians to make peace.[28] In spite of his more moderate stand, Francis was caught and hanged by the Americans when they invaded Florida in 1818.[29]

The British view of the situation was well stated by their minister to the United States, Charles Bagot. He reported to his superiors in early 1817

*Nicolls, who was supporting the whole party of Indians at his own expense, was having serious financial difficulties. Because of the unusual and unpopular nature of his service, he found it extremely difficult to get credit toward promotion and equally difficult to receive any funds. He was finally able to collect all or most of his money in May 1817, almost two years after bringing the Indians to England. Once Nicolls had collected his pay, there is no indication that he had any more direct dealings with the Creek or Seminole Indians. After much delay, he finally received his promotion to lieutenant colonel on August 12, 1819. In the course of his career in the Royal Marines Nicolls was wounded 107 times, and eventually rose to the rank of full general in November 1854. According to Cyril Field, " 'Fighting Nicolls' may fairly be claimed as having been *the* most distinguished officer the corps has had." Whatever Nicolls' faults, he was hardly the foolish braggart described by some American historians.

that under no circumstances did he wish to discuss with the United States the alleged violations of Article Nine of the Treaty of Ghent. Bagot was already engaged in the negotiations which led to the Rush-Bagot agreement for disarmament on the Great Lakes, and to have introduced the problem of the Creek Indians at that time would undoubtedly have delayed or wrecked such an agreement. As a result of this advice from Bagot (and many misgivings in London), the British government officially abandoned the Creek Nation to its inevitable fate at the hands of the United States.[30]

This ultimate British withdrawal could not have been predicted by the Americans, who, in spite of their brave front to the Indians, were clearly worried about the situation at Apalachicola. For several years, as a result, the British activities in Florida were viewed with much alarm in the United States, and a renewed Indian war was believed quite possible. In due time, in spite of threats by the Indians and constant rumors of impending attack, the new Creek boundary line was run, and the cession of land was made. The settlement of the boundary line did not end the difficulties, however; hostile Indians in Florida began a series of raids on Georgia which continued for several years. These Indians did not again resort to full-scale war, but there was no real peace on the Georgia-Florida boundary until after the invasion of Florida by Jackson in 1818.[31]

The Indians were not the only problem left by the war. There were numerous runaway slaves who had taken refuge around Apalachicola. During the war Nicolls claimed that he had raised a black fighting force of around 500 men at Apalachicola who, along with their families, had settled around the fort that had been built there. When the British finally evacuated Apalachicola, a number of these blacks chose to go with them and were taken for settlement to the British West Indian islands. Many of them chose to remain near the fort at Prospect Bluff.

When Nicolls finally evacuated with his troops, he left several hundred blacks, thousands of muskets, several cannon and a tremendous quantity of ammunition.[32] Because of this equipment, the Indian raids on the frontier were especially dangerous. But the factor which created the greatest alarm was the existence of a settlement of armed blacks close to the border of the United States.

Apalachicola was not exclusively a problem of the United States. The Spanish government was also interested in eliminating this settlement, especially since most of the blacks there were former slaves of Spaniards rather than Americans. As described, during the war the Spaniards were unable to do more than hold a few towns. Because of this weakness, Spanish representatives stated to the officials of both Britain and the United

States that they did not consider the territory around Apalachicola to belong to Spain. They regarded it instead as part of the Creek Indian Nation. Once the war had ended, the Spaniards quickly changed their position and insisted that the territory was indeed Spanish land, given to them by the Treaty of Paris of 1783. At this time, Spain belatedly protested the British forts and depots that had been established at Apalachicola and demanded that these installations be demolished and the British troops be withdrawn.[33] This new attitude represented an almost complete change in the Spanish position, but an examination of the Spanish records shows that the reason for this change was probably an attempt by the Spaniards to persuade the British to disarm the Indians and blacks who had been left at Apalachicola. The Spanish officials undoubtedly feared that the presence of such a base in their territory might invite an American attack and result in the seizure of Florida by the United States.[34]

Once the British forces evacuated Apalachicola, all but a few of the Indians left the fort; but the blacks remained and very soon had complete control of it.[35] The existence at Apalachicola of Negro Fort, as it came to be called, concerned the Americans more than anything else. General Edmund P. Gaines was ready to lead his troops against Apalachicola as early as May 1815, even before Nicolls had evacuated the place.[36]

The constant irritation caused by Indian and slave unrest convinced the governor of Georgia and other leaders to dispatch several small expeditions against Negro Fort. These expeditions proved to be too small to accomplish their objective. The main reason for the delay in destroying Negro Fort was the attempts by the United States to persuade the Spaniards to destroy the place, since it was on their soil.[37] Eventually, under pressure from the frontier, Andrew Jackson stretched his authority and ordered Negro Fort reduced.[38] The elimination of the structure was accomplished by a joint army-navy expedition under command of Colonel Duncan Clinch and Sailing Master Jairus Loomis. The actual destruction of the fort was accomplished on July 27, 1816, by a single shot which hit the main powder magazine and blew up the entire installation, killing most of its garrison.[39] The Spaniards made a mild protest of this action but unofficially were pleased to be rid of the fort.

The destruction of this base reduced the menace on the frontier, but did not end the Indian raids. Although the British government had officially washed its hands of the Creek Indians, there were a number of British citizens who were either ignorant of this new policy or believed that their country had violated its word. One such person was Alexander Arbuthnot, an elderly merchant and resident of New Providence. In spite of false rumors, the English merchant never encouraged the Indians to hostility, but he believed their lands could be recovered by legal action. Eventually he received the power of attorney for the Creek Nation (in Florida) and made a pest of himself by a barrage of protest letters which he sent to numerous British and American officials.[40] It was probably because of these protests that Americans commonly believed Arbuthnot was encouraging the Indians to renew hostilities. In any case his influence among the Creeks and Seminoles was ended when Jackson had him hanged in 1818.[41]*

The real efforts to persuade the Indians to continue hostilities against the Americans were made by George Woodbine and Robert C. Armbrister, former British officers with Nicolls' expedition. These men were trying to free Florida as an Indian state, hoping for a large land cession for themselves. They had visited the Indians in Florida, claiming to be the advance party of a British expedition being sent to restore their lands. Woodbine escaped but Ambrister, while leading a small body of armed men, was captured and shot by Jackson.[42] Although these men were opportunists, they probably expected to succeed while the British were still influential among the southern Indians. This expedition was also instrumental in bringing about the annexation of Florida and thus destroying the base of operations for both hostile Indians and adventurers.

*Jackson believed that Arbuthnot was encouraging the Indians to fight the Americans, and it was this effort to incite an Indian war that caused Jackson to have him hanged. Interestingly enough, Arbuthnot, a merchant, had always given the Indians a fair price for their deerskins, a practice which had nearly destroyed the business of his rival trader, William Hambly. Since the only really damaging testimony against Arbuthnot during his trial was given by Hambly, one can only suspect that Hambly was trying to eliminate the competition instead of telling the truth.

17

Significance of the War of 1812 on the Gulf Coast

THE WAR OF 1812 in the Gulf Coast region, like the conflict in the rest of the country, must be attributed to multiple causes. The inhabitants of this area were no doubt influenced by impressment, which clearly offended their sense of national honor. In a section where duels were still commonplace, the obligation to fight for national honor must have been strongly felt. Hostile sentiment can easily be identified in statements of southern leaders, as well as in numerous comments found in newspapers of the area. Impressment as such was only a psychological problem in the South where few persons were directly concerned with it. Probably of more immediate consequence was the agricultural depression affecting at least some parts of the region. Margaret K. Latimer's research clearly indicates that South Carolina, and probably most of the other southern states, were badly hurt economically by British trade restrictions.[1]

The Indian menace was one cause for the pro-war sentiment in the South. While there was no real Indian war until well after the outbreak of hostilities with Britain, atrocities and rumors of unrest were rampant. Tecumseh's visit to the Creek Indians in 1811 marked the beginning of uneasiness and occasional attacks on whites. The spring of 1812 saw several whites murdered by Creeks in Tennessee and in the Mississippi Territory. The offenders were often found in the company of northern Indians, and most whites in the region blamed the British as agitators. Tecumseh was commonly believed by contemporaries to be an English agent.[2]

This view was also held by many of the Indians themselves. Tecumseh had promised them that they would receive British arms at Pensacola. Because of this weight of American and Indian evidence, many historians have incorrectly assumed that the British and Spanish governments were engaged in stirring up Indian hostility before 1812. The contemporary importance of this information was that American leaders believed these rumors and acted accordingly, demanding war. Evidence from British and Spanish archives examined in this work indicates rather conclusively that neither of these governments attempted to arouse Indian hostility before the outbreak of general war in 1812. While there was probably some unofficial encouragement of Creek hostilities by merchants and minor officials, until the beginning of the war the British government at Nassau used its influence among the Creeks to keep the peace.[3]

The desire to annex Spanish Florida and Texas was intense in Georgia, Louisiana, Tennessee, and the Mississippi Territory. For years preceding the war, persons from these areas had engaged in every conceivable kind of political chicanery, intrigue, and even active filibustering to add these territories to the United States. Whatever the reasons, the southern and western demands for war in 1812 were far greater than in other parts of the country. These areas, which seem to have had a common interest, produced the "War Hawks" and later furnished the greatest support for the war. Therefore, since it was their war, the interests of the South and West in its unfolding would seem to have been more urgent than those of other parts of the country. The war with Britain furnished a good excuse to seize valuable territory from Spain, who was forced by weakness to ally herself with the British in order to defend her lands.[4]

It was the Spanish rather than the British who encouraged Indian hostility in the South. Ironically, the Spanish action was taken in desperation and was intended as a defensive move. After the seizure of Mobile in April 1813, Spanish officials became convinced that the Americans were planning to take all of Florida, and as a final diversion they encouraged their Indian allies to fight the United States. Unfortunately for the Creeks, the Spanish were so poorly supplied that they could furnish no arms for the Indians; their aid was limited to good wishes and a little powder and shot. Although the Americans held the British responsible for the Indian war, the truth was that London did not know that the Creeks were at war with the United States until the end of 1813. England could, therefore, supply no aid to the Indians until after their disastrous defeat at Horseshoe Bend.

The Creek War and the War of 1812 with Britain, starting as separate operations, eventually merged. After their landing at Apalachicola in the summer of 1814, the British reorganized the Indians with plans to use them as a major ally on the Gulf Coast. The British-armed Indians never actually got into any major engagements, but they did divert and disrupt substantial American troop strength from other duties.

Prior to 1813 the affairs of the Creeks had been well led and protected by Agent Benjamin Hawkins, who not only defended them against the white man's encroachments but also organized a popular form of government. Hawkins prevented any cession of Indian lands for several years, and he was usually able to secure justice for them. His introduction of agriculture among the Creeks had brought them prosperity, and they were gradually becoming assimilated into the white man's society. On the western frontiers between the Creek Nation and those settlements on the Alabama River, intermarriage was commonplace, and the two races lived in peace and friendship. Relations between the Creeks and the white settlers on the Georgia frontier were not as harmonious, but Hawkins saw to it that peace and justice were maintained.

Unknown to Hawkins and to most Creek chiefs, however, many conservative Indians resented the adoption of the white man's ways. This anti-white feeling remained submerged for years, since there was no serious hostility between the races to cause a flash point.[5]* In 1810 a federal road was opened between Georgia and the Alabama settlements, bringing many Creeks a measure of prosperity because of increased trade. Even so, the road was not popular; and the constant passage of whites to the west alarmed the conservative Creeks, who believed that their nation was threatened. When Tecumseh came in 1811 with his show of supernatural power and message of hate, the conservative faction listened to him. His comet and earthquake predictions and their fulfillment encouraged these Creeks to fight the pro-whites of their nation. A Creek civil war erupted and was stimulated by the Spanish call for war with the United States.

Early Indian successes at Burnt Corn and Fort Mims persuaded more Creeks to join the hostiles, and a full-scale Indian war developed. Only the Upper Creeks became openly hostile at this time. The Lower Creeks were divided between those loyal to the United States and those who were neutral. As events developed, the supposedly neutral Lower Creeks, who had always had close ties with the British, were only waiting for the arrival of their English allies; this group quickly joined the British when the latter landed at Apalachicola in the summer of 1814. Because the territory of the Lower Creeks was never invaded and the British at Apalachicola were never able to take much offensive action, scholars have not generally been aware of the existence of these hostile Indians. Those historians who knew of Indian support of the British landings have concluded that it came

*John K. Mahon rightly considers that Hawkins' successful effort to introduce the white man's way of life among the Creek Indians was a major cause of the war.

largely from the refugee Red Sticks whom the English rearmed and reorganized.[6]*

The campaigns of Jackson, Claiborne, Floyd, and others were fought against the Upper Creeks in the area of the Alabama River system. After their early successes, the hostile Creeks had no real chance of doing serious damage to the whites. They had no plans for a long-range war and were almost entirely without arms or good leadership. With the exception of Fort Mims, the attack on Floyd's army at Calabee Creek, and the attack on Jackson's army at Enitachopco Creek, the Indians waited in their towns for white armies to come and kill or starve them. Their defeats should not suggest that the Creeks were poor warriors. Properly led and armed, they were a formidable enemy; and the Indians who were later equipped by the British would almost certainly have been a dangerous foe had they been brought into action on a large scale.

The first part of the Creek War lasted about nine months, far longer than Jackson had anticipated. This delay in defeating these poorly armed Indians was due to the lack of transportation, the shortage of supplies, both food and arms, and short enlistments of the militia units. All of these factors prevented the armies of the United States from advancing against the enemy. Although many Creeks were killed during the numerous battles and skirmishes, probably the greatest damage to the nation was the policy of total war, that is, the burning of all food and shelter by the invading armies. By the spring of 1814 the whole Creek Nation was starving.

Although the Fort Mims massacre has been considered an Indian victory, it was actually a catastrophe for the Creek Nation. This event alone destroyed all possibility of good relations with the whites in Mississippi Territory. Immediately, there was a universal demand for the removal of all southern Indians. Had it not been for this disastrous massacre, it is possible that the Creeks and other southern Indians might have remained in the Southeast, where they would more readily have been assimilated into

*Glenn Tucker, Reginald Horsman, Robin Reilly, and John Mahon all have some discussion of the Indians at Apalachicola, but most of them assume that these Indians were almost entirely refugee Red Sticks from among the Upper Creeks. Only Mahon discusses some Lower Creeks and Seminoles among the hostiles at Apalachicola. Unfortunately, even Mahon identifies most of these Indians as individuals rather than Lower Creeks and Seminoles. The misleading factor in all of these accounts is that they all tend to overlook or play down the significance of the large numbers of undefeated Lower Creeks and Seminoles who joined the British cause at Apalachicola. Apalachicola, or more properly Prospect Bluff, was a major trade center for the Lower Creeks.

white society. Certainly they could never have held all or even most of their land, but with agriculture replacing hunting they would not have needed so much land. It should be remembered that these southern Indians have been largely assimilated in Oklahoma, a continuation of the process started before removal.[7]*

The Creek War was a disaster not only for the Indians but also for the British. Green American troops would have been hard put to fight the Indians and the British simultaneously, but the Creek War had led to a considerable buildup in the number of regular army troops in the Gulf states and had provided training time for inexperienced militia forces. Had the Upper Creeks not taken the warpath in the summer of 1813, had they instead sought British aid, as did their brothers living near Apalachicola, the British could have taken the entire Gulf area including New Orleans with little or no opposition. Had the Indians remained at peace, American forces would have lacked training and numbers, and the armament they used to defeat the British at New Orleans would almost certainly have been diverted to the Canadian frontier. Finally, had the Creeks remained at peace, the British might not have been drawn southward at all.

The dispute over command between General Flournoy and General Pinckney led to the resignation of Flournoy. Because of his Indian victories and the strong recommendations of General Pinckney, Jackson received the appointment to command the Seventh Military District. The citizens of Louisiana would never have fought well, if at all, under General Flournoy; and had he been in command at New Orleans at the time of the British attack, the city probably would have been lost.

The capture of New Orleans would have provided the British commanders with considerable plunder, but booty was not the main object in attacking the city. The British recognized the economic importance of this port to the South and West and what its loss would mean to the United States. These were after all the sections of the country who most wanted war. Contrary to some accounts, the British plan for an attack on the Gulf Coast and New Orleans was well conceived and should have been successful. Admiral Cochrane, who fully understood the great mobility of amphibious warfare, planned to scatter American forces and attack where they were weak. This plan could not be countered by any American commander lacking naval strength, unless he had had forces many times stronger than

*Fort Mims must be viewed as even more of a catastrophe for the Indians when one considers that a large part of the fight was between pro-white and anti-white factions of the Creek Nation itself. Robin Reilly claims that Samuel Mims himself was of mixed blood.

those of the British or had been fortunate enough to guess their landing point. Cochrane did succeed in diverting many American troops to the Atlantic Coast and elsewhere, thus preventing Jackson from making the massive buildup of troops needed for the defense of the Gulf region.

With an army too small to defend the entire coast, Jackson followed an aggressive campaign of spoiling operations and constant movement. Convinced that Jackson was committed to the Mobile and Pensacola area and finding that the secrecy of his plan had been compromised, Cochrane decided to make a direct attack on New Orleans, hoping to reach the city before the American general. If the British forces had arrived a week earlier, they could easily have occupied an undefended city; but Jackson's intelligence had warned him of the British change of plan, and by forced marches the general and his staff reached the city on December 1 and most of his army very soon thereafter.

Cochrane's error in judgment was in landing at an inaccessible point below New Orleans, but even this was not entirely his fault. Properly equipped with the shallow-draft vessels he had ordered, the British army could have landed through Lake Ponchartrain behind New Orleans and thus presented the Americans with a much greater defense problem. As it happened, the British landed in an area easily defended and utterly unsuited for offensive military operations. Cochrane's mistake occurred when he failed to withdraw and attack at another point when he discovered an American army in New Orleans.

The British admiral's second error in judgment was underestimating the fighting ability of American troops due to his earlier experience with United States ground forces at the Battle of Bladensburg. It is unlikely that Pakenham or any other British general would have disagreed with Cochrane's plan to reach New Orleans before Jackson, but they probably would have disagreed with the choice of a landing spot. However, Pakenham did not insist on relocating the point of attack against an enemy thought by all British officers to be weak.

Jackson's defense of the city was generally well conducted. His attack on the British advance party was an excellent plan; and had he succeeded in defeating them, the British might have ended the attack at that point. Even though Jackson did not gain an outright victory, his plan of harassment greatly weakened English morale.* But the British army might never have

*Wilburt Brown considers the battle of December 23 the most significant in the campaign and probably the engagement that won the ultimate victory for the Americans. Whether or not this battle was as important as Brown suggests, it was certainly one of the most critical actions of the New Orleans campaign (Brown, *Amphibious Campaign*, pp. 175–76).

breached all three of Jackson's defense lines even if its morale had been excellent. Much of the American army involved in the Battle of New Orleans was by that time a well-disciplined force. They were a heterogeneous lot, but they had had a considerable amount of training. Jackson's riflemen were expert in the use of their weapons, and his artillery was professional and performed better than that of the British. Most of the remaining American line forces had had some experience and used their muskets with good effect.

Jackson's decision not to counterattack the British army after his victory of January 8 was probably a wise one. Though the Americans had inflicted heavy casualties on the British, Jackson still faced a very strong foe. The continued arrival in the Gulf of new British regiments, whether or not they were able to land, resulted in the restoration of enemy strength. The British capture of Fort Bowyer, while it represented only a small victory, opened Mobile to easy siege. The British expected to capture Mobile, and in view of previous plans it is very likely that they hoped to make another attempt on New Orleans by an overland route. The news of peace brought an end to these maneuvers.

British action against Mobile and New Orleans was important in spite of the Treaty of Ghent. Neither of these areas was recognized by the English as American territory. The United States would eventually have taken possession of the Gulf Coast, since Britain was not planning to keep the territory and Spain was not strong enough to hold it; but with the Indian buffer state restored and the ports of entry returned to Spain, American annexation of Florida might have been delayed for years.

The War of 1812 is usually considered to have ended in a draw, but the extraordinary luck and iron will of Andrew Jackson brought an American victory in one area. In the eyes of southerners and westerners, the conflict ended in a smashing victory for the United States. Since the news of peace came after the great triumph at New Orleans, many Americans, especially in the South and the West, assumed that this defeat had caused the British to ask for peace. The claim of victory, however, rested on much more substantial grounds than the purely psychological value of winning the last major battle.

Most accounts of the War of 1812 remind us that, although impressment was not settled, it ceased to be an issue after the general peace. These accounts also note the fact that this war gave Britain respect for American arms and led to a more favorable British attitude toward the United States. At the same time, these works fail to take note of the fact that in the eyes of the British the peace settlement was not status quo ante-bellum. Such a settlement would have provided for the restoration of Louisiana and Mobile to Spain. In a conflict ending in a draw, a country does not normally add territory. Since the British had not captured these areas, they had to accept the American claim; by this tacit admission the settlement after the war did not return to the status quo ante-bellum.[8]*

An even greater factor supporting an American claim to victory was the destruction of the power of the Creek Nation and eventually of all of the southern Indians. In negotiating the Treaty of Fort Jackson, Andrew Jackson ignored the instructions of the War Department and forced the assembled friendly Creeks to cede about half of their land to the United States. When the English inserted Article Nine into the Treaty of Ghent, requiring the restoration of the land of their Indian allies, both the London and Washington governments expected the Creek lands to be returned. Jackson, again acting on his own authority and against the orders of the secretary of war, insisted that the Creeks had made peace at the Treaty of Fort Jackson and were not allies of the British at the time of the signing of the Treaty of Ghent.

After Jackson had initiated the removal of the Creeks from their land, the government, under pressure from western and southern states, hesitantly decided to accept the general's view of the Indian question. In taking this position, President Madison and his government were following a safe course; if the English had moved to force the return of the Indian lands, the United States could have blamed the misunderstanding on Jackson and his misleading reports. The London government, which probably wrote Article Nine of the Treaty of Ghent to protect its Indian allies in the North, did not discover the mistreatment of the Creeks until some months had passed. By this time, England was in the midst of negotiating new agreements with the United States and was committed to a policy of peace in America. The war-weary British had demobilized their forces, and recalling them would probably have been politically impossible. London was greatly embarrassed by the situation but, not wishing to risk a new conflict, saved face by tacitly accepting the American view that the Treaty of Fort Jackson exempted the Creeks from protection under the Treaty of Ghent.

*Relatively few historians have noted that Louisiana was not included in the Treaty of Ghent, and only Remini has mentioned the status of Mobile in this agreement. Even Robin Reilly argues that while the Battle of New Orleans "had no effect on the conduct of the war or the conditions of peace," it had lasting influence on history. Reilly's statement is somewhat contradictory since he strongly supports the idea that Louisiana was not included in the Treaty of Ghent and would have very likely been lost to the United States had Jackson failed to hold it.

This British surrender to expediency was a complete reversal of their previous policy, and it caused no end of confusion among British officials in the Western Hemisphere. Admiral Cochrane and the governors of Jamaica and the Bahamas had clearly expected the Creek lands to be evacuated and had notified the Creeks themselves to expect a return of their losses. Promises of British support were almost certainly a major cause of the continued Creek and Seminole hostility in Florida and along the Georgia frontier. The Ambrister and Arbuthnot episodes, caused by the British retreat from their former position, are examples of the confusion that existed and brought about continued hostility in Florida. This hostility did not end until Jackson invaded Florida in 1818.

The reduction of the Creek Nation made it possible to remove all the southern Indians from their lands east of the Mississippi. Without an Indian buffer state, defenseless Spanish Florida was annexed to the United States. Both the Creek cession and the annexation of Florida were credited to the actions of Andrew Jackson, adding still further to the general's reputation.

The War of 1812 had great significance to the South and especially to the states and territories west of the Appalachian Mountains. Support for the war had always been greatest in this area, and victory did much to place the transmontane West in the ascendency. The clearing out of vast areas of Indian territory for white settlement, the restlessness created by the war, and increased emigration resulting from a return of peace in Europe caused in the years immediately following the war a tremendous increase in the population of the West. As a result, many new western states were added to the Union, greatly enhancing that section's political power. When this power was added to the enthusiasm of a military victory and marshaled by a popular war hero–politician like Andrew Jackson, its momentum carried the general into the White House. Even the brief setback given by the election of John Quincy Adams ultimately helped the Tennessean win support with his slogans of "Kings Caucus" and "the Corrupt Bargain."

The path to new leadership was made smoother by the decline of the Virginia dynasty in the Southeast and the decrease of New England's influence. New England's refusal to support the war, when reinforced by threats of secession made by the Hartford Convention, left that section in an extremely weak position.

There would almost certainly have been an increase in western prestige even without a war in 1812, but there is no doubt that this conflict greatly added to western power and provided a new leader. If the war had not been fought, it is unlikely that history would have given Andrew Jackson the opportunity for great leadership. Without the war, the undisputed leader of the West was Henry Clay. In its unfolding, history has taught us that the impetus for great movements often is a result of the timing—the sequence within which events are free to happen.

Jacksonian Democracy eventually moved eastward, and the alleged ideals of the frontier found majorities who would support them, even in the East. The southern-western alliance dominated the country for many years, until it was finally submerged by the slavery controversy. While some changes might have taken place without a war, the whole phenomenon called Jacksonian Democracy and increasing western influence in the federal government would have been unlikely without an American victory in the War of 1812.

Notes

THE SHORT citations in the notes are tied alphabetically to the entries in the bibliography, where full bibliographical information is given, and the short citation is, where necessary, repeated at the end of each entry. The following abbreviations are used in the notes:

ADA	Alabama Department of Archives and History
AHN	Archivo Historico Nacional
Leg.	Legajo
AGI	Archivo General de Indias
PC	Papeles Procedentes de la Isla de Cuba
ASP	American State Papers
AU	Auburn University Archives
FHi	Florida Historical Society
GU	University of Georgia Library
GaDA	Georgia Department of Archives and History
IU	Lilly Library, Indiana University
LC	Library of Congress
LSM	Louisiana State Museum
LSU	Department of Archives, Louisiana State University

MDA Mississippi Department of Archives and History

MPL Mobile Public Library

NA National Archives

- RG Record Group
- AGO Records of the Adjutant General's Office
Record Group 94
- DLDS Domestic Letters of the Department of State
Record Group 59
- LSW Letters to the Secretary of War
Record Group 107
- LSWIA Letters sent by the Secretary of War, Indian Affairs
Record Group 75
- MSS Miscellaneous Letters of the Department of State
Record Group 59
- SWL Letters Sent Military Affairs
- LSW Letters sent by the Secretary of War
Record Group 107
- LSN-CO Letters to the Secretary of the Navy from Commanders 1804–1886
Record Group 45
- SNL-O Letters from the Secretary of the Navy to Officers
Record Group 45
- SNL-M Miscellaneous Letters sent by the Secretary of the Navy
Record Group 45

NLS National Library of Scotland

NMM National Maritime Museum

OU University of Oklahoma Library

PRO Public Record Office

- Adm Admiralty Office
- CO Colonial Office
- FO Foreign Office
- WO War Office

THi	Tennessee Historical Society
TSLA	Tennessee State Library and Archives
TUL	Special Collections, Howard-Tilton Memorial Library Tulane University
WHi	State Historical Society of Wisconsin

Chapter 1

1. Cotterill, *Old South*, pp. 85–88.
2. Boyd, "Prospect Bluff," pp. 55–59; Wright, *Bowles*, passim.
3. Boyd, "Prospect Bluff," pp. 55–59; John Bower [Bowyer] to F. L. Claiborne, Sept. 14, 1813, in Palmer, *Historical Register*, 4:332–33.
4. Dreisback to Draper, July 1874, Draper Collection, WHi.
5. Hopoiethle Micco to the King's Most Excellent Majesty, Sept. 1, 1811, Munnings to Hopoiethle Micco, Dec. 9, 1811, PRO CO 23/58.
6. Potts to Bathurst, Nov. 22, 1814, PRO WO 1/143.
7. Toulmin to Graham, Aug. 5, 1812, in Carter, *Mississippi*, pp. 306–7; Patrick, *Florida Fiasco*, passim.
8. Holmes to Monroe, May 5, 1813, in Carter, *Mississippi*, 6:364–65; Boyd, "Prospect Bluff," passim.
9. Pound, *Hawkins*, passim.
10. Tustunnuggee Hopi (Little Prince) to Hawkins, Mar. 14, 1809, Hawkins Papers, GaDA.
11. Hawkins to Hocohulthle Micco, July 18, 1810, NA LSW.
12. Hawkins to Secretary of War, Sept. 25, 1810, ibid.
13. Hoboheillhlee Micco to Luckett, undated, enclosure in Hawkins to Secretary of War, Nov. 5, 1810, ibid.
14. Hawkins to Secretary of War, May 22, 1811, ibid.
15. Hawkins to Hampton, Aug. 26, 1811, ibid.
16. Hawkins to Secretary of War, Nov. 25, 1811, ibid.; Horsman, *Expansion*, pp. 163–64.
17. Owsley, "Fort Mims Massacre," pp. 193–96, 203–4; Mahon, *War of 1812*, p. 232.

18. Tucker, *Tecumseh*, pp. 201–4, 206–9.
19. Abernethy, *South in the New Nation*, p. 367; Halbert and Ball, *Creek War*, pp. 58–84.
20. Hawkins to Secretary of War, Jan. 7, 1812, NA LSW.
21. Claiborne, *Mississippi*, p. 316.
22. Ibid., pp. 317–18.
23. Dreisback to Draper, July 1874, Draper Collection, WHi.
24. Pound, *Hawkins*, p. 212; George Stiggins MS, p. 43, Draper Collection, WHi.
25. Claiborne, *Mississippi*, p. 318.
26. Pound, *Hawkins*, p. 212.
27. Stiggins MS, pp. 43–44, Draper Collection, WHi.
28. Pickett, *Alabama*, pp. 246–47; Stiggins MS., pp. 44–46, Draper Collection, WHi.
29. Tucker, *Tecumseh*, pp. 171–72; Perkins, *Prologue to War*, pp. 95–96, 284–86.
30. Stiggins MS, pp. 47–52, Draper Collection, WHi.
31. Deposition of Samuel Manac, Aug. 2, 1813, enclosure in Flournoy to Secretary of War, Aug. 10, 1813, NA LSW.
32. Deposition of John Gill, April, 1812, enclosure in Caller to Secretary of War, Apr. 6, 1812, ibid.
33. Hawkins to Secretary of War, Apr. 6, July 25, 1812, ibid.
34. Hawkins to Secretary of War, May 25, July 13, 1812, ibid.
35. Doyle to Hawkins, May 3, 1813, in Lowrie, *ASP, Indian Affairs*, 2:883–84.
36. Robertson to Blount, Mar. 5, 1812, enclosure in Blount to Secretary of War, Mar. 15, 1812, NA LSW.
37. Hawkins to the Chiefs of the Creek Nation, June 12, 1812, ibid.; Hawkins to Cornells, Mar. 25, 1812, in Lowrie, *ASP, Indian Affairs*, 1:339.
38. Hawkins to Wilkinson, July 27, 1813, enclosure in F. L. Claiborne to Secretary of War, Aug. 12, 1813, NA LSW; *Augusta Chronicle*, July 30, 1813.
39. Carson to Gaines, Mar. 13, 1812, Bradley to Gaines, Mar. 14, 1812, enclosures in Gaines to Secretary of War, Mar. 14, 1812, NA LSW.
40. Tuskegee Tustunnuggee to Hawkins, Sept. 18, 1812, Hawkins Papers, GaDA; Hawkins to Secretary of War, Oct. 12, Nov. 2, 1812, NA LSW.
41. Pound, *Hawkins*, pp. 211–21; *Augusta Chronicle*, July 30, 1813.
42. Hawkins to Secretary of War, June 7, 1813, in Lowrie, *ASP, Indian Affairs*, 1:845–46.
43. Hawkins to Secretary of War, n.d., ibid., 1:840.
44. *Augusta Chronicle*, July 30, 1813; *Republican and Savannah Evening Ledger*, Nov. 12, 1812.
45. Deposition of Samuel Manac, Aug. 2, 1813, enclosure in Flournoy to Secretary of War, Aug. 10, 1813, NA LSW.
46. *Augusta Chronicle*, June 25, 1813; Hawkins to Wilkinson, July 27, 1813, enclosure in Claiborne to Secretary of War, Aug. 12, 1813, NA LSW.
47. Hawkins to Mitchell, July 27, 1813, NA LSW.
48. Mitchell to the Georgia House of Representatives, Nov. 3, 1812, Georgia House Journal, GaDA.

Chapter 2

1. Wright, "British Designs," pp. 265–84.

2. Jackson to Blount, July 13, 1813, in Lowrie, *ASP, Indian Affairs,* 1:850; W. C. C. Claiborne to Madison, Aug. 1, 1813, in Rowland, *Claiborne Letter Books,* 6:249–52.

3. Halsted to Hawkins, May 10, 1813, Records of the Creek Trading House, NA RG 75; Blount to Secretary of War, Aug. 15, 1813, NA LSW.

4. Hopoiethle Micco, First Chief and Speaker of the United Nations of the Chickesaus, Choctaus, Cherokees, and Muskogee tribes of Indians to the Kings Most Excellent Majesty, 1 Sept. 1811 (this is the request for aid against the Americans); W. Vesey Munnings, president and commander-in-chief of the Bahama Islands, to Hopoiethle Micco, 9 Sept. 1811 (this is the refusal of the request for aid); unsigned but dated Downing Street to President Munnings, 29 Feb. 1812 (this letter agrees with Munnings' action in refusing aid); all in PRO CO 23/58.

5. Handfield to Cameron, Oct. 28, 1813, PRO CO 23/60.

6. James Stirling to Charles Stirling, Nov. 15, 1812, in Murdock, "British Report," pp. 43–51; Wilkinson to Hawkins, Sept. 16, 1812, in Carter, *Mississippi,* pp. 321–23.

7. Horsman, "British Indian Policy," pp. 51–67.

8. Extract from Minutes of Georgia legislature, April 9, 1813, Indian Letters, 1782–1839, pp. 171–72, GaDA; *Republican and Savannah Evening Ledger,* Nov. 10, 1812.

9. Bowyer to F. L. Claiborne, Sept. 14, 1813, in Palmer, *Historical Register,* 2:332–33; Doyle to James Innerarity, July 14, 1813, transcript in Indian Letters, GaDA; Shipping Returns, Nassau, 1813, PRO CO 27/15.

10. Doyle to James Innerarity, Nov. 2, 1812, Forbes Papers, MPL; Durant to Governor of New Providence (Charles Cameron), Sept. 11, 1813, PRO CO 23/60.

11. McKee to Hawkins, Mar. 25, 1812, Indian Letters, GaDA.

12. Baron de Carondelet to Luis de las Casas, May 23, 1793, AGI PC, Leg. 1447.

13. Whitaker, *Spanish-American Frontier,* pp. 201–22; Billington, *Westward Expansion,* pp. 230–45, 270–72.

14. Harrison, "Indians," passim.

15. Luis Onís to Monroe, April 4, 1812, Dec. 8, 1813, in Notes from the Spanish Legation, NA RG 59; Franco, *Política,* pp. 31–32, 44–45.

16. Cox, *West Florida,* pp. 89–101, 388–486, 604–5; "Juan Ventura Morales to Alexandro Ramírez," Nov. 3, 1817, *Boletín del Archivo Nacional,* 13 (Jan.–Feb. 1914):9–21.

17. Zuñiga to Ruiz Apodaca, April 8, 1813, AGI PC, Leg 1794; Proclamation of David Holmes, Governor of the Mississippi Territory, in Carter, *Mississippi,* pp. 305–6; Cox, *West Florida,* pp. 605–12.

18. Brady to Toulmin, Oct. 2, 1812, Toulmin to Wilkinson, Oct. 6, 1812, Toulmin to Pérez, Oct. 5, 1812, and Pérez to Toulmin, Oct. 5, 1812, enclosures in Wilkinson to Secretary of War, Oct. 6, 1812, NA LSW.

19. Secretary of War to Wilkinson, Feb. 16, 1813, NA SWL, vol. 7.

20. Secretary of War to Wilkinson, May 27, 1813, ibid.

21. James Innerarity to Forbes, April 24, 1813, Greenslade Papers, FHi; Re-

port of James Wilkinson, April 28, 1813, in *Niles' Weekly Register*, Vol. 14, June 5, 1813.

22. Wilkinson to Commanding Officer of the Spanish Garrison in the town of Mobile, Mississippi Territory, Apr. 12, 1813, and Articles of Capitulation for Mobile, enclosures in Zuñiga to Ruiz Apodaca, May 2, 1813, AGI PC, Leg. 1794.

23. Onís to Monroe, June 4, 1813, Notes from the Spanish Legation, NA, RG 59: Onís to Labrador, Oct. 8, 1813, AHN, Estado, Leg. 5639; Onís to San Carlos, Sept. 16, 1814, Expediente 25, AHN, Estado, Leg. 5557; Griffin, *United States*, pp. 29–36, 40–41.

24. Ruiz Apodaca to Minister of War, Oct. 1, 1813, March 23, 1814, AGI PC, Leg. 1856.

25. González Manrique to Ruiz Apodaca, May 15, Dec. 18, 1813, AGI PC, Leg. 1794; Holmes, *Honor and Fidelity*, pp. 74–78.

26. Ruiz Apodaca to Minister of War, June 16, 1813, AGI PC, Leg. 1856.

27. Expedition against New Orleans (undated memorandum), PRO WO 1/142; González Manrique to Ruiz Apodaca, Aug. 23, 1813, AGI PC, Leg. 1794.

28. Zuñiga to Ruiz Apodaca, April 18, 1813, AGI PC, Leg. 1794; Ruiz Apodaca to Minister of War, Aug. 6, 1813, AGI PC, Leg. 1856; González Manrique to Creeks [Josiah Francis], Sept. 29, 1813, in Claiborne, Letterbook F, MDA.

29. Toulmin to Blount, July 28, 1813, NA LSW; Deposition of Samuel Manac, Aug. 2, 1813, enclosure in Flournoy to Secretary of War, Aug. 10, 1813, ibid.

30. González Manrique to Creeks [Josiah Francis], Sept. 29, 1813, González Manrique to Friends and Brothers, Nov. 15, 1813, in Claiborne, Letterbook F, MDA.

31. González Manrique to Creeks, Sept. 29, 1813, González Manrique to Friends and Brothers, Nov. 15, 1813, Deposition of James Cornells, Aug. 1, 1813, ibid.

32. Letter to the Editor, Apr. 18, 1813, in *Niles' Weekly Register*, May 29, 1813; González Manrique to Ruiz Apodaca [Sept. 1813], Alva to González Manrique, Sept. 30, 1813, AGI PC, Leg. 1794; Deposition of David Tait, Aug. 2, 1813, in Claiborne, Letterbook F, MDA.

33. González Manrique to Ruiz Apodaca, June 1813, AGI PC, Leg. 1794.

34. Doyle to Hawkins, May 3, 1813, Lowrie, *ASP, Indian Affairs*, 1:843–44; *Niles' Weekly Register*, June 12, 1813.

35. González Manrique to Ruiz Apodaca, May 18, July 23, Aug. 16, 1813, AGI PC, Leg. 1794.

36. Stiggins MS, pp. 24–27, Draper Collection, WHi.

37. Deposition of David Tait, Aug. 2, 1813, in Claiborne, Letterbook F, MDA.

38. Nicolls to Cochrane, Mar. 1, 1816, PRO WO 1/144; John Innerarity to James Innerarity, July 27, 1813, in West, "Prelude," pp. 249–66; Doyle to James Innerarity, July 14, 1813, Creek Letters, GaDA.

39. John Innerarity to James Innerarity, July 27, 1813, in West, "Prelude," pp. 249–66; González Manrique to Ruiz Apodaca [Sept. 1813], Alva to González Manrique, Sept. 30, 1813, AGI PC, Leg. 1794; Statement of William Pierce, Aug. 1, 1813, enclosure in Flournoy to Secretary of War, Aug. 10, 1813, NA LSW.

40. Forbes to Castlereagh, May 29, 1815, Forbes Papers, MPL.

41. González Manrique to Ruiz Apodaca [Sept. 1813], Alva to González Manri-

que, Sept. 30, 1813, AGI PC, Leg. 1794; Ruiz Apodaca to Minister of War, Aug. 6, 1813, AGI PC, Leg. 1856.

42. González Manrique to Ruiz Apodaca, Jan. 8, 1814, AGI PC, Leg. 1795.

43. Sworn Statement of William Hambly, July 24, 1818, in Lowrie, *ASP, Foreign Affairs*, 4:577.

44. *Niles' Weekly Register*, Oct. 16, 1813.

45. John Innerarity to James Innerarity, July 27, 1813, in West, "Prelude," pp. 249–66; Handfield to Cameron, Oct. 28, 1813, PRO CO 23/60.

46. Handfield to Cameron, Oct. 28, 1813, Cameron to Bathurst, Oct. 28, 1813, PRO CO 23/60.

47. Durant, Noah Hoeo, Captain William Perryman, and Thomas Perryman, head chief, Creek Nation, to His Excellency the Governor of Providence, Sept. 11, 1813, ibid.

48. Ibid.; Durant to Your Excellency Governor of Providence, Sept. 11, 1813, ibid.

49. Cameron to Bathurst, Oct. 28, 1813, ibid.

50. Bathurst to Cameron, Jan. 21, 1814, PRO CO 24/17.

Chapter 3

1. Statement of William Pierce, Aug. 1, 1813, enclosure in Flournoy to Secretary of War, Aug. 10, 1813, NA LSW; Carson to F. L. Claiborne, July 29, 1813, Miscellaneous Correspondence, TSLA.

2. Pickett, *Alabama*, p. 258.

3. Stiggins MS, pp. 52–55, Draper Collection, WHi.

4. Toulmin to Blount, July 28, 1813, enclosure in Blount to Secretary of War, Sept. 7, 1813, NA LSW.

5. Pickett, *Alabama*, p. 259; Stiggins MS, pp. 54–55, Draper Collection, WHi.

6. Stiggins MS, pp. 54–55, Draper Collection, WHi; Carson to F. L. Claiborne, July 30, 1813, enclosure in Flournoy to Secretary of War, Aug. 10, 1813, NA LSW.

7. Lipscomb to Gaines, Aug. 21, 1813, loose folder of letters on Creek War, NA LSW.

8. Stiggins MS, pp. 54–55, Draper Collection, WHi.

9. Holmes to Flournoy, Sept. 6, 1813, in Holmes Journal, MDA.

10. Holmes to Caller, July 21, 1813, ibid.

11. Toulmin to Blount, July 28, 1813, enclosure in Blount to Secretary of War, Sept. 7, 1813, NA LSW; Holmes to Secretary of War, Aug. 30, 1813, in Carter, *Mississippi*, pp. 396–97.

12. Stiggins MS, pp. 55–60, Draper Collection, WHi.

13. Pickett, *Alabama*, pp. 267–68; *Woodward's Reminiscences*, pp. 94–96.

14. Hawkins to Governor of Georgia, July 28, 1813, Hawkins Papers, GaDA.

15. Hammond to Blount, July 28, 1813, enclosure in Blount to Secretary of War, NA LSW.

16. Stiggins MS, pp. 57–60, Draper Collection, WHi.

17. Gaines to Blount, July 23, 1813, enclosure in Blount to Secretary of War,

Aug. 18, 1813, NA LSW; Holmes to F. L. Claiborne, Aug. 11, 1813, in Holmes' Journal, MDA.

18. F. L. Claiborne to Secretary of War, Aug. 12, 1813, NA LSW.

19. Stiggins MS, pp. 58–63, Draper Collection, WHi.

20. Claiborne, *Mississippi*, pp. 322–23.

21. Doster, "Fort Mims," pp. 269–70.

22. F. L. Claiborne to Secretary of War, Aug. 12, 1813, NA LSW.

23. Andrew Montgomery to Samuel Montgomery, Sept. 4, 1813, in Doster, "Fort Mims," p. 283.

24. F. L. Claiborne to Editors, *Mississippi Republican*, Mar. 25, 1814.

25. Stiggins MS, pp. 58–64, Draper Collection, WHi.

26. F. L. Claiborne to Secretary of War, Aug. 28, 1813, NA LSW.

27. Beasley to F. L. Claiborne, Aug. 30, 1813, in Doster, "Fort Mims," pp. 281–82.

28. *Woodward's Reminiscences*, pp. 98–99.

29. Pickett, *Alabama*, pp. 269–70.

30. Stiggins MS, pp. 60–63, Draper Collection, WHi.

31. Pickett, *Alabama*, pp. 271–72.

32. Stiggins MS, pp. 64–65, Draper Collection, WHi.

33. Pickett, *Alabama*, p. 274.

34. Stiggins MS, pp. 64–65, Draper Collection, WHi; Pickett, *Alabama*, p. 274; Claiborne, *Mississippi*, p. 324.

35. Pickett, *Alabama*, p. 275.

36. Kennedy to F. L. Claiborne, Sept. 26, 1813, in Palmer, *Historical Register*, 4:332.

37. F. L. Claiborne to the Editors, *Mississippi Republican*, Mar. 25, 1814; *Augusta Chronicle*, Oct. 1, 1813.

38. Circular to Colonels of Militia from Governor William C. C. Claiborne, Sept. 8, 1813, in Rowland, *Claiborne Letter Books*, 6:265–66.

39. Kennedy to F. L. Claiborne, Sept. 26, 1813, in Palmer, *Historical Register*, 4:332.

40. Stiggins MS, pp. 63–67, Draper Collection, WHi.

41. Circular to Colonels of Militia from Governor W. C. C. Claiborne, Sept. 8, 1813, in Rowland, *Claiborne Letter Books*, 6:265–66.

42. Hawkins to Secretary of War, Sept. 21, 1813, in Lowrie, *ASP, Indian Affairs*, 1:853–54; Holmes to Flournoy, Aug. 2, 1813, in Holmes' Journal, MDA.

43. Gaines to Blount, Sept. 4, 1813, enclosure in Blount to Secretary of War, Oct. 1813, NA LSW.

44. Carson to F. L. Claiborne, Sept. 6, 1813, Miscellaneous Correspondence TSLA; Halbert and Ball, *Creek War*, pp. 175–99.

45. W. C. C. Claiborne to Madison, Aug. 1, 1813, in Rowland, *Claiborne Letter Books*, 6:249–52; Lanier to Mitchell, Sept. 13, 1813, Creek Letters, GaDA.

46. Jackson to Blount, July 13, 1813, in Lowrie, *ASP, Indian Affairs*, 1:850.

47. Jackson to Coffee, Sept. 29, 1813, André de Coppet Collection, Princeton University.

48. Halbert and Ball, *Creek War*, p. 257.

49. Onís to Labrador, Oct. 8, 1813, AHN, Estado, Leg. 5639.

50. Owsley, "Fort Mims Massacre," pp. 203–5.

CHAPTER 4

1. Holmes to Clinch, Sept. 17, 1813, in Holmes' Journal, MDA; Jackson to Coffee, Sept. 29, 1813, Coppet Collection, Princeton; Journal of John McKee, Sept. 1813–Jan. 1815, Jackson Papers, LC.

2. Meigs to Secretary of War, Aug. 6, 1813, Hicks to Meigs, Aug. 19, 1813, enclosure in Meigs to Secretary of War, Aug. 23, 1813, NA LSW.

3. Holmes to Brashears, Aug. 3, 1813, in Holmes' Journal, MDA; McKee to Blount, Nov. 4, 1813, enclosure in Blount to Secretary of War, Dec. 12, 1813, NA LSW.

4. Neelly to Secretary of War, Apr. 24, 1812, NA LSW.

5. McKee to Pitchlynn, Sept. 14, 1813, Jackson Papers, LC; Dinsmore to Armstrong, Aug. 4, 1813, in Carter, *Mississippi*, pp. 391–92; Meigs to Secretary of War, Dec. 4, 1811, NA LSW.

6. Secretary of War to Hawkins, July 22, 1813, NA LSW-IA.

7. Monroe to Mitchell, Oct. 27, 1813, Graham to Mitchell, Nov. 8, 1813, NA DLDS.

8. Blount to Mitchell, Aug. 8, 1813, enclosure in Blount to Secretary of War, Aug. 13, 1813, NA LSW; Pinckney to Jackson, Nov. 16, 1813, Bassett, *Correspondence*, 1:352–53.

9. Pinckney to Jackson, Nov. 16, 1813, Bassett, *Correspondence*, 1:351–52.

10. Pinckney to Flournoy, Apr. 5, 1814, Pinckney to Secretary of War, Apr. 5, 1814, NA LSW.

11. Secretary of War to Flournoy, Oct. 18, 1813, Secretary of War to Pinckney, Oct. 18, 1813, Feb. 28, 1814, NA SWL, vol. 7.

12. Claiborne, *Mississippi*, p. 337.

13. F. L. Claiborne to Isler, Oct. 29, 1813, *Mississippi Republican*, Dec. 15, 1813.

14. Pickett, *Alabama*, pp. 308–15; Halbert and Ball, *Creek War*, pp. 229–40.

15. F. L. Claiborne to Flournoy, Nov. 8, 1813, in Claiborne, *Mississippi*, p. 338.

16. F. L. Claiborne to Editors, *Mississippi Republican*, Mar. 25, 1814; Claiborne, *Mississippi*, pp. 227–28.

17. F. L. Claiborne to Editors, *Mississippi Republican*, Mar. 25, 1814.

18. F. L. Claiborne to Secretary of War, Jan. 1, 1814, NA LSW.

19. Halbert and Ball, *Creek War*, p. 249.

20. Stiggins MS, pp. 68–69, Draper Collection, WHi.

21. Claiborne, *Mississippi*, pp. 329–30.

22. F. L. Claiborne to Secretary of War, Jan. 1, 1814, NA LSW.

23. Pickett, *Alabama*, pp. 322–24.

24. *Niles' Weekly Register*, Feb. 19, 1814; Halbert and Ball, *Creek War*, p. 258.

25. Pickett, *Alabama*, p. 324; Halbert and Ball, *Creek War*, pp. 253–55.

26. Stiggins MS, p. 71, Draper Collection, WHi.

27. Halbert and Ball, *Creek War*, p. 257; F. L. Claiborne to Gaines, Dec. 26, 1813, unidentified newspaper clipping in AGI PC, Leg. 1795.

28. González Manrique to the Creek Indians, Sept. 29, 1813, in Claiborne, Letterbook F, MDA.

29. F. L. Claiborne to Secretary of War, Jan. 1, 1814, NA LSW.

30. Pickett, *Alabama*, pp. 325–26; Claiborne, *Mississippi*, p. 330.

31. F. L. Claiborne to Jackson, Nov. 12, 1813, Jackson to F. L. Claiborne, Dec. 18, 1813, Jackson Papers, LC.

32. Pinckney to Russell, Feb. 1, 1814, enclosure in Pinckney to Secretary of War, Feb. 3, 1814; Russell to Pinckney, Mar. 17, 1814, enclosure in Pinckney to Secretary of War, Apr. 3, 1814, both in NA LSW.

33. Russell to F. L. Claiborne, Jan. 12, 16, 1814, enclosures in Pinckney to Secretary of War, Feb. 3, 1814, NA LSW; Russell to Claiborne, Jan. 15, 1814, in Claiborne, Letterbook F, MDA.

34. Russell to the Officer in Command of forces destined to act against the Creeks [Pinckney], Jan. 16, 1814, enclosure in Pinckney to Secretary of War, Feb. 3, 1814; Russell to Pinckney, Feb. 21, 1814, enclosure in Pinckney to Secretary of War, Mar. 10, 1814; both in NA LSW.

35. McKee to Blount, Dec. 1, 1813, enclosure in Blount to Secretary of War, Dec. 12, 1813, NA LSW.

36. Russell to Pinckney, Feb. 21, 1814, enclosure in Pinckney to Secretary of War, Mar. 10, 1814, ibid.

37. Pickett, *Alabama*, pp. 327–28.

38. Russell to Pinckney, Feb. 21, 1814, enclosure in Pinckney to Secretary of War, Mar. 10, 1814, NA LSW.

39. Russell to McKee, Feb. 21, 1814, transcript in Military Section, Book 207, ADA.

40. McKee to Russell, Mar. 31, 1814, Jackson Papers, LC.

Chapter 5

1. Mitchell to Blount, July 29, 1813, Blount to Mitchell, Aug. 13, 1813, enclosures in Blount to Secretary of War, Aug. 13, 1813, NA LSW.

2. John Floyd to Mary Floyd, Sept. 19, 1813, Floyd Letters, GaDA.

3. Blount to Mitchell, Aug. 8, 1813, enclosure in Blount to Secretary of War, Aug. 13, 1813, NA LSW; Pinckney to Jackson, Nov. 16, 1813, Bassett, *Correspondence*, 1:352–53.

4. General Orders, Nov. 12, 1813, Executive Minutes, GaDA.

5. Mitchell to Adams, Aug. 5, 1813, Governors' Letterbook, and General Order of the Commander in Chief, Executive Minutes, both in GaDA.

6. Adams to Early, Dec. 24, 1813, Military Affairs, ibid.

7. Mitchell to Floyd, Sept. 17, 1813, Governors' Letterbook, ibid.

8. Floyd to Secretary of War, Dec. 4, 1813, in Palmer, *Historical Register*, 4:340–43.

9. Floyd to Mary Floyd, Oct. 7, 1813, Floyd Letters, and Early to Floyd, Nov. 28, 1813, Governors' Letterbook, both in GaDA.

10. Barton to Mitchell, Oct. 8, 1813, Military Affairs, ibid.

11. Floyd to Mitchell, Oct. 7, 1813, Big Warrior, William McIntosh, and Little Prince to Floyd, Nov. 18, 1813, Creek Letters, ibid.

12. Unsigned letter from Milledgeville, Ga., Oct. 20, 1813, in *Royal Gazette and Bahama Advertiser*, Dec. 15, 1813.

13. Floyd to Mary Floyd, Nov. 18, 1813, Floyd Letters; Floyd to Early, Nov. 23, 1813, Military Affairs, both in GaDA.

14. Floyd to Pinckney, Dec. 4, 1813, enclosure in Pinckney to Secretary of War, Dec. 7, 1813, NA LSW; Floyd to Mary Floyd, Dec. 5, 1813, Floyd Letters, GaDA.

15. Pinckney to Secretary of War, Dec. 7, 1813, NA LSW.

16. Floyd to Pinckney, Dec. 4, 1813, enclosure in Pinckney to Secretary of War, Dec. 7, 1813, ibid.

17. Floyd to Mary Floyd, Dec. 5, 1813, Floyd Letters, GaDA.

18. Stiggins MS, pp. 72–78, Draper Collection, WHi.

19. *Augusta Chronicle*, Dec. 24, 1813.

20. Carter to Pinckney, Dec. 1, 1813, Pinckney to Secretary of War, Dec. 7, 1813, NA LSW.

21. Floyd to Pinckney, Jan. 2, 1814, enclosure in Pinckney to Secretary of War, Jan. 13, 1814, ibid.

22. Floyd to Pinckney, Jan. 3, 1814, Pinckney to Secretary of War, Jan. 17, 1814, ibid.

23. Floyd to Pinckney, Dec. 11, 1813, enclosure in Pinckney to Secretary of War, Jan. 17, 1814, ibid.

24. Huger to Commanding Officer of the Georgia Troops, Dec. 31, 1813; Floyd to Pinckney, Jan. 9, 11, 1814, enclosures in Pinckney to Secretary of War, Jan. 17, 1814; all ibid.

25. Stiggins MS, pp. 76–80, Draper Collection, WHi; González Manrique to Ruiz Apodaca, Jan. 8, 1814, AGI PC, Leg. 1795.

26. Stiggins MS, pp. 76–80, Draper Collection, WHi.

27. Account of the Battle of Calabee by the son of Allen Brooks, a participant, as written down by H. S. Halbert, and a second unidentified account also written down by H. S. Halbert; accounts are enclosed with Halbert to Draper, Jan. 4, 1886, Tecumseh Papers, Draper Collection, WHi.

28. Floyd to Pinckney, Jan. 27, 1814, in *Niles' Weekly Register*, Feb. 12, 1814.

29. Second account in Halbert to Draper, Jan. 4, 1886, Tecumseh Papers, Draper Collection, WHi.

30. Brooks' Account, ibid.

31. Halbert to Draper, June 16, 1886, ibid.

32. Floyd to Pinckney, Jan. 28, 1814, *Mississippi Republican*, Feb. 28, 1814; Report of Charles Williamson, Creek Letters, GaDA.

33. Floyd to Pinckney, Jan. 31, 1814, enclosure in Pinckney to Secretary of War, Feb. 6, 1814, NA LSW.

34. Floyd to Pinckney, Feb. 1, 1814, enclosure ibid.

35. Floyd to Pinckney, Feb. 2, 1814, enclosure in Pinckney to Secretary of War, Feb. 2, 1814, ibid.

36. Floyd to Pinckney, Feb. 3, 1814, enclosure in Pinckney to Secretary of War, Feb. 6, 1814, ibid.

37. Pinckney to Secretary of War, Jan. 7, 1814, ibid.

38. Pinckney to Secretary of War, Feb. 3, 1814, ibid.

39. Floyd to Pinckney, Feb. 6, 1814, enclosure in Pinckney to Secretary of War, Feb. 11, 1814, ibid.

40. Floyd to Pinckney, Feb. 16, 1814, MIlton to Pinckney, Feb. 16, 1814, enclosures in Pinckney to Secretary of War, Feb. 20, 1814, ibid.

41. Pinckney to Milton, Feb. 19, 1814, Pinckney to Floyd, Feb. 19, 1814, enclosures in Pinckney to Secretary of War, Feb. 20, 1814, ibid.

42. Milton to Pinckney, Feb. 27, 1814, enclosure in Pinckney to Secretary of War, Mar. 10, 1814, ibid.

43. Milton to Pinckney, Mar. 2, 1814, enclosure in Pinckney to Secretary of War, Mar. 18, 1814, ibid.

44. Pinckney to Milton, Mar. 6, 1814, Milton to Pinckney, Mar. 10, 1814, enclosures in Pinckney to Secretary of War, Mar. 17, 1814, ibid.

45. Pinckney to Milton, Mar. 23, 1814, enclosure in Pinckney to Secretary of War, Apr. 3, 1814, ibid.

46. Milton to Pinckney, Apr. 4, 1814, enclosure in Pinckney to Secretary of War, Apr. 22, 1814, ibid.

47. Pinckney to Milton, Apr. 7, 1814, Milton to Pinckney, Apr. 12, 1814, enclosures in Pinckney to Secretary of War, Apr. 18, 1814, ibid.

Chapter 6

1. Jackson to Blount, June 4, 1812, Bassett, *Correspondence*, 1:225–26.

2. Blount to Secretary of War, July 22, 1813, Graham to Blount, Aug. 28, 1813, enclosures in Blount to Secretary of War, Sept. 3, 1813, NA LSW; Leach, "John Gordon," p. 334.

3. Blount to Mitchell, Aug. 8, 13, 1813, enclosures in Blount to Secretary of War, Aug. 13, 1813; Blount to Parker, Sept. 8, 1813; all in NA LSW.

4. Mason to Blount, July 1, 12, 1812, enclosures in Blount to Secretary of War, July 25, 1812, ibid.

5. Blount to Secretary of War, Sept. 28, 1813, ibid.; Remini, *Andrew Jackson*, pp. 184–86.

6. Jackson to Coffee, Sept. 25, 1813, Bassett, *Correspondence*, 1:321; Pitchlyn to Blount, Sept. 18, 1813, Military Section, Book 207, ADA.

7. Coffee to Jackson, Oct. 4, 1813, Bassett, *Correspondence*, 1:326.

8. Strother to Jackson, Oct. 9, 1813, Jackson Papers, LC.

9. Jackson to Coffee, Oct. 7, 1813, Bassett, *Correspondence*, 1:328–29.

10. Strother to Jackson, Oct. 9, 1813, Jackson Papers, LC.

11. Jackson to Coffee, Oct. 13, 1813, ibid.; John Donelson, Jr., to John Donelson, Oct. 15, 1813, Miscellaneous Files, THi.

12. Coffee to Jackson, Oct. 22, 1813, Bassett, *Correspondence*, 1:334.

13. Coffee to Mary Coffee, Oct. 24, 1813, Coffee Papers, THi.

14. Coffee to Mary Coffee, Oct. 25, 1813, ibid.; Jackson to Blount, Oct. 24, 1813, Jackson Papers, LC.

15. Reid MS, pp. 32–33, THi.

16. Path Killer to Jackson, Oct. 22, 1813, Jackson Papers, LC.

17. Jackson to Blount, Oct. 24, 1813, ibid.
18. Jackson to Generals White and Cocke, Oct. 31, 1813, ibid.; Reid MS, pp. 42–44, THi.
19. Coffee to Jackson, Nov. 4, 1813, in Palmer, *Historical Register*, 1:333–35; Alex Donelson to John Donelson, Nov. 5, 1813, Miscellaneous Files, THi.
20. Coffee to Mary Coffee, Nov. 4, 1813, Coffee Papers, THi.
21. Jackson to Pope, Nov. 4, 1813, Bassett, *Correspondence*, 1:341.
22. Jackson to Blount, Nov. 11, 1813, Jackson Papers, LC.
23. Roberts to Jackson, Nov. 14, 1813, ibid.
24. Reid MS, pp. 46–47, THi; Jackson to Chennabee, Oct. 19, 1813, Bassett, *Correspondence*, 1:334.
25. Jackson to Blount, Nov. 15, 1813, Jackson Papers, LC; Coffee to Mary Coffee, Nov. 12, 1813, Coffee Papers, THi.
26. Coffee to John Donelson, Nov. 12, 1813, Miscellaneous Files, THi.
27. James, *Jackson*, p. 171.
28. Parton, *Jackson*, 1:452; Cocke to Jackson, Nov. 14, 1813, Jackson Papers, LC.
29. White to Cocke, Nov. 24, 1813, in *Niles' Weekly Register*, Dec. 25, 1813; Cocke to Jackson, Nov. 27, 1813, Jackson Papers, LC.
30. Morgan to Meigs, Nov. 23, 1813, enclosure in Meigs to Secretary of War, Nov. 28, 1813; Meigs to Secretary of War, Dec. 4, 1813; both in NA LSW.
31. Jackson to Blount, Nov. 11, 1813, Jackson Papers, LC.
32. Lowry to Jackson, Nov. 7, 1813, ibid.; Parton, *Jackson*, 1:452–57.
33. Grierson to Jackson, Nov. 13, 1813, Jackson Papers, LC.
34. Jackson to the Hillabees [peace terms], Nov. 17, 1813, ibid.
35. Jackson to Cocke, Nov. 18, 1813, ibid.
36. Cocke to Jackson, Nov. 27, 1813, Bassett, *Correspondence*, 1:361.
37. Pinckney to Jackson, Nov. 16, 1813, ibid., 1:352–53; Grayson Manuscript of 1917, Smock Collection, OU.
38. Reid MS, pp. 52–54, THi.
39. James, *Jackson*, pp. 171–72.
40. Reid MS, pp. 55–56, THi.
41. Jackson to Blount, Nov. 14, 1813, Bassett, *Correspondence*, 1:345–46.
42. Jackson to Hall, Nov. 15, 1813, Jackson Papers, LC.
43. Reid MS, p. 61, THi.
44. Ibid.; Jackson to Cocke, Nov. 18, 1813, Jackson Papers, LC.
45. Reported by Matthew D. Cooper to his son, William F. Cooper, Cooper Letterbook, TSLA.
46. Reid MS, pp. 61–64, THi.
47. James, *Jackson*, p. 173.
48. Jackson to Coffee, Dec. 11, 1813, Bassett, *Correspondence*, 1:382–83.
49. Cannon, Alcorn, and Five Other Officers to Jackson, Dec. 8, 1813, ibid., 1:374–75.
50. Jackson to Pinckney, Dec. 11, 1813, enclosure in Pinckney to Secretary of War, Dec. 28, 1813, NA LSW.
51. Cocke to Jackson, Dec. 13, 1813, enclosure, ibid.
52. Jackson to Cocke, Dec. 15, 1813, Bassett, *Correspondence*, 1:393–95.
53. James, *Jackson*, pp. 174–75.

Chapter 7

1. James, *Jackson*, p. 176.
2. Jackson to Coffee, Dec. 23, 1813, Jackson Papers, LC.
3. Jackson to Coffee, Dec. 27, 1813, Bassett, *Correspondence*, 1:412.
4. James, *Jackson*, pp. 176–77.
5. Reid MS, pp. 79–88, THi.
6. Bassett, *Correspondence*, 1:423*n*.
7. Jackson to Blount, Dec. 26, 1813, ibid., 1:409–11.
8. Jackson to Reid, Jan. 3, 1814, Jackson Papers, LC.
9. Blount to Secretary of War, Jan. 5, 1814, NA LSW.
10. Jackson to Pinckney, Jan. 2, 1814, ibid.
11. Jackson to John Williams, Jan. 7, 1814, Bassett, *Correspondence*, 1:438.
12. Jackson to Blount, Dec. 29, 1813, ibid., 1:416.
13. Jackson to Coffee, Dec. 29, 1813, ibid., 1:421–22.
14. F. L. Claiborne to Jackson, Dec. 5, 1813, ibid., 1:425.
15. Jackson to Williams, Jan. 7, 1814, ibid., 1:438.
16. Jackson to Williams, Jan. 15, 1814, ibid., 1:442.
17. Jackson to Pinckney, Jan. 29, 1814, ibid., 1:447.
18. Reid MS, p. 115, THi.
19. Stephen "Forgotten Army," pp. 126–29.
20. Jackson to Pinckney, Jan. 29, 1814, Bassett, *Correspondence*, 1:447–54.
21. Reid MS, p. 117, THi.
22. Jackson to Pinckney, Jan. 29, 1814, Bassett, *Correspondence*, 1:447–54; Coffee to John Donelson, Jan. 28, 1814, Miscellaneous Files, THi.
23. Jackson to Mrs. Jackson, Jan. 28, 1814, Bassett, *Correspondence*, 1:444–47; Coffee to his wife, Jan. 30, 1814, Coffee Papers, THi.
24. James, *Jackson*, pp. 177–79.
25. Pinckney to Secretary of War, Jan. 13, 1814, NA LSW; Coffee to his wife, Jan. 8, 1814, Coffee Papers, THi.
26. Parton, *Jackson*, 1:498.
27. Pinckney to Jackson, Jan. 9, 1814, Bassett, *Correspondence*, 1:338–40; Pinckney to Jackson, Feb. 9, 1814, Jackson Papers, LC.
28. Jackson to Pinckney, Jan. 29, 1814, enclosure in Pinckney to Secretary of War, Feb. 11, 1814, NA LSW.
29. Jackson to Pinckney, Feb. 17, 1814, enclosure in Pinckney to Secretary of War, Mar. 10, 1814, ibid.
30. Jackson to Pinckney, Feb. 5, 1814, Bassett, *Correspondence*, 1:456; Jackson to Pinckney, Jan. 31, 1814, enclosure in Pinckney to Secretary of War, Feb. 16, 1814, NA LSW.
31. Pinckney to Jackson, Feb. 17, 1814, Bassett, *Correspondence*, 1:466–68.
32. Jackson to Blount, Mar. 10, 1814, ibid., 1:476.
33. Doherty to Jackson, Mar. 2, 1814, enclosure in Pinckney to Secretary of War, Mar. 17, 1814, NA LSW.
34. Jackson to Pinckney, Mar. 6, 1814, enclosure in Pinckney to Secretary of War, Mar. 17, 1814; Doherty to Jackson, Mar. 6, 1814, enclosure in Pinckney to Secretary of War, Apr. 3, 1814; both in NA LSW.

35. Pinckney to Jackson, Mar. 11, 1814, enclosure in Pinckney to Secretary of War, Mar. 17, 1814, ibid.

36. Bassett, *Correspondence,* 1:476*n.*

37. Parton, *Jackson,* 1:505–8; Jackson to Pinckney, Feb. 26, 1814, enclosure in Pinckney to Secretary of War, Mar. 10, 1814, NA LSW.

38. Pinckney to Jackson, Feb. 26, 1814, Jackson to Pinckney, Mar. 4, 1814, enclosures in Pinckney to Secretary of War, Mar. 17, 1814, NA LSW.

39. James, *Jackson,* p. 181; Jackson to Pinckney, Mar. 14, 1814, enclosure in letter (letter missing), NA LSW.

40. Jackson to Pinckney, Mar. 22, 1814, enclosure in Pinckney to Secretary of War, Apr. 3, 1814, NA LSW.

41. Stiggins MS, p. 107, Draper Collection, WHi.

42. Jackson to Pinckney, Feb. 26, 1814, enclosure in Pinckney to Secretary of War, Mar. 10, 1814; Jackson to Pinckney, Mar. 14, 1814, enclosure in Pinckney to Secretary of War, date and cover missing; both in NA LSW.

43. Jackson to Pinckney, Mar. 25, 1814, enclosure in Pinckney to Secretary of War, Apr. 3, 1814; Pinckney to Jackson, Mar. 23, 1814, enclosure in Pinckney to Secretary of War, Mar. 31, 1814; both ibid.

44. Jackson to Baxter, Mar. 23, 1814, Jackson Papers, LC; Jackson to Blount, Mar. 31, 1814, Jackson Papers, TSLA.

45. Jackson to Pinckney, Mar. 28, 1814, *Niles' Weekly Register,* Apr. 23, 1815.

46. Coffee to Jackson, Apr. 1, 1814, enclosure in Jackson to Secretary of War, Apr. 2, 1814, NA LSW.

47. Jackson to Blount, Mar. 31, 1814, Jackson Papers, TSLA; Jackson to Pinckney, Mar. 28, 1814, in *Niles' Weekly Register,* Apr. 23, 1814; Coffee to his wife, Apr. 1, 1814, Coffee to Donelson, Apr. 1, 1814, Coffee Papers, THi.

48. Coffee to Jackson, Apr. 1, 1814, in *Niles' Weekly Register,* Apr. 30, 1814.

49. Coffee to Donelson, Apr. 1, 1814, Coffee to his wife, Apr. 1, 1814, Coffee Papers, THi; Grayson MS, p. 34, Smock Collection, OU.

50. Coffee to Donelson, Apr. 1, 1814, Coffee Papers, THi; Jackson to his wife, Apr. 1, 1814, Bassett, *Correspondence,* 1:492.

51. John Donelson, Jr., to John Donelson, Apr. 1, 1814, Miscellaneous Files, THi; Jackson to Secretary of War, Apr. 2, 1814, NA LSW.

52. Stiggins MS, passim, Draper Collection, WHi; Hawkins to Floyd, Oct. 4, 1813, in Lowrie, *ASP, Indian Affairs,* 1:855.

53. Parton, *Jackson,* 1:524–25; Jackson to Secretary of War, Apr. 2, 1814, NA LSW.

54. Smith to Jackson, Apr. 4, 1814, Bassett, *Correspondence,* 1:395.

55. Jackson to Pinckney, Apr. 5, 1814, enclosure in Pinckney to Secretary of War, Apr. 18, 1814, NA LSW.

56. Coffee to his wife, Apr. 2, 1814, Coffee Papers, THi.

57. Coffee to his wife, Apr. 6, 1814, ibid.

58. Jackson to Pinckney, Apr. 3, 1814, Bassett, *Correspondence,* 1:495–96; Pinckney to Jackson, Apr. 7, 14, 1814, enclosures in Pinckney to Secretary of War, Apr. 18, 1814, NA LSW.

59. Pinckney to Jackson, Apr. 14, 1814, Jackson to Pinckney, Apr. 14, 1814,

Pinckney to Jackson, Apr. 16, 1814, all enclosures in Pinckney to Secretary of War, Apr. 18, 1814, NA LSW.

60. Pinckney to Jackson, Apr. 16, 1814, enclosure ibid.

61. Pinckney, General Orders, Apr. 21, 1814, Jackson Papers, LC.

62. Smith to Jackson, Apr. 14, 1814, Jackson to Pinckney, Apr. 18, 1814, enclosures in Pinckney to Secretary of War, Apr. 22, 1814, NA LSW.

63. Jackson to Pinckney, Apr. 14, 1814, Pinckney to Jackson, Apr. 17, 1814, enclosures in Pinckney to Secretary of War, Apr. 18, 1814, ibid.; Coffee to his wife, Apr. 18, 1814, Coffee to Donelson, Apr. 25, 1814, Coffee Papers, THi.

64. Royall, *Letters*, pp. 91–92.

65. Pickett, *Alabama*, 2:348–51.

66. Stiggins MS, passim, Halbert to Draper, June 16, 1886, Tecumseh Papers, both in Draper Collection, WHi.

67. Driesback to Draper, July 1874, Georgia Papers, ibid.

68. Pinckney to Secretary of War, Apr. 8, 1814, Pinckney to Secretary of War, Apr. 28, 1814, NA LSW.

69. Jackson to Blount, Apr. 25, 1814, in *Niles' Weekly Register*, June 4, 1814.

70. Pinckney to Secretary of War, Apr. 28, 1814, NA LSW.

Chapter 8

1. Pound, *Hawkins*, pp. 234–35.
2. Pinckney to Hawkins, Apr. 23, 1814, Bassett, *Correspondence*, 2:1–2.
3. Secretary of War to Pinckney, Mar. 17, 1814, NA SWL, vol. 7.
4. Jackson to Pinckney, May 18, 1814, Bassett, *Correspondence*, 2:1–4.
5. Secretary of War to Jackson, May 22, 1814, ibid., 2:4.
6. Secretary of War to Jackson, May 24, 1814, ibid., 2:4–5.
7. Secretary of War to Jackson, May 28, 1814, ibid., 2:5.
8. Parton, *Jackson*, 1:531–61.
9. Secretary of War to Jackson, May 24, 1814, Jackson to Secretary of War, June 13, 1814, Toulmin to Jackson, June 22, 1814, all in Bassett, *Correspondence*, 2:4–5, 6–8, 9–11.
10. Jackson to Secretary of War, July 24, 1814, Aug. 10, 1814, NA LSW.
11. Parton, *Jackson*, 1:551–61.
12. Floyd to Pinckney, Jan. 8, 1814, enclosure in Pinckney to Secretary of State, Jan. 17, 1814, NA MSS.
13. Secretary of War to Jackson, June 25, 1814, Bassett, *Correspondence*, 2:11–12.
14. Jackson to Secretary of War, June 27, 1814, NA LSW.
15. Jackson to Hawkins, July 11, 1814, Bassett, *Correspondence*, 2:15–16.
16. Jackson to Blount, Aug. 9, 1814, ibid., 2:24.
17. Jackson to Hawkins, July 11, 1814, ibid., 2:14–15; Parton, *Jackson*, 1:549–51.
18. Talk of Tustunnuggee Thlucco to Jackson, Aug. 8, 1814, in Lowrie, *ASP, Indian Affairs*, 1:838.

19. *Augusta Chronicle*, Aug. 26, 1814.
20. Reid and Eaton, *Jackson*, pp. 172–73.
21. Tustunnuggee Thlucco and Other Chiefs to Andrew Jackson Representing the United States, Aug. 9, 1814, in Lowrie, *ASP*, *Indian Affairs*, 1:838.
22. Parton, *Jackson*, 1:555–57.
23. Hawkins to Meigs, Aug. 7, 1814, typed copy, Hawkins Letters, GaDA.
24. Hawkins to Early, Aug. 23, 1814, *Niles' Weekly Register*, Oct. 6, 1815.
25. Hawkins to Secretary of War, Aug. 16, 1814, LSW.
26. Hawkins to McIntosh, Nov. 26, 1814, original, LC, typescript, GaDA.
27. James, *Jackson*, p. 190.
28. *Royal Gazette and Bahama Advertiser*, Aug. 13, 1814.
29. Patrick, *Florida Fiasco*, pp. 281–84, 300.
30. Notes and documents enclosed in Hawkins to Early, Nov. 15, 1814, Cuyler Collection, GU; Hawkins to McIntosh, Nov. 26, 1814, typescript, GaDA, original, LC; Durant, et al. to the Governor of New Providence, Sept. 11, 1813, Cameron to Bathurst, Oct. 28, 1813, Nov. 30, 1813, and enclosures, PRO CO 23/60.
31. Hawkins to Big Warrior, Little Prince and other Chiefs of the Creek Nation, June 16, 1814, in Lowrie, *ASP*, *Indian Affairs*, 1:845.
32. Boyd, "Prospect Bluff," pp. 55–68.
33. Mahon, "British Strategy," p. 92.
34. Jackson to Secretary of War, Aug. 10, 1814, W. C. C. Claiborne to Jackson, Aug. 29, 1814, Jackson Papers, LC; Edward Nicolls, "Return of Creek Indians who have not joined the British and Return of Miscogee Indians Under Command of Lieut. Nicolls" (not dated, probably Feb. 1815), PRO WO 1/143.
35. Floyd to Pinckney, Jan. 9, 17, 1814, enclosures in Pinckney to Secretary of War, Jan. 17, 1814, NA LSW.
36. Woodbine to Hope, May 31, 1814, MS 2328, Cochrane Papers, NLS; Codrington to his wife, Dec. 14, 1814, Codrington Papers, NMM.
37. Nicolls, "Return of the Creek Indians Who Have Not Joined the British," PRO WO 1/143; Tustunnuggee Thlucco, Tustunnuggee Hopooie, and John Steddam to Hawkins, June 1814, Cuyler Collection, GU.
38. Toulmin to Jackson, June 22, 1814, Jackson Papers, LC.
39. Gannie to Jackson, July 19, 1814, Hinson to Toulmin, July 19, 1814, Gordon to [Jackson], July 29, 1814, Jackson Papers, LC; Robinson and Muir to Jackson, July 28, 1814, Bassett, *Correspondence*, 2:21–22.
40. Coles, *War of 1812*, p. 203.
41. *Royal Gazette and Bahama Advertiser*, Aug. 17, 1814; Doyle to James Innerarity, May 25, 1814, enclosure in James Innerarity to McKee, June 16, 1814, NA LSW.
42. de Grummond, "Platter of Glory," pp. 316–58.
43. Jones to Benton, July 4, 1814, enclosure in Jackson to Secretary of War, July 30, 1814, NA LSW.
44. Jackson to Blount, Aug. 27, 1814, *Augusta Chronicle*, Oct. 7, 1814.
45. Extract of Letter received by Samuel Acre from Pedro Alva, July 16, 1812 [1814], enclosure in Jackson to Secretary of War, July 30, 1814, NA LSW.
46. W. C. C. Claiborne to Jackson, Aug. 24, 1814, Bassett, *Correspondence*, 2:29–30.

Chapter 9

1. Coles, *War of 1812*, pp. 121–22, 150–51, 163–81; Bathurst to Ross, Sept. 28, 1814, PRO WO 6/2; "The Expedition against New Orleans," PRO WO 1/142.

2. Cameron to Bathurst, Oct. 28, 1813, PRO WO 23/60; Reilly, *British at the Gates*, pp. 170–71.

3. Gordon to Cameron, Apr. 13, 1814, and enclosures, PRO CO 23/61.

4. Cameron to Bathurst, Nov. 30, 1813, and enclosures, PRO CO 23/60; Young, "Memoir," pp. 21–23, MS in APS, microfilm copy, GU.

5. Bathurst to Cameron, Jan. 21, 1814, PRO CO 24/17.

6. Warren to Melville, Nov. 18, 1812, Feb. 25, 1813, Warren Papers, NMM.

7. Bathurst to Beckwith, Mar. 1813, MS 2326, Cochrane Papers, NLS.

8. Mahon, "British Strategy," p. 285.

9. Cameron to Bathurst, Apr. 17, 1814, PRO CO 23/61.

10. Pigot to Cochrane, Apr. 13, 1814, MS 2328, Cochrane Papers, NLS; Memorandum from Governor Charles Cameron, dated Feb. 1, 1818, enclosure in Popham to Bathurst, Apr. 12, 1818, PRO Adm. 1/269.

11. Pigot to Woodbine, May 5, 10, 1814, MS 2328, Cochrane Papers, NLS.

12. Pigot to Cochrane, Apr. 13, 1814, ibid.

13. Pigot to Cochrane, June 8, 1814, PRO Adm. 1/506; Durant and Ten Indian Chiefs to Cochrane [May 1814], PRO Adm. 1/4360; Pigot to Woodbine, May 10, 1814, MS 2328, Cochrane Papers, NLS.

14. Woodbine to Pigot, May 25, 1814, Woodbine to Hope, May 31, 1814, MS 2328, Cochrane Papers, NLS.

15. Pigot to Cochrane, June 8, 1814, PRO Adm. 1/506.

16. Cochrane to Croker, June 20, 1814, ibid.; Bathurst to Ross, Sept. 10, 1814, PRO WO 6/2.

17. Pigot to Cochrane, June 8, 1814, PRO Adm. 1/506.

18. Bassett, *Correspondence*, 2:4*n*.

19. Pigot to Cochrane, Apr. 13, June 8, 1814, PRO Adm. 1/506.

20. Wheeler to John Innerarity, June 6, 1814, Cruzat Papers, FHi.

21. Murdoch, "British Report," pp. 36–51.

22. Cochrane to Croker, June 20, 1814, PRO Adm. 1/506; "Expedition against New Orleans," PRO WO 1/142; Cochrane to Bathurst, Sept. 2, 1814, PRO WO 1/141.

23. Jackson to Secretary of War, Feb. 10, 1815, Jackson Papers, LC; Floyd to Mary Floyd, Oct. 7, 1813, Floyd Letters, GaDA; Floyd to Pinckney, Jan. 3, 1814, enclosure in Pinckney to Secretary of War, Jan. 17, 1814, NA LSW.

24. Reilly, *British at the Gates*, pp. 170–73; Cochrane to Croker, June 20, 1814, PRO Adm. 1/506; Cochrane to Bathurst, July 14, 1814, PRO WO 1/141; "Expedition against New Orleans," PRO WO 1/142.

25. Fortescue, *British Army*, 10:151.

26. Flournoy to the Secretary of War, Jan. 31, March 14, 1814, NA LSW; *New Orleans Gazette*, Jan. 14, 1814.

27. "Expedition against New Orleans," PRO WO 1/142.

28. Cochrane to Bathurst, Sept. 2, 1814; "Expedition against New Orleans"; both in PRO WO 1/141.

29. Cochrane to Croker, Jan. 5, 1814, PRO Adm. 1/506.

30. Field, *Britain's Sea Soldiers*, 1:248.

31. "A Proclamation to the Indian Chiefs Signed by Alexander Inglis Cochrane KB," July 1, 1814, PRO WO 1/143; Cochrane to Croker, July 29, 1814, PRO Adm. 1/506.

32. Cochrane to Nicolls, Dec. 28, 1814, PRO Adm. 1/505.

33. Cochrane to Nicolls, July 4, 1814, PRO Adm. 1/506.

34. Woodbine to the Creeks, May 28, 1814, MS 2328, Cochrane Papers, NLS; Cochrane to Nicolls, July 4, 1814, PRO Adm. 1/506.

35. Cochrane to Nicolls, July 4, 1814, PRO Adm. 1/506.

36. Cochrane to Percy, July 5, 1814, ibid.

37. Cochrane to Cameron, July 4, 1814, PRO CO 23/61.

38. Nicolls to Cochrane, July 27, 1814, MS 2328, Cochrane Papers, NLS.

39. Cochrane to Cameron, July 4, 1814, PRO CO 23/61.

40. Cameron to Ruiz Apodaca, July 29, 1814, ibid.

41. Nicolls to Cochrane, Aug. 4, 1814, MS 2328, Cochrane Papers, NLS.

42. González Manrique to Jackson, July 26, 1814, Bassett, *Correspondence*, 2:20–21.

43. Ruiz Apodaca to the Governor of East Florida, Dec. 10, 1813, Ruiz Apodaca to Juan O. Donoju, June 6, 1814, AGI PC, Leg. 1856.

44. Fernan-Nuñez to Castlereagh, Dec. 8, 1815, PRO FO 72/180.

45. Percy to Cochrane, Sept. 9, 1814, PRO Adm. 1/505.

46. Woodbine to Pigot, May 25, 31, 1814, MS 2328, Cochrane Papers, NLS.

47. Francis and Hopoyhisckyhotta to the Commander of British forces at Apalachicola, June 1, 1814, unsigned to Samuel Jackson, July 19, 1814, ibid.

48. Lockyer to Woodbine, July 19, 1814, Woodbine to Smith, July 20, 1814, ibid.

49. Woodbine to Lockyer, July 30, 1814, Woodbine to Cameron, Aug. 9, 1814, ibid.

50. Nicolls to Cochrane, Nov. 17, 1814, Report Journal from Aug. 12, 1814, to Nov. 17, 1814, ibid.

51. Ibid.

52. Percy to Cochrane, Sept. 9, 1814, PRO Adm. 1/505.

Chapter 10

1. Mauricio Zuñiga to Ruiz Apodaca, Apr. 8, 1813, González Manrique to Ruiz Apodaca, Oct. 19, 1813, AGI PC, Leg. 1794.

2. John Innerarity to James Innerarity, July 27, 1813, in West, "Prelude," pp. 249–60; Ruiz Apodaca to Minister of War, Oct. 1, 1813, AGI PC, Leg. 1856.

3. Ruiz Apodaca to Minister of War, June 16, Aug. 6, 1813, AGI PC, Leg. 1856; González Manrique to Ruiz Apodaca, June 13, 1813, AGI PC, Leg. 1794; Onís to Labrador, Oct. 8, 1813, AHN, Estado, Leg. 5639.

4. John Innerarity, "Narrative of the Operations of the British in the Floridas," MS dated 1815, Cruzat Papers, FHi; Nicolls to Cochrane, Report, Aug. 12 to Nov. 17, 1814, MS 2328, Cochrane Papers, NLS.

5. Innerarity, "Narrative," Cruzat Papers, FHi.

6. Gonźalez Manrique to Ruiz Apodaca, Sept. 10, 1814, enclosure in Jackson to Gonźalez Manrique, Aug. 30, 1814, AGI PC, Leg. 1795.

7. Tucker, *Poltroons*, 2:640; Ruiz Apodaca to Minister of War, June 6, Sept. 24, 1814, AGI PC, Leg. 1856.

8. Nicolls to Cochrane, Report, Aug. 12 to Nov. 17, 1814, MS 2328, Cochrane Papers, NLS.

9. Ibid.

10. Gonźalez Manrique to Ruiz Apodaca, Sept. 10, 1814, AGI PC, Leg. 1795.

11. Latour, *Memoir*, pp. 12–25; Nicolls to Jean Laffite (copy), Aug. 31, 1814, AGI PC, Leg. 1795.

12. Pigot to Cochrane, June 8, 1814, PRO Adm. 1/506.

13. "Expedition against New Orleans," PRO WO 1/142; Cochrane to Nicolls, July 4, 1814, PRO Adm. 1/506.

14. Lockyer to Percy, Sept. 11, 1814, MS 2328, Cochrane Papers, NLS; Latour, *Memoir*, pp. 15–19.

15. Laffite to Blanque, Sept. 4, 1814, in Latour, *Memoir*, appendix, p. xii.

16. Nicolls to Laffite, Aug. 31, 1814, AGI PC, Leg. 1795, letter reprinted ibid., appendix, p. ix.

17. Latour, *Memoir*, pp. 21–25; de Grummond, *Baratarians*, pp. 35–36.

18. Nicolls to Laffite, Aug. 31, 1814, AGI PC, Leg. 1795; Latour, *Memoir*, pp. 19–25; Kenner to Minor, Nov. 11, 1814, Kenner Papers, LSU.

19. Nicolls to Cochrane, Aug. 12, Nov. 17, 1814, MS 2328, Cochrane Papers, NLS.

20. Percy to Cochrane, Sept. 9, 1814, PRO Adm. 1/505.

21. Nicolls to Cochrane, Aug. 12, Nov. 17, 1814, MS 2328, Cochrane Papers, NLS; "The Memorial of Edward Nicolls, Major Brevet in the Royal Marines, to the Right Honorable Lord Melville, First Lord of the Admiralty," May 5, 1817, PRO WO 1/144.

22. Henry to Nicolls, Sept. 20, 1814, MS 2328, Cochrane Papers, NLS.

23. Percy to Cochrane, Sept. 16, 1814, PRO Adm. 1/505; Henry to Nicolls, Sept. 20, 1814, Nicolls to Cochrane, Nov. 17, 1814, MS 2328, Cochrane Papers, NLS.

24. Nicolls to Cochrane, Aug. 12, Nov. 17, 1814, MS 2328, Cochrane Papers, NLS.

25. Jackson to Monroe, Sept. 17, 1814, Bassett *Correspondence*, 2: 50–51; *Mississippi Republican*, Nov. 16, 1814.

26. Latour, *Memoir*, pp. 32–34.

27. A. P. Hayne, General Orders, Sept. 17, 1814, in Lowrie, *ASP, Indian Affairs*, 1:860; "Tatum's Journal," pp. 79–84, LSM.

28. Jackson to Secretary of War, Sept. 16, 1814, NA LSW.

29. Woodruff to Jackson, Sept. 18, 1814, Military Section, Book 205, ADA.

30. Jackson to Williams, Sept. 21, 1814, Jackson Papers, LC.

31. Butler to Kennedy, Sept. 17, 1814, ibid.

32. Owsley, "Jackson's Capture," pp. 175–79.

33. Jackson to Monroe, Oct. 26, 1814, NA LSW.

34. Latour, *Memoir*, p. 45.

35. McAlister, "Pensacola," pp. 316–17.

36. Campbell to Milton, May [June?] 7, 1814, enclosure in Pinckney to Armstrong, July 2, 1814, NA LSW; Holmes, *Honor and Fidelity*, pp. 75–78.

37. Zuñiga to Ruiz Apodaca, Apr. 21, 1813, Report of the Louisiana Regiment,

May 1813, Gonźalez Manrique to Ruiz Apodaca, May 15, 1813, in AGI PC, Leg. 1794; Campbell to Milton, May [June?] 7, 1814, enclosure in Pinckney to Secretary of War, July 2, 1814, NA LSW; Cox, *West Florida*, pp. 614–15.

38. Engineer's report dated Aug. 23, 1813, Gonźalez Manrique et al. to Ruiz Apodaca, Dec. 18, 1813, AGI PC, Leg. 1794; Ruiz Apodaca to Minister of War, Mar. 25, 1814, AGI PC, Leg. 1856.

39. Forbes to Castlereagh, May 20, 1815, Forbes Papers, MPL.

40. Jones to Benton, July 4, 1814, enclosure in Jackson to Armstrong, July 30, 1813, NA LSW.

41. Gonźalez Manrique to Ruiz Apodaca, Dec. 6, 1814, AGI PC, Leg. 1795.

42. Nicolls to Cochrane, Nov. 17, 1814, MS 2328, Cochrane Papers, NLS; Forbes to Castlereagh, May 20, 1815, Forbes Papers, MPL.

43. Gonźalez Manrique to Ruiz Apodaca, Jan. 8, July 23, 1814, AGI PC, Leg. 1795; González Manrique et al. to Ruiz Apodaca, Dec. 18, 1813, AGI PC, Leg. 1794; "Tatum's Journal," MS, pp. 86–87, LSM.

44. Milton to Pinckney, June 9, 1814, enclosure in Pinckney to Secretary of War, July 2, 1814, NA LSW.

45. Innerarity, "Narrative," Cruzat Papers, FHi; Ruiz Apodaca to Minister of War, Oct. 1, 1813, June 6, 1814, AGI PC, Leg. 1856.

46. Franco, *Politica*, pp. 44–46.

47. "Expedition against New Orleans," PRO WO 1/142.

48. González Manrique to Ruiz Apodaca, Sept. 10, 1814, AGI PC, Leg. 1795; Ruiz Apodaca to Minister of War, Oct. 1, 1813, June 6, 1814, AGI PC, Leg. 1856.

49. Nicolls to Cochrane, Report, Aug, 12 to Nov. 17, 1814, MS 2328, Cochrane Papers, NLS; Nicolls to Melville, May 5, 1817, PRO WO 1/144; Gordon and Nicolls to González Manrique, Nov. 2, 1814, PRO FO 72/219; Ruiz Apodaca to Minister of War, Oct. 9, 1814, AGI PC, Leg. 1856.

50. Greenslade, "Innerarity," pp. 90–95; Gordon to James Innerarity, Feb. 17, 1817, Forbes Papers, MPL; Nicolls to Cochrane, Mar. 1, 1816, PRO WO 1/144; John Innerarity to James Innerarity, June 9, 1814, James Innerarity to McKee, June 16, 1814, NA LSW.

51. Forbes to Castlereagh, May 20, 1815, Forbes Papers, MPL; Henry to Nicolls, Sept. 20, 1814, Nicolls to Cochrane, Nov. 17, 1814, MS 2328, Cochrane Papers, NLS; Potts to Bathurst. Nov. 22, 1815, PRO WO 1/143; Certificate of citizenship recorded by Don Joseph E. Caro, Keeper of the Public Spanish Archives of West Florida, Oct. 6, 1812, Greenslade Papers, FHi.

52. Innerarity, "Narrative," Cruzat Papers, FHi; "Tatum's Journal," p. 87, LSM.

53. González Manrique to Ruiz Apodaca, Dec. 5, 1814, AGI PC, Leg. 1795.

54. Doyle to [John Innerarity], 1817 [no other date], Greenslade Papers, FHi; Cockburn to Kindelan, Feb. 13, 1815, Butler to Harrison, Jan. 26, 1816, PRO WO 1/144; Report of Lieutenant Jose Urcerllo to Gonźalez Manrique, Jan. 23, 1815, Forbes Papers, MPL.

55. John Innerarity to James Innerarity, May 10, 1815, Forbes Papers, MPL.

56. Gordon to Cochrane, Nov. 18, 1814, PRO Adm. 1/505; Gonźalez Manrique to Ruiz Apodaca, Nov. 15, 1814, AGI PC, Leg. 1795.

57. Gordon and Nicolls to González Manrique, Nov. 2, 1814, PRO FO 72/219.

58. Gordon to Cochrane, Nov. 18, 1814, PRO Adm. 1/505.

59. John Innerarity to James Innerarity, Nov. 10, 1814; Yonge, "Innerarity Letters," pp. 127–30.

60. Coffee to his wife, Nov. 15, 1814, Coffee Papers, THi.

61. McAlister, "Pensacola," p. 317.

62. Coffee to his wife, Nov. 15, 1814, Coffee Papers, THi.

63. Jackson to Monroe, Nov. 14, 1814, NA LSW; McAlister, "Pensacola," p. 317; "Tatum's Journal," pp. 99–105, LSM.

64. González Manrique to Ruiz Apodaca, Nov. 14, 1814, AGI PC, Leg. 1795.

65. Jackson to Monroe, Nov. 14, 1814, NA LSW.

66. Gordon to Cochrane, Nov. 18, 1814, PRO Adm. 1/505.

67. Coffee to his wife, Nov. 15, 1814, Coffee Papers, THi.

68. Cochrane to Croker, Dec. 7, 1814, PRO Adm. 1/508; "Juan Ventura Morales to Alexandro Ramírez, Nov. 3, 1817," *Boletín del Archivo Nacional* 13 (Jan.–Feb. 1914): 15–16.

69. Jackson to Monroe, Nov. 14, 1814, NA LSW; Latour, *Memoir*, p. 48.

70. Cochrane to Lambert, Feb. 3, 1815, PRO WO 1/143.

71. "Tatum's Journal," pp. 111–12, LSM.

72. John Innerarity to James Innerarity, Nov. 10, 29, 1814, Greenslade Papers, FHi.

73. Innerarity, "Narrative," Cruzat Papers, FHi.

Chapter 11

1. Anonymous letter from Havana to an unknown addressee, Aug. 8, 1814, Latour, *Memoir*, appendix, pp. v–vii; anonymous letter from Havana to unknown addressee, Aug. 13, 1814, Jackson Papers, LC.

2. Anonymous letter from Havana, Aug. 13, 1814, Jackson Papers, LC.

3. Cochrane to Nicolls, July 4, 1814, PRO Adm. 1/506; Cochrane to Croker, June 20, 1814, PRO WO 1/142.

4. Jackson to Secretary of War, July 26, 1814, Jackson Papers, LC.

5. Jackson to Secretary of War, Aug. 5, 1814, NA LSW.

6. Jackson to Patterson, Aug. 27, 1814, Patterson to Jackson, Sept. 2, 1814, enclosures in Patterson to Jones, NA LSN-CO.

7. Jackson to Patterson, Oct. 23, 1814, Bassett, *Correspondence*, 2:80–81.

8. Jackson to Secretary of War, July 31, Aug. 18, 1814, Jackson Papers, LC; Brown, *The Amphibious Campaign*, p. 48.

9. Secretary of War to Jackson, June 25, July 18, 1814, NA SWL, vol. 7.

10. Secretary of War to Jackson, Aug. 10, Sept. 27, Oct. 10, 1814, ibid.; Jackson to Blount, Aug. 27, 1814, in *Augusta Chronicle*, Oct. 7, 1814; Adams, *History*, bk. 8, pp. 311–32.

11. Jackson to Secretary of War, Oct. 14, 1814, Bassett, *Correspondence*, 2:72–73.

12. Jackson to Secretary of War, Dec. 13, 1814, NA LSW; Blount to Hynes, Dec. 23, 1814, Hynes Papers, TUL.

13. Cochrane to Croker, June 20, 1814, PRO Adm. 1/506; Cochrane to [Melville], Nov. 22, 1814, War of 1812, IU; Cochrane to Croker, Dec. 7, 1814, PRO

Adm. 1/508; "Memorial of Edward Nicolls to the Right Honorable Lord Melville," May 5, 1817, PRO WO 1/144.

14. Adams, *History*, bk. 8, pp. 311–12, 332; Codrington to his wife, Jan. 23, 1815, Codrington Pappers, NMM.

15. Coffee to his wife, Nov. 18, 21, 1814, Coffee Papers, THi.

16. Gray to Jackson, Dec. 30, 1826, Feb. 14, 1827, Jackson Papers, LC.

17. Jackson, "General Orders," Nov. 16, 1814, Bassett, *Correspondence*, 2:100–101.

18. Jackson to Secretary of War, Dec. 13, 1814, NA LSW; Cochrane to Croker, Dec. 7, 1814, PRO Adm. 1/508; "Juan Ventura Morales to Alexandro Ramírez, Nov. 3, 1817," *Boletín del Archivo Nacional* 13 (Jan.–Feb. 1914): 9–21; de Grummond, *Baratarians*, p. 34.

19. Jackson to Winchester, Nov. 18, 1814, Jackson to Secretary of War, Dec. 2, 1814, Jackson Papers, LC; "Tatum's Journal," pp. 117–26, LSM.

20. James, *Jackson*, pp. 221–22; Coles, *War of 1812*, pp. 210–12; Cochrane to Croker, Dec. 7, 1814, PRO Adm. 1/508.

21. Hayne to Jackson, Dec. 1, 1814, Bassett, *Correspondence*, 2:107–8.

22. Jackson to Winchester, Dec. 11, 1814, Jackson Papers, LC; Jackson to Secretary of War, Dec. 13, 1814, NA LSW.

23. James, *Jackson*, pp. 222–23; Jackson to Reynolds, Dec. 22, 1814, Jackson Papers, LC; Jackson to Secretary of War, Dec. 10, 27, 1814, Bassett, *Correspondence*, 2:126–28.

24. Coles, *War of 1812*, p. 213.

25. Latour, *Memoir*, pp. 52–53; James, *Jackson*, pp. 226–27.

26. Flournoy to Secretary of War, Jan. 31, 1814, NA LSW.

27. Flournoy to Secretary of War, Mar. 14, 1814, ibid.

28. Message of the Louisiana Senate in Answer to the Governor of the State, signed J. Poydras, President of the Senate, *New Orleans Gazette*, Jan. 14, 1814.

29. Resolution by the Senate of Louisiana, signed J. Poydras, Mar. 5, 1814, enclosure in W. C. C. Claiborne to Secretary of War, Apr. 16, 1814; Wittle to Flournoy, Aug. 20, 1813, enclosure in Flournoy to Secretary of War, Jan. 20, 1814; all in NA LSW.

30. Marigny, "Reflections," pp. 63–64.

31. Hunt, *Memoir*, pp. 53–54.

32. Kenner to Minor, Dec. 2, 1814, Kenner Papers, LSU; Hynes to Carswell, Jan. 6, 1815, Hynes Papers, TUL.

33. Proclamation signed by Alexander Cochrane, July 1, 1814, PRO WO 1/143.

34. Butler to Blount, Oct. 30, 1814, Jackson Papers, LC.

35. Jackson to McIntosh, Nov. 16, 1815, ibid.

36. Coles, *War of 1812*, p. 218.

37. Marigny, "Reflections," pp. 65–75; Coles, *War of 1812*, p. 218; James, *Jackson*, pp. 228–29; Latour, *Memoir*, pp. 71–72; de Grummond, *Baratarians*, pp. 54–71; Hunt, *Livingston*, pp. 195–210; Hatcher, *Livingston*, p. 203.

38. Patterson to Jackson, Jan. 18, 1815, Jackson Papers, LC.

39. Patterson to Jackson, Jan. 15, 1815, Bassett, *Correspondence*, 2:132; Coles, *War of 1812*, pp. 218–19.

40. Lambert to Bathurst, Jan. 28, 1815, PRO WO 1/141.

41. Hamilton to Helms, July 8, 1814, NA SNL-M.

Chapter 12

1. "Expedition against New Orleans," PRO WO 1/142; Mahon, "Command Decisions," pp. 53–76; James, *Jackson*, passim; Coles, *War of 1812*, pp. 208–9; Horsman, *War of 1812*, pp. 223–30; Mahon, *War of 1812*, pp. 235, 340–46; Reilly, *British at the Gates*, pp. 171–73.

2. Croker to Cochrane, Aug. 10, 1814, Bathurst to Ross, Aug. 10, 1814, PRO WO 6/2.

3. Brooks, *Siege*, p. 34; Brown, *Amphibious Campaign*, pp. 6–8, 13–14; Coles, *War of 1812*, pp. 184–85.

4. Bathurst to Ross, Sept. 6, 1814, PRO WO 6/2.

5. Coles, *War of 1812*, pp. 214–15.

6. Mahon, "Command Decisions," pp. 68–69.

7. "Expedition against New Orleans," PRO WO 1/142.

8. Memorial of Edward Nicolls to Lord Melville, May 5, 1817, PRO WO 1/144; Cochrane's Journal, Dec. 3, 1814, PRO Adm. 50/122.

9. Bathurst to Ross, Aug. 10, 1814, and memorandum enclosed in Bathurst to Ross, Sept. 10, 1814, PRO WO 6/2; "Expedition against New Orleans," PRO WO 1/142; Cameron to Cochrane, Aug. 2, 1814, MS 2328, Cochrane Papers, NLS.

10. Hawkins to Winchester, Dec. 27, 1814, Winchester Papers, THS; *Augusta Chronicle*, Dec. 30, 1814; Blackshear to Floyd, Feb. 2, 1815, in Blackshear, *Memoir*, pp. 457–58.

11. Cochrane to Bathurst, July 14, 1814, PRO WO 1/141; Cochrane to Prevost, Oct. 5, 1814, PRO Adm. 1/508; "Expedition against New Orleans," PRO WO 1/142.

12. Cochrane to Bathurst, July 14, 1814, PRO WO 1/141.

13. Cockburn to Cochrane, Apr. 2, 1814, MS 2574, Cochrane Papers, NLS.

14. Adams, *History*, bk. 9, pp. 62–63; Ramsay to Cockburn, Feb. 16, 1815, Somerville to Cockburn, Jan. 14, 1815, Cockburn to Cochrane, Oct. 10, 1814, MS 2334, Cochrane Papers, NLS.

15. Floyd to Mary Floyd, Dec. 28, 1814, Floyd Letters, GaDA; Brown, *Amphibious Campaign*, p. 171.

16. Floyd to Early, Nov. 26, 1814, Floyd Papers, GaDA; Blackshear to Floyd, Feb. 2, 1815, Pinckney to Blackshear, Feb. 13, 1815, in Blackshear, *Memoir*, pp. 457–58.

17. Bathurst to Ross, July 30, 1814, PRO WO 6/2.

18. Bathurst to Pakenham, Oct. 24, 1814, ibid.; Brown, *Amphibious Campaign*, pp. 14–17.

19. Bathurst to Ross, Aug. 10, 1814, PRO WO 6/2; Cochrane to Croker, Dec. 7, 16, 1814, Jan. 26, 1815, PRO Adm. 1/508; Croker to Cochrane, Oct. 3, 1814, MS 2344, Cochrane Papers, NLS.

20. Cochrane to Croker, Dec. 7, 1814, PRO Adm. 1/508.

21. Ibid.; de Grummond, "Platter of Glory," pp. 324–25.

22. Cochrane to Croker, Dec. 16, 1814, PRO Adm. 1/508; List of Schooners Hired by Captain Spencer, Dec. 4, 1814, MS 2330, Cochrane Papers, NLS.

23. Cochrane to Croker, Dec. 16, 1814, PRO Adm. 1/508.

24. Jones to Patterson, Mar. 12, 1815, in Latour, *Memoir*, appendix, pp.

xxxiii–xxxvi; Lockyer to Cochrane, Dec. 16, 1814, and enclosure, PRO Adm. 1/508.

25. Jones to Patterson, Mar. 12, 1815, in Latour, *Memoir*, appendix, pp. xxxiii–xxxv.

26. Lockyer to Cochrane, Dec. 16, 1814, PRO Adm. 1/508.

27. Enclosure in Jones to Patterson, Mar. 12, 1815, in Latour, *Memoir*, appendix, pp. xxxiii–xxxvi.

28. "List of Killed and wounded in the Boats of His Majesty's Ships at the Capture of the American gun vessels near New Orleans," enclosure in Cochrane to Croker, Dec. 28, 1814, PRO Adm. 1/508.

29. Jones to Patterson, Oct. 18, 1813, NA SNL-O; Patterson to Jones, Nov. 22, 1813, NA LSN-CO.

30. Cochrane to Croker, Jan. 24, 1815, PRO Adm. 1/508.

31. Jackson to Winchester, Dec. 16, 1814, Jackson Papers, LC.

32. Jackson to Secretary of War, Dec. 27, 1814, Bassett, *Correspondence*, 2:126–28.

33. Forester, *Fighting Sail*, pp. 267–69.

34. Kenner to Minor, Dec. 17, 1814, Kenner Papers, LSU; Thomas to Hicky, Dec. 28, 1814, Hicky Papers, LSU.

35. Brown, *Amphibious Campaign*, pp. 80–81.

36. Jones to Patterson, Oct. 18, 1813, Mar. 7, 1814, NA SNL-O.

37. Patterson to Jones, Jan. 25, 1814, NA LSN-CO.

38. Cochrane to Croker, Jan. 18, 1815, PRO Adm. 1/508.

39. Keane to Packenham, Dec. 26, 1814, PRO WO 1/141.

40. Cochrane to Croker, Dec. 16, 1814, PRO Adm. 1/508.

41. Mahon, "Command Decisions," pp. 71–72; Coles, *War of 1812*, p. 214.

42. de Grummond, *Baratarians*, p. 65.

43. Cochrane to Croker, Dec. 16, 1814, PRO Adm. 1/508.

44. Keane to Packenham, Dec. 26, 1814, PRO WO 1/141; Coles, *War of 1812*, pp. 214–15; de Grummond, *Baratarians*, pp. 75–76.

45. Coles, *War of 1812*, p. 216.

46. de Grummond, *Baratarians*, pp. 85–86.

47. Latour, *Memoir*, p. 88.

48. Patterson to Secretary of the Navy, Dec. 28, 1814, in Latour, *Memoir*, appendix, p. xlii.

49. Jones to Patterson, July 8, 1814, NA SNL-O; de Grummond, *Baratarians*, pp. 86, 90.

50. Henley to Patterson, Dec. 28, 1814, in Latour, *Memoir*, appendix, pp. xlvii–xlviii; Coles, *War of 1812*, p. 219.

Chapter 13

1. Jackson to Secretary of War, Dec. 27, 1814, Bassett, *Correspondence*, 2:126–27; Brown, *Amphibious Campaign*, pp. 98–99.

2. John Coffee to [?], Jan. 25, 1815, Miscellaneous Files, THi.

3. Latour, *Memoir*, pp. 91–92.

4. Adams, *History*, bk. 8, pp. 346–47.

5. Jackson to Secretary of War, Dec. 27, 1814, Bassett, *Correspondence*, 2:126–27.

6. Patterson to Secretary of War, Dec. 28, 1814, in Latour, *Memoir*, appendix, pp. xlii–xliii; Keane to Pakenham, Dec. 26, 1814, PRO WO 1/141; Patterson to Jackson, Jan. 7, 1815, Bassett, *Correspondence*, 2:331.

7. Coffee to [?], Jan. 25, 1814, Miscellaneous Files, THi.

8. Latour, *Memoir*, pp. 95–101; James, *Jackson*, pp. 242–43; Adams, *History*, bk. 8, pp. 346–48; Jackson to Secretary of War, Dec. 27, 1814, Bassett, *Correspondence*, 2:126–27; Keane to Pakenham, Dec. 26, 1814, PRO WO 1/141; "Tatum's Journal," pp. 139–41, LSM; Copy of the diary of Benjamin Story, as a British prisoner of war during the Battle of New Orleans, 1814–1815, Louisiana Collection, TUL; Jim Brundige to [?], Dec. 31, 1814, Hynes Papers, TUL.

9. Return of Casualties in the army under the command of Major General Keane in Action with the enemy near New Orleans on 23 Dec. 1814, PRO WO 1/141.

10. Latour, *Memoir*, pp. 102–3; Report of the Killed, Wounded and Missing of the Army of Major General Andrew Jackson in the action of Dec. 23 and 25, 1814, and Jan. 1 and 8, 1815, Jackson Papers, LC.

11. Adams, *History*, bk. 8, pp. 351–57; Keane to Pakenham, Dec. 26, 1814, PRO WO 1/141; Coffee to [?], Jan. 25, 1815, Miscellaneous Files, THi; Latour, *Memoir*, pp. 104–13.

12. de Grummond, *Baratarians*, p. 100; Butler to Kemper, Dec. 29, 1814, Jackson Papers, LC.

13. Extract from the Journal of the Quartermaster, signed C. R. Forrest, Major 34th Regiment, Assistant Quartermaster General, PRO WO 1/141; de Grummond, *Baratarians*, p. 97; Latour, *Memoir*, p. 115; Brown, *Amphibious Campaign*, pp. 101–24.

14. de Grummond, *Baratarians*, pp. 97–103; Fortescue, *British Army*, 10:162–63.

15. Henley to Patterson, Dec. 28, 1814, Latour, *Memoir*, appendix, pp. xlvii-xlviii; "Tatum's Journal," pp. 146–47, LSM; Brown, *Amphibious Campaign*, pp. 112–13.

16. de Grummond, *Baratarians*, p. 101.

17. Butler to Morgan, Dec. 25, 1814, Jackson Papers, LC; Latour, *Memoir*, p. 113.

18. de Grummond, *Baratarians*, p. 101.

19. Ibid., pp. 96–105; Latour, *Memoir*, pp. 106–15; "Tatum's Journal," pp. 147–49, LSM; Livingston to Jackson, Dec. 25, 1814, Bassett, *Correspondence*, 2:125.

20. de Grummond, *Baratarians*, pp. 103–5.

21. Coffee to [?], Jan. 25, 1815, Miscellaneous Files, THi.

22. Extract from the Journal of the Quartermaster, signed C. R. Forrest, Major, 34th Regiment, Assistant Quartermaster General, PRO WO 1/141; de Grummond, *Baratarians*, pp. 106–7; "Tatum's Journal," pp. 149–50, LSM.

23. Return of Casualties in the Army under Command of Major General the Honorable Sir Edward Pakenham KB in Action with the enemy near New Orleans between the 25th and 31st Dec. 1814, PRO WO 1/141.

24. Latour, *Memoir*, appendix, p. lix.

25. Pakenham to Cochrane, Dec. 28, 1814, MS 2330, Cochrane Papers, NLS.

26. Latour, *Memoir*, pp. 114–17; Jackson to LaCoste, Dec. 25, 1814, Jackson Papers, LC.

27. Latour, *Memoir*, pp. 147–48.

28. Ibid., pp. 126–27.

29. Extract from the Journal of the movements of the Army, employed on the Southern Coast of North America, signed C. R. Forrest, Assistant Quartermaster General, Major, 34th Regiment, PRO WO 1/141; there are two Journals of C. R. Forrest, and they differ slightly in content.

30. Extract of the Journal of the Quartermaster, signed C. R. Forrest, Major, 34th Regiment, Assistant Quartermaster General, PRO WO 1/141; de Grummond, *Baratarians*, p. 117.

31. de Grummond, *Baratarians*, pp. 115–16; Reilly, *British at the Gates*, pp. 280–81, 355–56; Brooks, *Siege*, pp. 201–2.

32. Coles, *War of 1812*, p. 224.

33. Brown, *Amphibious Campaign*, p. 124; Extract from the Journal of the Quartermaster, signed C. R. Forrest, etc., PRO WO 1/141; Pakenham to Cochrane, Dec. 28, 1814, MS 2330, Cochrane Papers, NLS; Coles, *War of 1812*, p. 225.

34. de Grummond, *Baratarians*, p. 117.

35. Adams, *History*, bk. 8, pp. 363–66.

36. Reilly, *British at the Gates*, pp. 281–82.

37. Coffee to [?], Jan. 25, 1815, Miscellaneous Files, THi.

38. Latour, *Memoir*, appendix, p. lix.

39. Return of Casualties in the Army under the Command of Major General, the Honorable Sir Edward Pakenham KB, in action with the enemy before New Orleans between the 1st and 7th of Jan. 1815, PRO WO 1/141.

40. de Grummond, *Baratarians*, pp. 119–20; Latour, *Memoir*, pp. 135–37; Jackson to Secretary of War, Jan. 3, 1815, Bassett, *Correspondence*, 2:130.

41. de Grummond, *Baratarians*, p. 115; Latour, *Memoir*, appendix map; "Tatum's Journal," pp. 153–54, LSM.

42. Marigny, "Reflections," pp. 66–68; Dent to Jackson, Jan. 6, 1815, Bassett, *Correspondence*, 2:131; de Grummond, *Baratarians*, pp. 109–10.

43. Cochrane to Croker, Jan. 18, 1815, PRO Adm. 1/508; Extract from the Journal of the Quartermaster, signed C. R. Forrest, PRO WO 1/141; Brown, *Amphibious Campaign*, pp. 129–32.

44. Thornton to Pakenham, Jan. 7–8, 1815, PRO WO 1/141.

45. Report of J. Mitchell to Colonel Thornton, Jan. 8, 1815, ibid.

46. Return of Casualties in the Army under the command of Major General, the Honorable Edward M. Pakenham KB in action with the enemy near New Orleans on the 8th of Jan. 1815, ibid.

47. de Grummond, *Baratarians*, p. 129.

48. Latour, *Memoir*, pp. 165–66.

49. de Grummond, *Baratarians*, pp. 127–28.

50. Patterson to Jackson, Jan. 7, 1815, Bassett, *Correspondence*, 2:331.

51. de Grummond, *Baratarians*, pp.. 128–30.

52. "Morgan's Defense," pp. 17–21.

53. Patterson to Secretary of the Navy, Jan. 13, 1815, in Latour, *Memoir*, appendix, pp. lx–lxiv; Jonathan Rees to David Rees, Jan. 1815, Rees Papers, TUL.

54. Thornton to Pakenham, Jan. 8, 1815, in Latour, *Memoir*, appendix, pp. clvii–clix.

Chapter 14

1. Adams, *History*, bk. 8, p. 367; de Grummond, *Baratarians*, p. 129.
2. Lambert to Bathurst, Jan. 10, 1813, in Latour, *Memoir*, appendix, pp. clix–clxiii; Adams, *History*, bk. 8, pp. 372–73.
3. de Grummond, *Baratarians*, p. 131.
4. Donald Daniel McL., Lieutenant, Royal Scots Fusiliers to [?], Jan. 6, 1815, Jackson Papers, LC; Jamaica *Royal Gazette*, in de Grummond, "Platter of Glory," pp. 324, 326; Coles, *War of 1812*, pp. 226–27.
5. Adams, *History*, bk. 8, pp. 373–74; de Grummond, *Baratarians*, pp. 130–36; Brown, *Amphibious Campaign*, p. 142.
6. Rankin, *New Orleans*, pp. 13–14.
7. Latour, *Memoir*, appendix, pp. cxlix–cliii; Adams, *History*, bk. 8, pp. 374–75; Brown, *Amphibious Campaign*, pp. 137, 234–35; Brooks, *Siege*, pp. 234–35.
8. Report of the Rank and file of the Army under the Immediate Command of Major General Jackson at New Orleans, Jan. 8, 1815, Jackson Papers, LC.; "Tatum's Journal," pp. 161–62, LSM; Brown, *Amphibious Campaign*, p. 137.
9. Lambert to Bathurst, Jan. 10, 1815, in Latour, *Memoir*, appendix, pp. cxlix–cliii; "Contemporary Account," p. 11; Adams, *History*, bk. 8, pp. 374–75; Report of the Rank and File of the Army under the Immediate Command of Major General Jackson at New Orleans, Jan. 8, 1815, Jackson Papers, LC; Coles, *War of 1812*, pp. 228–29; de Grummond, *Baratarians*, pp. 134–41; Battle of New Orleans, pp. 107–18; Marigny, "Reflections," pp. 74–76; "Tatum's Journal," pp. 161–62, LSM; Brown, *Amphibious Campaign*, p. 137.
10. "Tatum's Journal," pp. 161–62, LSM.
11. James, *Jackson*, pp. 265–67; Mayhew to Susan [?], Jan. 26, 1815, in "Massachusetts," pp. 30–31; Lambert to Bathurst, Jan. 28, 1815, PRO WO 1/141.
12. "Contemporary Account," pp. 11–12.
13. Parton, *Jackson*, 2:208.
14. Latour, *Memoir*, appendix, p. lx; Return of Casualties in the Army under the Command of Major General the Honorable Edward M. Pakenham KB in Action with the enemy near New Orleans on the 8th of Jan. 1815, PRO WO 1/141; Battle of New Orleans, p. 104.
15. James, *Jackson*, p. 262.
16. de Grummond, *Baratarians*, p. 153; "Tatum's Journal," pp. 146–47, LSM; Jackson to Morgan, Jan. 8, 1815, Jackson Papers, LC.
17. Tousard to Stocker, Jan. 20, 1815, in Wilkinson, "Assaults," p. 53.
18. Carroll to Jackson, Dec. 21, 1814, Bassett, *Correspondence*, 2:123; Coffee to Jackson, Dec. 17, 1814, ibid., 2:117; de Grummond, *Baratarians*, p. 120; McGehee to Porter, May 17, 1813, Cuyler Collection, GU.
19. Lambert to Bathurst, Jan. 29, 1815, PRO WO 1/141.
20. Quoted in James, *Jackson*, p. 231.

21. Patterson to Jackson, Jan. 7, 1815, Patterson to Jones, Jan. 13, 1815, NA LSN-CO.
22. Jackson to Morgan, Jan. 8, 1814, Jackson Papers, LC.
23. Brooks, *Siege*, pp. 250, 256.
24. Patterson to Jones, Jan. 13, 1815, NA LSN-CO.
25. Lambert to Bathurst, Jan. 10, 1815, in Latour, *Memoir*, appendix, p. clii.
26. Brooks, *Siege*, p. 249.
27. Lambert to Bathurst, Jan. 28, 1815, PRO WO 1/141.
28. Rankin, *New Orleans*, pp. 21–44.
29. Jackson to Secretary of War, Jan. 9, Feb. 13, 1815, Bassett, *Correspondence*, 2:136–38, 164–70; Horsman, *War of 1812*, p. 248; Reilly, *British at the Gates*, pp. 307–9; Ritchie, "Louisiana Campaign," pp. 26–32.
30. Lambert to Bathurst, Jan. 28, 29, 1815, PRO WO 1/141; Brooks, *Siege*, p. 249.
31. Cochrane to Croker, Jan. 18, 1815, PRO Adm. 1/508.
32. Latour, *Memoir*, pp. 187–90.
33. Ibid., pp. 187–97; Overton to Jackson, Jan. 19, 1815, enclosure in Jackson to Secretary of War, Feb. 17, 1815, NA LSW; Patterson to Jones, Jan. 20, 1815, NA LSN-CO.
34. Latour, *Memoir*, p. 179.
35. Lambert to Bathurst, Jan. 28, 1815, PRO WO 1/141; Malcolm to Cochrane, Jan. 28, 1815, PRO Adm. 1/508; Cochrane to Croker, Jan. 18, 1815, in London *Times*, Mar. 11, 1815.
36. Patterson to Secretary of Navy, Jan. 20, 1815, NA LSN-CO.
37. Shields to Patterson, Jan. 25, 1815, enclosure in Patterson to Secretary of Navy, Jan. 27, 1815, ibid.; Latour, *Memoir*, pp. 181–83; Jackson to Hays, Feb. 4, 1815, Bassett, *Correspondence*, 2:157.
38. *Royal Gazette and Bahama Advertiser*, Feb. 8, 1815.

Chapter 15

1. Brooks, *Siege*, pp. 263–64.
2. Latour, *Memoir*, pp. 202–3.
3. de Grummond, *Baratarians*, p. 147; Secretary of War to Thomas S. Jesup, Nov. 26, 1814, SWC, NA RG 107.
4. Jackson to Winchester, Jan. 31, 1815, Winchester Papers, THi.
5. Jackson to Winchester, Jan. 10, 1815, Jackson Papers, LC.
6. Cochrane to Lambert, Feb. 3, 1815, PRO WO 1/143.
7. Ibid.
8. Lambert to Bathurst, Jan. 29, 1815, PRO WO 1/141.
9. Ibid.
10. Lambert to Bathurst and enclosures, Feb. 14, 1815, ibid.; Rickett to Cochrane, Feb. 8, 15, 1815, Cochrane to Croker, Feb. 14, 1815, PRO Adm. 1/508.
11. Rickett to Cochrane, Feb. 15, 1815, PRO Adm. 1/508; Lambert to Bathurst and enclosures, Feb. 14, 1815, PRO WO 1/141.
12. Lawrence to Jackson, Feb. 12, 1815, in *Niles' Weekly Register*, Mar. 25, 1815.

13. Latour, *Memoir*, pp. 212–14.

14. Overton to Jackson, Jan. 19, 1815, and Comment from the *National Intelligencer*, in *Niles' Weekly Register*, Mar. 25, 1815.

15. Jackson to Winchester, Dec. 11, 1814, Winchester to Jackson, Dec. 17, 1814, Jackson Papers, LC.

16. Coulter to Winchester, Feb. 8, 1815; "Winchester's Defense of his conduct at Mobile," undated document; "Morning Report of the Troops stationed at Fort Charlotte," Feb. 15, 1815; "Consolidated Morning Report of the Troops Commanded by General Nathaniel Taylor and Lt. Colonel Peter Perkins at Camp Montville," Feb. 12, 1815; all in Winchester Papers, THi; McIntosh to Winchester, Feb. 8, 1815, Jackson to Winchester, Feb. 23, 1815, Jackson Papers, LC.

17. Winchester to Jackson, Mar. 7, 1815, Jackson Papers, LC; Jackson to Secretary of War, Feb. 24, 1815, NA LSW.

18. McKinzie to Winchester, Feb. 4, 1815, Hobart to Winchester, Feb. 6, 1815, Powell to Winchester, Feb. 16, 1815, Winchester Papers, THi; "Journal of Lieutenant M. M. McKinzie, Jan. 5, 1815–Jan. 13, 1815," Claybrooke Papers, THi.

19. Johnston to Winchester, Feb. 6, 1815, Winchester Papers, THi; Winchester to Jackson, Feb. 17, 1815, Jackson Papers, LC.

20. Fisher to Winchester, Feb. 21, 1815, Winchester Papers, THi.

21. Jackson to Winchester, Feb. 23, 1815, Jackson Papers, LC; Jackson to Lawrence, Apr. 6, 1815, Hurja Collection, THi.

22. Winchester to Jackson, Feb. 20, 1815, Jackson Papers, LC.

23. Gaines to Winchester, Feb. 26, 1815, Winchester Papers, THi; Winchester to Lambert, Mar. 2, 1815, enclosure in Lambert to Bathurst, Mar. 8, 1815, PRO WO 1/141.

24. Cochrane to Croker, Feb. 14, 1815, PRO Adm. 1/508; Lambert to Cochrane, Feb. 18, 1815, PRO Adm. 1/509.

25. Winchester to Jackson, Dec. 1, 1814, Blue to Jackson, Dec. 7, 1814, Jackson Papers, LC; "Tatum's Journal," pp. 113–14, LSM.

26. Blue to Jackson, Dec. 18, 27, 1814, Jackson Papers, LC; McIntosh to Early, Dec. 12, 1814, Creek Letters, GaDA.

27. Jackson to Winchester, Jan. 10, 1815, Jackson Papers, LC.

28. Jackson to McIntosh, Nov. 16, 1814, ibid.; Hawkins to Jackson, Nov. 4, 1814, typed transcript, AU, original in LC.

29. McIntosh to Jackson, Dec. 18, 1814, Winchester Papers, THi.

30. Early to Blackshear, Jan. 6, 1815, Governors' Letterbook, 18 May, 1814 to 30 Oct. 1821, GaDA.

31. Early to Blackshear, Jan. 19, 1815, ibid.

32. Hawkins to Jackson, Dec. 27, 1814, Feb. 27, 1815, typed transcript, AU, original in LC.

33. Nicolls to Cochrane [ca. Nov. 17, 1814], MS 2328, Cochrane Papers, NLS.

34. Nicolls to Cochrane, Dec. 5, 1814, ibid.; Codrington to his wife, Dec. 31, 1814, Codrington Papers, NMM.

35. Nicolls to Cochrane, Dec. 5, 1814, MS 2328, Cochrane Papers, NLS.

36. Alexander Cochrane's Journal, Admirals' Journals, Dec. 3, 1814, PRO Adm. 50/122; Henry to Governor of Pensacola, Jan. 12, 1815, Cruzat Papers, FHI; Codrington to his wife, Dec. 31, 1814, Codrington Papers, NMM.

37. Henry to Rawlins, Dec. 18, 1814, MS 2328, Cochrane Papers, NLS.

38. Rawlins to Cochrane, Jan. 15, 1815, MS 2328, ibid.

39. Cochrane's Journal, Admirals' Journals, Jan. 5, 10, 18, 1815, PRO Adm. 50/122.

40. Bartholomew to Cochrane, Jan. 31, 1815, MS 2328, Cochrane Papers, NLS.

41. Cochrane to Lambert, Feb. 3, 1815, PRO WO 1/143.

42. Hawkins to Secretary of War, Aug. 16, 1814, in Lowrie, *ASP*, *Indian Affairs*, 1:860; "Return of Muscogee Indians under the Command of Lieutenant Colonel Nicolls," undated, PRO WO 1/143; Boyd, "Prospect Bluff," pp. 68–70.

43. Hawkins to McIntosh, Nov. 26, 1814, Military Section, ADA.

44. Rawlins to Malcolm, Feb. 26, 1815, MS 2336, Cochrane Papers, NLS.

45. Hawkins to Secretary of War, Mar. 1, 1815, NA LSW; Cochrane to Nicolls, Feb. 14, 1815, PRO Adm. 1/508.

Chapter 16

1. Bathurst to Ross, Sept. 6, 1814, PRO WO 6/2; Memorandum, "Expedition against New Orleans," PRO WO 1/142; Brown, *Amphibious Campaign*, pp. 166–69; Reilly, *British at the Gates*, pp. 174–75, 342–43.

2. Onís to San Carlos, Mar. 11, 1815, Expediente 25, AHN, Estado, Leg. 5557.

3. Malcolm to Nicolls, Mar. 5, 29, 1815, Cochrane to Nicolls, Mar. 9, 1815, Ratification of Article 9 of the Treaty of Ghent signed by the Chiefs of the Muscogee Nation, Apr. 2, 1815, all in PRO FO 5/139.

4. Cochrane to Lambert, Feb. 17, 1815, PRO WO 1/143; Lambert to Cochrane, Feb. 25, 1815, PRO WO 1/141.

5. Cochrane to Malcolm, General Instructions, Feb. 17, 1815, Special Indian Instructions, Feb. 17, 1815, PRO WO 1/143.

6. Ibid.

7. Cochrane to Malcolm, Special Indian Instructions, Feb. 17, 1815, ibid.

8. Ibid.

9. Cochrane to Nicolls, Feb. 14, 1815, PRO Adm. 1/508.

10. Malcolm to Nicolls, Mar. 5, 1815, PRO FO 5/139.

11. Malcolm to Nicolls, Mar. 29, 1815, ibid.

12. Secretary of War to Jackson, June 12, 1815, NA SWL, vol. 8.

13. James, *Jackson*, p. 190.

14. Nicolls to Barker, his BMs Chargé d'Affaires, June 12, 1815, PRO FO 5/139; Spencer to Cochrane, Feb. 17, 1816, Nicolls to Cochrane, Mar. 1, 1816, Cochrane to Bathurst, Mar. 12, 1816, all in PRO WO 1/144.

15. Hawkins to Nicolls, Mar. 24, 1815, Nicolls to Hawkins, May 12, 1815, Hawkins to Nicolls, May 28, 1815, all in *Niles' Weekly Register*, June 24, 1815; Nicolls to Hawkins, Apr. 28, 1815, PRO WO 1/143.

16. Nicolls to Croker, Aug. 15, 1815, PRO WO 1/143.

17. Bathurst to Hidlis Hadjo, Sept. 21, 1815, PRO FO 5/140; Nicolls to Morier, Sept. 25, 1815, PRO WO 1/143.

18. Nicolls to Morier, Nov. 16, 1815, Croker to Goulburn, Nov. 28, 1815, PRO WO 1/143.

19. Bunbury to Barrow, Sept. 7, 1815, PRO FO 5/140; Nicolls to Cochrane, Mar. 1, 1816, Spencer to Cochrane, Feb. 17, 1816, Cochrane to Bathurst, Mar. 12, 1816, all in PRO WO 1/144.

20. Nicolls to Goulburn, Jan. 15, 1816, Nicolls to Cochrane, Aug. 14, 1816, PRO WO 1/144.

21. Estimate of Agricultural and Household Instruments for the Creek Indian Chief Hidlis Hadjo and Estimate of Clothing, enclosure in Nicolls to Goulburn, Jan. 15, 1816, and Nicolls to Goulburn, Oct. 8, 1816, both in PRO WO 1/144.

22. Nicolls to Goulburn, Jan. 7, 1817, ibid.

23. Nicolls to Gordon, Sept. 24, 1816, ibid.

24. Nicolls to Bathurst, Sept. 23, 1817, ibid. For additional information about Nicolls, see Nicolls to Goulburn, June 23, 1816, Jan. 27, 1817, Nicolls to Bathurst, May 5, 1817, Lushington to Goulburn, May 16, 1817, ibid.; Field, *Britain's Sea Soldiers*, 1:248.

25. Boyd, "Prospect Bluff," p. 85.

26. Doyle to John Innerarity, June 17, 1817, Yonge, ed., "The Panton, Leslie Papers," pp. 61–63.

27. Doyle to John Innerarity, July 11, 1817, ibid., pp. 135–38.

28. Boyd, "Prospect Bluff," p. 89.

29. Jackson to the Secretary of War, Apr. 8, 1818, in Lowrie, *ASP, Indian Affairs*, 1:699–700.

30. Goulburn to Hamilton, May 17, 1816, Apr. 2, 1817, PRO CO 138/146.

31. *Augusta Chronicle*, Nov. 3, 1815; Whitehead to Mitchell, Feb. 17, 1816, Powell to Rabun, Mar. 14, 1818, Cuyler Collection, GU.

32. Deposition to Samuel Jarvis, May 9, 1815, enclosure Gaines to Secretary of War, NA LSW, Note on total Indian arms.

33. Fernán-Núñez to Castlereagh, Dec. 8, 1815, PRO FO 72/180.

34. Petition of the Pensacola Citizens to his Excellency the Governor of West Florida, Mar. 1815, MS 2328, Cochrane Papers, NLS; González Manrique to Cochrane, Dec. 5, 1814, Urcerllo to González Manrique, Jan. 23, 1815, Forbes Papers, MPL; Cochrane to González Manrique, Feb. 10, 1815, Cruzat Papers, FHi; Ruiz Apodaca to Minister of War, May 6, June 15, 1815, AGI PC Leg. 1856.

35. Boyd, "Prospect Bluff," pp. 75–76.

36. Gaines to Secretary of War, May 22, 1815, NA LSW; Freeman to Meigs, Apr. 12, 1816, in Carter, *Mississippi*, pp. 677–78.

37. Boyd, "Prospect Bluff," p. 75; Early to Kindelan, May 24, 1815, Estrada to Early, June 14, Sept. 11, 1815, Governors' Letterbook, GaDA.

38. Boyd, "Prospect Bluff," p. 77.

39. Ibid., pp. 74–80; Clinch to Butler, Aug. 2, 1816, NA AGO.

40. Gaines to Secretary of War, Oct. 14, 1815, NA LSW; Arbuthnot to Nicolls, Aug. 26, 1817, in Parton, *Jackson*, 2:414–16; Arbuthnot to Cameron, undated, Arbuthnot to his son, Apr. 2, 1818, in Lowrie, *ASP, Indian Affairs*, 1:722–23.

41. Parton, *Jackson*, 2:417–18; Boyd, "Prospect Bluff," pp. 83–84.

42. James, *Jackson*, pp. 313–14; enclosure in Popham to Bathurst, Apr. 12, 1818, PRO Adm. 1/269; Petition of James Ambrister to His Honor William Vesey Munnings, June 19, 1818, enclosure in Munnings to Bagot, June 20, 1818, PRO FO 5/133; Memorial of James Ambrister, *Mobile Gazette*, Nov. 3, 1818.

Chapter 17

1. Latimer, "South Carolina," passim.

2. Hawkins to Secretary of War, May 25, 1812, Deposition of John Gill, Apr. 1812, NA LSW.

3. Hopoiethle Micco to the King's Most Excellent Majesty, Sept. 1, 1811, Munnings to Hopoiethle Micco, Dec. 9, 1811, PRO CO 23/58.

4. Cox, *West Florida*, passim; Pratt, *Expansionists*, passim.

5. Mahon, *War of 1812*, pp. 21, 232.

6. Tucker, *Poltroons*, 2:640–41; Horsman, *War of 1812*, pp. 224–31; Reilly, *British at the Gates*, pp. 170–71; Mahon, *War of 1812*, pp. 340–42.

7. Reilly, *British at the Gates*, pp. 110–11.

8. Ibid., pp. 344–46; Remini, *Andrew Jackson*, pp. 306–7.

Bibliography

THE SHORT citations used in the notes are, where necessary, given in brackets.

MANUSCRIPT COLLECTIONS

Alabama Department of Archives and History, Montgomery, Alabama [ADA]

Manuscript Section
The John Coffee Papers
The Henry S. Halbert Papers
The A. B. Meek Manuscript, "History of Alabama"
The Albert J. Pickett Papers
Military Section, Books 205 and 207 (typed copies of letters relating to the Creek War) [Military Section]

American Philosophical Society Library, Philadelphia, Pennsylvania [APS]

Young, H. "A Topographical Memoir on East and West Florida with Itineraries" (microfilm copy in the University of Georgia Library) [Young, "Memoir"]

Archivo General de Indias, Seville, Spain [AGI]

Papeles Procedentes de Cuba, Legajos 1447, 1794–95, 1856 (photostats in Library of Congress, Washington, D.C.) [PC]

Archivo Histórico Nacional, Madrid, Spain [AHN]

Estado, Legajo 5557, 5639 (photostats in Library of Congress, Washington, D.C.)

Auburn University Archives, Auburn, Alabama [AU]

Collection of typed transcripts of Hawkins letters

Florida Historical Society, University of South Florida, Tampa, Florida [FHi]

The Cruzat Papers
The Greenslade Papers

Georgia Department of Archives, Atlanta, Georgia [GaDA]

Collected letters of Benjamin Hawkins (typed copies from originals located here and in other archives) [Hawkins Letters]
Copies of letters written during the War of 1812–14 by General John Floyd to his daughter Mary Hazzard Floyd, presented to the General John Floyd Chapter, National Society of the Daughters of 1812, by Laura E. Blackshear (originals in private hands, copies in these archives) [Floyd Letters]
Governors' Letterbook, Nov. 28, 1809, to May 18, 1814, and May 18, 1814, to Oct. 30, 1827 [Governors' Letterbook]
Executive Minutes, Oct. 4, 1812, to Apr. 10, 1814, Governor David Bridie Mitchell and Governor Peter Early [Executive Minutes]
Georgia Military Affairs, vol. 3, 1801–13 [Military Affairs]
Georgia House Journal
Creek Letters, talks, and treaties, 1705–1839 (a collection of typed copies) [Creek Letters]
The John Floyd Papers [Floyd Papers]
The Benjamin Hawkins Papers [Hawkins Papers, GaDA]
Indian Letters, 1782–1839 [Indian Letters]

Indiana University, Bloomington, Indiana, Lilly Library [IU]

War of 1812 manuscripts collection [War of 1812]

Library of Congress, Washington, D.C. [LC]

The Andrew Jackson Papers [Jackson Papers, LC]
The Benjamin Hawkins Papers [Hawkins Papers, LC]

Louisiana State Museum, New Orleans, Louisiana [LSM]

"Major Howell Tatum's Journal While Acting Topographical Engineer (1814) to General Jackson Commanding 7th Military District" ["Tatum's Journal"]

Louisiana State University, Baton Rouge, Louisiana [LSU]

Kenner Papers
Daniel and Philip Hicky Papers [Hicky Papers]

Mississippi Department of Archives and History, Jackson, Mississippi [MDA]

J. F. H. Claiborne Collection, "Letters relating to the Indian Wars, 1812–1816," Letterbook F [Claiborne, Letterbook F]
Executive Journal of David Holmes, Governor of the Mississippi Territory, 1810–14 [Holmes Journal]

Mobile Public Library, Mobile, Alabama [MPL]

The John Forbes Papers [Forbes Papers]

National Archives, Washington, D.C. [NA]

Record Group 45 [RG 45]
Letters sent by the Secretary of the Navy to Officers [SNL-O]
Miscellaneous Letters Sent by the Secretary of the Navy [SNL-M]
Letters Received by the Secretary of the Navy from Commanders, 1804–86 [LSN-CO]
Letters Received by the Secretary of the Navy from Captains [SNL-C]
Record Group 59 [RG 59]
Notes from the Spanish Legation, vol. 3
Miscellaneous Letters of the Department of State [MSS]
Domestic Letters to the Department of State [DLDS]
Record Group 75 [RG 75]
Records of the Creek Trading House, 1795–1816
Letters sent by Secretary of War, Indian Affairs 1800–1824 [LSW-IA]
Record Group 94 [RG 94]
Records of the Adjutant General's Office [AGO]
Record Group 107 [RG 107]
Letters Sent, Military Affairs, vols. 7–8 [SWL]
Letters to the Secretary of War [LSW]
Register of Letters received by the Secretary of War, vol. 8 [RLS]
Records of the Office of the Secretary of War, Confidential and Unofficial Letters Sent, 1814–47 [SWC]
Letters Sent to the President by the Secretary of War, 1800–1863, vol. 1

National Library of Scotland, Edinburgh, Scotland [NLS]

The Papers of Admiral Alexander Forrester Inglis Cochrane, MSS 2326, 2328, 2330, 2334, 2336, 2344, 2374, 2574 [Cochrane Papers]

National Maritime Museum, Greenwich, England [NMM]

Admiral Sir Edward Codrington Papers, MS 9278 [Codrington Papers]
Admiral Sir John B. Warren Papers, MS 9622 [Warren Papers]

Princeton University Library

André de Coppet Collection

Public Record Office, London, England [PRO]

Admiralty Office 1, vols. 269, 505–9, 4360 [PRO Adm. 1]
Admiralty Office 50, vols. 87, 122 [PRO Adm. 50]
Colonial Office 23, vols. 58–61 [PRO CO 23]
Colonial Office 24, vol. 17 [PRO CO 24]
Colonial Office 27, vol. 15 [PRO CO 27]
Colonial Office 138, vol. 146 [PRO CO 138]
Foreign Office 5, vols. 133, 139–40 [PRO FO 5]
Foreign Office 72, vols. 180, 219 [PRO FO 72]
War Office 1, vols. 141–44 [PRO WO 1]
War Office 6, vol. 2 [PRO WO 6]

State Historical Society of Wisconsin, Madison, Wisconsin [WHi]

The Lyman Draper Manuscript Collection [Draper Collection]
The Georgia, Alabama, and South Carolina Papers, series V, vol. 1 [Georgia Papers]
The Tecumseh Papers, series YY, vols. 1–13 [Tecumseh Papers]

Tennessee Historical Society, Nashville, Tennessee [THi]

The John Coffee Papers [Coffee Papers]
The Emil Hurja Collection [Hurja Collection]
The Andrew Jackson Papers
Miscellaneous Files (many letters on the Creek War)
The John Reid Manuscript, "Life of Andrew Jackson" [Reid MS]
James Winchester Papers [Winchester Papers]
Claybrooke Papers

Tennessee State Library and Archives, Nashville, Tennessee [TSLA]

The Joseph Carson Papers
The Andrew Jackson Papers [Jackson Papers, TSLA]
Letterbook of William F. Cooper
Miscellaneous Correspondence

Tulane University, New Orleans, Louisiana, Howard-Tilton Memorial Library [TUL]

Andrew Hynes Collection [Hynes Papers]
Louisiana Historical Association Collection [Louisiana Collection]
David Rees Collection [Rees Papers]

University of Florida, Gainesville, Florida [FHi]

Transcripts of Cruzat Papers
Transcripts of Greenslade Papers
Elizabeth H. West Collection

University of Georgia, Athens, Georgia [GU]

The Telamon Cuyler Collection [Cuyler Collection]

University of Oklahoma, Norman, Oklahoma

Grayson Manuscript of 1917, Eloise D. Smock Collection [Smock Collection]

Published Documents

Adams, John Quincy. *The Duplicate Letters, the Fisheries, and the Mississippi. Documents Relating to Transactions at the Negotiation of Ghent.* Washington: Davis and Force, 1822.

Bassett, John S., ed. *Correspondence of Andrew Jackson.* 6 vols. Washington: Carnegie Institution, 1926–33. [Bassett, *Correspondence*]

Carter, Clarence E., ed. *The Territorial Papers of the United States*. Vol. 6: *The Territory of Mississippi; 1809–1817*. Washington: Government Printing Office, 1938. [Carter, *Mississippi*]

Lowrie, Walter, et al., eds. *The American State Papers*. Vol. 1: *Indian Affairs*. Washington: Gales and Seaton, 1832. [Lowrie, *ASP, Indian Affairs*]

Palmer, Thomas H. *The Historical Register of the United States*. 4 vols. Washington: G. Palmer, 1816. [Palmer, *Historical Register*]

Ponce de León, Julio C., director. *Boletín del Archivo Nacional*. Vol. 13, no. 1. Jan.–Feb. 1914. Havana, Cuba: De Aurelio Miranda, 1914.

Richardson, James D., ed. *A Compilation of the Messages and Papers of the Presidents, 1789–1897*. 10 vols. Washington: Government Printing Office, 1896–99.

Rowland, Dunbar, ed. *Official Letter Books of W. C. C. Claiborne, 1801–1816*. 6 vols. Jackson: Mississippi State Department of Archives and History, 1917. [Rowland, *Claiborne Letter Books*]

Yonge, Julien C., ed. "Letters of John Innerarity." *Florida Historical Quarterly* 9 (January 1931): 127–34.

———, ed. "The Panton Leslie Papers." *Florida Historical Quarterly* 18 (July 1939): 61–63; 18 (October 1939): 135–40.

Secondary Works: Books

Abernethy, Thomas P. *The South in the New Nation, 1789–1819*. Baton Rouge: Louisiana State University Press, 1961. [Abernethy, *South in the New Nation*]

Adams, Henry. *History of the United States of America during the Administration of James Madison*. 2 vols. containing books 5–9 of *History of the United States of America during the Administration of Thomas Jefferson and James Madison*. 4 vols. New York: Albert and Charles Boni, 1930. [Adams, *History*]

Armstrong, John. *Notices of the War of 1812*. 2 vols. New York: Wiley and Putnam, 1840.

Arthur, Stanley Clisby. *The Story of the Battle of New Orleans*. New Orleans: Louisiana Historical Society, 1915.

———. *Jean Laffite: Gentleman Rover*. New Orleans: Harmonson, 1952.

Ball, T. H. *A Glance into the Great South-East; Or, Clarke County, Alabama, and Its Surroundings from 1540 to 1877*. Tuscaloosa, AL: Willo Publishing Co., 1962.

Bancroft, George. *History of the United States of America, from the Discovery of the Continent*. 6 vols. New York: D. Appleton, 1888.

Bassett, John S. *The Life of Andrew Jackson*. 2 vols. Garden City, NY: Doubleday, Page, 1911.

Battle of New Orleans Sesquicentennial Celebration Commission, *Battle of New Orleans Sesquicentennial Celebration, 1815–1965*. Washington: Government Printing Office, 1965. [Battle of New Orleans]

Beirne, Francis F. *The War of 1812*. New York: E. P. Dutton, 1949.

Berkhofer, Robert F., Jr. *The White Man's Indian*. New York: Alfred A. Knopf, 1978.

Bernardo, C. Joseph, and Bacon, E. H. *American Military Policy*. Harrisburg, PA: Military Service Publishing Co., 1955.

Billington, Ray Allen. *Westward Expansion: A History of the Frontier.* 2d ed. New York: Macmillan, 1960. [Billington, *Westward Expansion*]

Blackshear, David. *Memoir of General David Blackshear, Including Letters from Governors Irwin, Jackson, Mitchell, Early, and Rabun, and from Major General McIntosh, Brigadier-General Floyd, and Other Officers of the Army in the War of 1813–14, on the Frontier and Sea-Coast of Georgia; and Also Letters from Members of Congress, Dr. Moses Waddel, and Others: Together with a Muster Roll of Troops Under his Command.* Edited by Stephen F. Miller. Philadelphia: J. B. Lippincott, 1858. [Blackshear, *Memoir*]

Brackenridge, H. M. *History of the Late War.* Philadelphia: James Kay, Jr., 1839.

Brannan, John. *Official Letters of the Military and Naval Officers of the United States, During the War with Great Britain in the years 1812, 13, 14, and 15.* Washington: Way and Gideon, 1823.

Brant, Irving. *James Madison: Commander-in-Chief.* Indianapolis: Bobbs-Merrill, 1961.

Brewer, Willis. *Alabama: Her History, Resources, War Record, and Public Men.* Montgomery: Barrett and Brown, 1872.

Brooks, Charles. *The Siege of New Orleans.* Seattle: University of Washington Press, 1961. [Brooks, *Siege*]

Brown, John P. *Old Frontiers; the Story of the Cherokee Indians from the Earliest Times to the Date of Their Removal West, 1838.* Kingsport, TN: Southern Publishers, 1938.

Brown, Roger H. *The Republic in Peril: 1812.* New York: Columbia University Press, 1964.

Brown, Wilburt S. *The Amphibious Campaign for West Florida and Louisiana, 1814–1815.* University: University of Alabama Press, 1969. [Brown, *Amphibious Campaign*]

Brown, William Horace. *The Glory Seekers: The Romance of the Would-be Founders of Empire in the Early Days of the Great Southwest.* New York: A. C. McClurg, 1906.

Buchan, John. *The History of the Royal Scots Fusiliers: 1678–1918.* London: Thos. Nelson & Sons, 1925.

Buckmaster, Henrietta. *The Seminole Wars.* New York: Collier Books, 1966.

Buell, Augustus C. *A History of Andrew Jackson.* 2 vols. New York: Charles Scribner's Sons, 1904.

Burt, A. L. *The United States, Great Britain, and British North America from the Revolution to the Establishment of Peace after the War of 1812.* New Haven: Yale University Press, 1940.

Butler, Lewis. *Annals of the King's Royal Rifle Corps.* 4 vols. London: John Murray, 1923.

Carter, Samuel, III. *Blaze of Glory: The Fight for New Orleans, 1814–1815.* New York: St. Martin's Press, 1971.

Caughey, John W. *McGillivray of the Creeks.* Norman: University of Oklahoma Press, 1959.

Chapelle, Howard I. *The History of the American Sailing Navy.* New York: W. W. Norton, 1949.

Chidsey, D. B. *The Battle of New Orleans.* New York: Crown, 1961.

Christian, Marcus. *Negro Soldiers in the Battle of New Orleans.* New Orleans: Louisiana Landmarks Society, 1965.

Claiborne, John Francis Hamtramck. *Life and Times of Gen. Sam Dale, the Mississippi Partisan.* New York: Harper and Brothers, 1860.

———. *Mississippi as a Province, Territory and State with Biographical Notices of Eminent Citizens.* Jackson: Power and Barksdale, 1880. [Claiborne, *Mississippi*]

Claiborne, Nathaniel Herbert. *Notes on the War in the South; with Biographical Sketches of the Lives of Montgomery, Jackson, Sevier, the Late Gov. Claiborne, and Others.* Richmond: William Ramsay, 1819.

Clowes, William Laird. *The Royal Navy: A History from the Earliest Time to the Present.* 7 vols. London: Sampson, Low, Marston, and Co., 1887–1903.

Cobbett, William. *Life of Andrew Jackson.* New York: Harper and Brothers, 1834.

Codrington, Sir Edward. *Memoirs of Admiral Sir Edward Codrington.* 2 vols. Edited by Lady Jane B. Bouchier. London: Longmans, Green, 1873.

Coles, Harry L. *The War of 1812.* Chicago: University of Chicago Press, 1965. [Coles, *War of 1812*]

Cooke, John Henry. *A Narative of Events in the South of France and of the Attack on New Orleans.* London: T. & W. Boone, 1835.

Cooper, James, and Sherman, Charles. *Secret Acts, Resolutions, and Instructions under which East Florida was Invaded by the United States Troops, Naval Forces, and Volunteers, in 1812 and 1813: Together with the Official Correspondence of the Agents and Officers of the Government, Showing That the Pretended Revolution Was Excited by the Agents of the United States as a Cover to the Seizure of the Province: and that the Executive Government Secretly Sanctioned and Abetted the Said Invasion, and Is Justly Responsible for All Injuries Which Resulted from It; and That Active Hostilities Were Carried on from March, 1812, until the Middle of May, 1813.* Washington: George S. Gideon, 1860.

Cooper, John Spencer. *Rough Notes of Seven Campaigns.* 2d ed. Carlisle, England: G. & T. Coward, 1914 (originally published 1869).

Cotterill, Robert S. *The Old South.* Glendale, CA: Arthur H. Clark Co., 1937. [Cotterill, *Old South*]

———. *The Southern Indians; The Story of the Civilized Tribes before Removal.* Norman: University of Oklahoma Press, 1954.

Cox, Isaac Joslin. *The West Florida Controversy, 1798–1813: A Study in American Diplomacy.* Baltimore: Johns Hopkins Press, 1918; reprint, Gloucester, MA: Peter Smith, 1967. [Cox, *West Florida*]

Cullum, G. W., ed. *Campaigns of the War of 1812–15.* New York: Miller, 1879.

Davis, Virgil S. *A History of the Mobile District U.S. Army Corps of Engineers, 1815–1971.* Mobile: Mobile District, South Atlantic Division, Corps of Engineers, U.S. Army, 1975.

Dawson, H. B. *Battles of the United States by Sea and Land.* 2 vols. New York: Johnson, Fry, 1858.

de Grummond, Jane L. *The Baratarians and the Battle of New Orleans.* Baton Rouge: Louisiana State University Press, 1961. [de Grummond, *Baratarians*]

Dixon, Richard R. *The Battle on the West Bank.* New Orleans: Louisiana Landmarks Society, 1965.

Drake, Benjamin. *Life of Tecumseh, and His Brother the Prophet: with a Historical Sketch of the Shawnoe Indians.* Cincinnati: E. Morgan, 1841.

Eggleston, George Cary. *Red Eagle and the Wars with the Creek Indians of Alabama.* New York: Dodd, Mead, 1878.

Eller, E. M., Morgan, W. J., and Basoco, R. M. *Sea Power and the Battle of New Orleans.* New Orleans: Louisiana Landmarks Society, 1965.

Fay, H. A. *Collection of the Official Accounts, in Detail, of All the Battles Fought by Sea and Land Between the Navy and Army of Great Britain, During the Years 1812, 13, 14 and 15.* New York: E. Conrad, 1817.

Field, Cyril. *Britain's Sea Soldiers: History of the Royal Marines and Their Predecessors and of Their Services in Action.* 2 vols. Liverpool: Lyceum Press, 1924. [Field, *Britain's Sea Soldiers*]

Forester, C. S. *The Age of Fighting Sail.* Garden City, NY: Doubleday, 1956. [Forester, *Fighting Sail*]

Fortescue, J. W. *A History of the British Army.* 13 vols. London: Macmillan Co., 1899–1930. [Fortescue, *British Army*]

Fortier, Alcee. *A History of Louisiana.* 4 vols. New York: Goupil, 1903.

Foster, Laurence. *Negro-Indian Relationships in the Southeast.* Philadelphia: University of Pennsylvania Press, 1935.

Franco, José L. *Politica Continental América de España en Cuba, 1812–1830.* Havana: Archivo Nacional de Cuba, 1947. [Franco, *Política*]

Gatschet, Albert Samuel. *A Migration Legend of the Creek Indians, with a Linguistic, Historic, and Ethnolographic Introduction.* 2 vols. Philadelphia: D. G. Brinton, 1884–88.

Gayarré, Charles. *History of Louisiana.* 4 vols. New York: William D. Widdon, 1866.

Gleig, George R. *The Campaigns of the British Army at Washington and New Orleans.* London: John Murray, 1847.

Goodwin, Philo A. *Biography of Andrew Jackson, President of the United States.* New York: R. H. Towner, 1833.

Griffin, Charles Carroll. *The United States and the Disruption of the Spanish Empire, 1810–1822: A Study of the Relations of the United States with Spain and with the Rebel Spanish Colonies.* New York: Columbia University Press, 1937. [Griffin, *United States*]

Halbert, H. S., and Ball, T. H. *The Creek War of 1813 and 1814.* Chicago: Donohue and Henneberry, 1895; reprint, edited by Frank L. Owsley, Jr., University: University of Alabama Press, 1969. [Halbert and Ball, *Creek War*]

Hatcher, William B. *Edward Livingston: Jeffersonian Republican and Jacksonian Democrat.* Baton Rouge: Louisiana State University Press, 1940. [Hatcher, *Livingston*]

Holmes, Jack D. L. *Honor and Fidelity: The Louisiana Infantry Regiment and the Louisiana Militia Companies, 1766–1821.* Louisiana Collection Series, edited by Jack D. L. Holmes. Vol. 1. Birmingham, AL: privately printed, 1965. [Holmes, *Honor and Fidelity*]

Horsman, Reginald. *The Causes of the War of 1812.* Philadelphia: University of Pennsylvania Press, 1962.

———. *Expansion and American Indian Policy 1812–1813.* East Lansing: Michigan State University Press, 1967. [Horsman, *Expansion*]

———. *The Origins of Indian Removal, 1815–1824*. East Lansing: Michigan State University Press, 1970. [Horsman, *Indian Removal*]

———. *The War of 1812*. New York: Alfred A. Knopf, 1969. [Horsman, *War of 1812*]

Huber, Leonard V. *New Orleans as It Was in 1814–1815*. New Orleans: Louisiana Landmarks Society, 1965.

Hunt, Charles H. *Life of Edward Livingston*. New York: D. Appleton, 1864. [Hunt, *Livingston*]

Hunt, Louise Livingston. *Memoir of Mrs. Edward Livingston, with Letters Hitherto Unpublished*. New York: Harper and Brothers, 1886. [Hunt, *Memoir*]

Jacobs, James R. *Tarnished Warrior: Major General James Wilkinson*. New York: Macmillan, 1938.

Jacobs, James R., and Tucker, Glenn. *The War of 1812: A Compact History*. New York: Hawthorn Books, 1969.

James, Marquis. *Andrew Jackson: The Border Captain*. Indianapolis: Bobbs Merrill, 1933. [James, *Jackson*]

James, William. *A Full and Correct Account of the Military Occurrences of the Late War between Great Britain and the United States of America*. 2 vols. London: Privately printed, 1818.

———. *The Naval History of Great Britain from the Declaration of War by France in 1793, to the Accession of George IV*. 6 vols. London: Privately printed, 1826.

Johns, Richard, and Nicolas, P. H. *The Naval and Military Heroes of Great Britain or Calendar of Victory*. London: Henry G. Bohn, 1860.

Johnson, Gerald W. *Andrew Jackson: An Epic in Homespun*. New York: Milton Balch, 1927.

King, G. *Creole Families of New Orleans*. New York: Macmillan, 1921.

Knox, Dudley W. *A History of the United States Navy*. New York: G. P. Putnam's Sons, 1936.

Laffite, Jean. *The Journal of Jean Laffite; the Privateer–Patriot's Own Story*. New York: Vantage Press, 1958.

Latour, A. Lacarrière. *Historical Memoir of the War in West Florida and Louisiana in 1814–15*. Translated by H. P. Nugent. Philadelphia: John Conrad & Co., 1816; reprint, Gainesville: University of Florida Press, 1964. [Latour, *Memoir*]

Leckie, Robert. *The Wars of America*. New York: Harper and Row, 1968.

Lossing, Benson John. *The Pictorial Field–Book of the War of 1812, or, Illustrations, by Pen and Pencil, of the History, Biography, Scenery, Relics, and Traditions of the Last War for American Independence*. New York: Harper and Brothers, 1868.

McAfee, Robert B. *History of the Late War in the Western Country*. Bowling Green, OH: 1919; reprint from 1816 version Historical Publications Company.

Mahan, A. T. *Sea Power in Its Relations to the War of 1812*. 2 vols. Boston: Little, Brown, 1905.

Mahon, John K. *The War of 1812*. Gainesville: University of Florida Press, 1972. [Mahon, *War of 1812*]

Martin, Francois-Xavier. *The History of Louisiana*. New Orleans: James A. Gresham, 1882.

A Narrative of the Life and Death of Lieut. Joseph Morgan Willcox, Who Was Massa-

cred by the Creek Indians, on the Alabama River (Miss. Ter.) on the 15th of January, 1814. Marietta, OH: R. Prentiss, 1816.

Nolte, Vincent. *The Memoirs of Vincent Nolte: Reminiscences in the Period of Anthony Adverse*. Translated from the German. New York: G. Howard Watt, 1934. (Originally published in the U.S., 1854.)

Parton, James. *Life of Andrew Jackson*. 3 vols. New York: Mason Bros., 1861. [Parton, *Jackson*]

Patrick, Rembert. *Florida Fiasco: Rampant Rebels on the Georgia-Florida Border*. Athens: University of Georgia Press, 1954. [Patrick, *Florida Fiasco*]

Perkins, Bradford, ed. *The Causes of the War of 1812, National Honor or National Interest*. New York: Holt, Rinehart and Winston, 1962.

———. *Prologue to War*. Berkeley: University of California Press, 1963. [Perkins, *Prologue to War*]

Pickett, Albert James. *History of Alabama, and Incidentally of Georgia and Mississippi, from the Earliest Period*. Vol. 2. Charleston, SC: Walker and James, 1851. [Pickett, *Alabama*]

Pound, Merritt B. *Benjamin Hawkins, Indian Agent*. Athens: University of Georgia Press, 1951. [Pound, *Hawkins*]

Pratt, Julius W. *Expansionists of 1812*. New York: Macmillan Co., 1925; reprint, Gloucester, MA: Peter Smith, 1957. [Pratt, *Expansionists*]

Prucha, Francis Paul. *American Indian Policy in the Formative Years*. Lincoln: University of Nebraska Press, 1970.

———. *A Bibliographical Guide to the History of Indian-White Relations in the United States*. Chicago: University of Chicago Press, 1977.

———. *The Indian in American History*. New York: Holt, Rinehart, and Winston, 1971.

———. *The Sword of the Republic: The United States Army on the Frontier, 1783–1846*. New York: Macmillan, 1969.

Ramsay, David. *History of the United States, from Their First Settlement as English Colonies, in 1607 to the Year 1808, or the Thirty-third of Their Sovereignty and Independence*. 3 vols. Philadelphia: M. Carey and Son, 1818.

Rankin, Hugh, ed. *The Battle of New Orleans: A British View*. New Orleans: Hauser Press, 1961. [Rankin, *New Orleans*]

Reid, John, and Eaton, John H. *The Life of Andrew Jackson, Major General, in the Service of the United States, Comprising a History of the War in the South, from the Commencement of the Creek Campaign, to the Termination of Hostilities before New Orleans*. Philadelphia: M. Carey and Son, 1817. [Reid and Eaton, *Jackson*]

Reilly, Robin. *The British at the Gates: The New Orleans Campaign in the War of 1812*. New York: G. P. Putnam's Sons, 1974. [Reilly, *British at the Gates*]

Remini, Robert V. *Andrew Jackson*. New York: Harper and Row, 1969.

———. *Andrew Jackson and the Course of American Empire, 1767–1821*. New York: Harper and Row, 1977.

Rogin, Michael Paul. *Fathers and Children*. New York: Vintage Books, 1975.

Roosevelt, Theodore. *The Naval War of 1812*. 4th ed. New York: G. P. Putnam's Sons, 1889.

Rowland, Mrs. Dunbar. *Andrew Jackson's Campaign against the British*. New York: Macmillan, 1926.

Royall, Anne Newport. *Letters from Alabama, 1817–1822*. Edited by Lucille Griffith. University: University of Alabama Press, 1969. [Royall, *Letters*]

Sanders, Daniel Clark. *History of the Indian Wars with the First Settlers of the United States to the Commencement of the Late War; Together with an Appendix Not Before Added to This History, Containing Interesting Accounts of the Battles Fought by General Andrew Jackson*. Rochester, NY: Edwin Scranton, 1828.

Satz, Ronald N. *American Indian Policy in the Jackson Era*. Lincoln: University of Nebraska Press, 1975.

Scott, Valerie M. (Lady Pakenham). *Major-General Sir Edward Pakenham*. New Orleans: Louisiana Landmarks Society, 1965.

Silver, James W. *Edmund Pendleton Gaines: Frontier General*. Baton Rouge: Louisiana State University Press, 1949.

Sinclair, H. *The Port of New Orleans*. Garden City, NY: Doubleday, 1942.

Smith, Zachary F. *The Battle of New Orleans*. Filson Club Publications, No. 19. Louisville, KY: John P. Morton, 1904.

Snelling, William Joseph. *A Brief and Impartial History of the Life and Actions of Andrew Jackson*. Boston: Stimpson and Clapp, 1831.

Starkey, Marion L. *The Cherokee Nation*. New York: A. A. Knopf, 1946.

Stoddard, William Osborn. *Andrew Jackson and Martin Van Buren*. New York: F. A. Stokes, 1887.

Surtees, William. *Twenty-five Years in the Rifle Brigade*. Edinburgh: Wm. Blackwood, 1833.

Tucker, Glenn. *Poltroons and Patriots: A Popular Account of the War of 1812*. 2 vols. Indianapolis: Bobbs-Merrill, 1954. [Tucker, *Poltroons*]

———. *Tecumseh: Vision of Glory*. Indianapolis: Bobbs-Merrill, 1956. [Tucker, *Tecumseh*]

Van Ness, William Peter. *A Concise Narrative of General Jackson's First Invasion of Florida, and of His Immortal Defence of New Orleans*. New York: E. M. Murden and A. Ming, Jr., 1827.

Waldo, Samuel Putnam. *Memoirs of Andrew Jackson, Major General in the Army of the United States; and Commander in Chief of the Division of the South*. Hartford: S. Andrus, 1819.

Walker, Alexander. *Jackson and New Orleans*. New York: J. C. Derby, 1856.

Ward, John William. *Andrew Jackson, Symbol for an Age*. New York: Oxford University Press, 1955.

Watson, Thomas E. *Life and Times of Andrew Jackson*. Thompson, GA: Jeffersonian Publishing Co., 1912.

Whitaker, Arthur P. *The Spanish-American Frontier: 1783–1795*. Boston: Houghton Mifflin, 1927. [Whitaker, *Spanish-American Frontier*]

White, Leonard D. *The Jeffersonians: A Study in Administrative History, 1801–1829*. New York: Macmillan, 1951.

White, Patrick C. T. *A Nation on Trial: America and the War of 1812*. New York: John Wiley & Sons, 1965.

Wilkinson, James. *Memoirs of My Own Times*. 3 vols. Philadelphia: Abraham Small, 1816.

Wilson, Samuel, Jr. *Plantation Houses on the Battlefield of New Orleans*. New Orleans: Louisiana Landmarks Society, 1965.

Woodward, Grace S. *The Cherokees*. Norman: University of Oklahoma Press, 1963.

Woodward, Thomas S. *Woodward's Reminiscences of the Creek, or Muscogee Indians, Contained in Letters to Friends in Georgia and Alabama.* Montgomery, AL: Barrett and Wimbish, 1859; reprint, Tuscaloosa, AL: Alabama Bookstore, 1939. [*Woodward's Reminiscences*]

Wright, J. Leitch, Jr. *William Augustus Bowles, Director General of the Creek Nation.* Athens: University of Georgia Press, 1967. [Wright, *Bowles*]

Secondary Works: Articles

Adams, Reed McC. B. "New Orleans and the War of 1812." *Louisiana Historical Quarterly* 16 (April, July, Oct. 1933): 221–34, 478–503, 681–703; 17 (January, April, July 1934):169–82, 349–63, 502–23.

Ainsworth, Walden L. "An Amphibious Operation that Failed." *United States Naval Institute Proceedings* 71 (Feb. 1945):193–202.

Barbour, Violet. "Privateers and Pirates of the West Indies." *American Historical Review* 17 (Apr. 1911):543–65.

Brooks, Philip C. "Spain's Farewell to Louisiana, 1803–1821." *Mississippi Valley Historical Review* 27 (July 1940):29–42.

Boyd, Mark F. "Events at Prospect Bluff on the Apalachicola River, 1808–1818." *Florida Historical Quarterly* 14 (Oct. 1937):55–96. [Boyd, "Prospect Bluff "]

Cable, George W. "The Creoles in the American Revolution." *Century Magazine* 25 (Feb. 1883):538–50.

———. "The End of Foreign Dominion in Louisiana." *Century Magazine* 25 (Mar. 1883):643–54.

———. "Plotters and Pirates of Louisiana." *Century Magazine* 25 (April 1883):852–66.

———. "Who Are the Creoles?" *Century Magazine* 25 (Jan. 1883):384–98.

Calkins, Carlos G. "The Repression of Piracy in the West Indies, 1814–1825." *United States Naval Institute Proceedings* 37 (Dec. 1911):1187–98.

Carpenter, Edwin H., Jr. "Latour's Report on Spanish-American Relations in Southwest." *Louisiana Historical Quarterly* 30 (July 1947):715–17.

"A Contemporary Account of the Battle of New Orleans by a Soldier in the Ranks." *Louisiana Historical Quarterly* 9 (Jan. 1926):11–15. ["Contemporary Account"]

Cusacks, Gaspar. "Lafitte, the Louisiana Pirate and Patriot." *Louisiana Historical Quarterly* 2 (Oct. 1919):418–38.

Dart, Henry P., ed. "Andrew Jackson and Judge D. A. Hall." *Louisiana Historical Quarterly* 5 (Oct. 1922):509–70.

———. "Jackson and the Louisiana Legislature, 1814–15." *Louisiana Historical Quarterly* 9 (Apr. 1926):221–30.

de Grummond, Jane L. "Platter of Glory." *Louisiana History* 3 (Fall 1962):316–58. [de Grummond, "Platter of Glory"]

Dickson, Colonel Sir Alexander. "Artillery Services in North America in 1814 and

1815." *Journal of the Society for Army Historical Research* 8 (Apr., July, Oct. 1929):79–112, 147–78, 213–26.

Doster, James F., ed. "Letters Relating to the Tragedy of Fort Mims: August –September, 1813." *Alabama Review* 14 (Oct. 1961):269–85. [Doster, "Fort Mims"]

Espy, William, ed. "General Court-Martial Held at the Royal Barracks, Dublin, for the Trial of Brevet Lieutenant Colonel Hon. Thomas Mullins, Captain of the 44th Regiment of Foot, July 11 to August 1, 1815." *Louisiana Historical Quarterly* 9 (Jan. 1926):33–110.

Faye, Stanley. "Privateers of Guadeloupe and Their Establishment in Barataria." *Louisiana Historical Quarterly* 23 (Apr. 1940):428–44.

———. "Privateersmen of the Gulf and Their Prizes." *Louisiana Historical Quarterly* 22 (Oct. 1929):1012–94.

Fisher, Ruth A. "The Surrender of Pensacola as Told by the British." *American Historical Review* 54 (Jan. 1949):326–29.

Forrester, Cecil S. "Victory at New Orleans." *American Heritage* 8 (Aug. 1957):4–9, 106–8.

Galpin, William F. "American Grain Trade to the Spanish Peninsula." *American Historical Review* 28 (Oct. 1922):24–44.

Gayarré, Charles E. "Historical Sketch of Pierre and Jean Lafitte." *Magazine of American History* 10 (Oct., Nov. 1883):284–98, 389–96.

[Gleig, George R.] "Subaltern in America." *Blackwood's Edinburgh Magazine* 21 (Jan.–June 1827):243–53, 417–33, 531–43, 719–26; 22 (July–Dec. 1827):74–82, 316–28.

Goodrich, Caspar F. "Our Navy and the West Indian Pirates." *United States Naval Institute Proceedings* 42 (Jan. 1916):1459–75.

Greenslade, Marie Taylor. "John Innerarity, 1783–1854." *Florida Historical Quarterly* 9 (Oct. 1930):90–95. [Greenslade, "Innerarity"]

Hardin, J. Fair. "The First Great River Captain." *Louisiana Historical Quarterly* 10 (Jan. 1927):27–28.

Henry, Robert S. "Tennesseans and Territory." *Tennessee Historical Quarterly* 12 (Sept. 1953):195–203.

Holland, James W. "Andrew Jackson and the Creek War: Victory at the Horseshoe." *Alabama Review* 21 (October 1968):243–75.

Horsman, Reginald. "British Indian Policy in the Northwest, 1807–1812." *Mississippi Valley Historical Review* 45 (Apr. 1958):51–67. [Horsman, "British Indian Policy"]

Latimer, Margaret K. "South Carolina—A Protagonist of the War of 1812." *American Historical Review* 61 (July 1956):914–29. [Latimer, "South Carolina"]

Leach, Douglas E. "John Gordon of Gordon's Ferry." *Tennessee Historical Quarterly* 18 (1959):322–44. [Leach, "John Gordon"]

Liljegren, Ernest R. "Jacobinism in Spanish Louisiana, 1792–1797." *Louisiana Historical Quarterly* 22 (Jan. 1939):47–97.

Lister, Walter B. "Portrait of a Pirate." *American Mercury* 7 (Feb. 1926):214–19.

McAlister, L. N. "Pensacola during the Second Spanish Period." *Florida Historical Quarterly* 32 (Jan.–Apr. 1959):281–327. [McAlister, "Pensacola"]

McClellan, Edwin. "The Navy at New Orleans." *United States Naval Institute Proceedings* 50 (Dec. 1924):2041–60.

Maclay, Edgar S. "Battle of New Orleans Half Won at Sea." *Magazine of History* 16 (Jan. 1913):29–34.

Mahon, John K. "British Command Decisions Relative to the Battle of New Orleans." *Louisiana History* 6 (Winter 1965):53–76. [Mahon, "Command Decisions"]

———. "British Strategy and Southern Indians: War of 1812." *Florida Historical Quarterly* 44 (Apr. 1966):285–302. [Mahon, "British Strategy"]

Marigny, Bernard. "Reflections on New Orleans Campaign." Edited and translated by Grace King. *Louisiana Historical Quarterly* 6 (Jan. 1923):61–85. [Marigny, "Reflections"]

"A Massachusetts Volunteer at the Battle of New Orleans." *Louisiana Historical Quarterly* 9 (Jan. 1926):30–31. ["Massachusetts"]

Mills, Colonel Dudley, Royal Engineers. "The Duke of Wellington and the Peace Negotiations at Ghent." *Canadian Historical Review* 2 (Mar. 1921):19–32.

Morgan, David B. "General David B. Morgan's Defense of the Conduct of the Louisiana Militia in the Battle on the Left Side of the River." *Louisiana Historical Quarterly* 9 (Jan. 1926):16–29. ["Morgan's Defense"]

Murdock, Richard K., ed. "A British Report on West Florida and Louisiana, November 1812." *Florida Historical Quarterly* 43 (July 1964):36–51. [Murdock, "British Report"]

Owsley, Frank L., Jr. "British and Indian Activities in Spanish West Florida during the War of 1812." *Florida Historical Quarterly* 46 (Oct. 1967):111–23.

———. "The Fort Mims Massacre." *Alabama Review* 24 (July 1971):192–204. [Owsley, "Fort Mims Massacre"]

———. "Jackson's Capture of Pensacola." *Alabama Review* 19 (July 1966):175–85. [Owsley, "Jackson's Capture"]

———. "The Role of the South in the British Grand Strategy in the War of 1812." *Tennessee Historical Quarterly* 31 (Spring 1972):22–38.

Parsons, Edward A. "Jean Lafitte in the War of 1812: A Narative Based on the Original Documents." *Proceedings of the American Antiquarian Society* 50 (Oct. 1940):205–24.

Pratt, Julius. "Western Aims in the War of 1812." *Mississippi Valley Historical Review* 12 (June 1925):38–50.

Prucha, Francis Paul. "Andrew Jackson's Indian Policy: A Reassessment." *Journal of American History* 56 (Dec. 1969):527–39.

Risjord, Norman K. "1812: Conservatives, War Hawks, and the Nation's Honor." *William and Mary Quarterly* 18 (Apr. 1961):196–210.

Ritchie, Carson I. A. "The Louisiana Campaign." *Louisiana Historical Quarterly* 44 (Jan.–Apr. 1961):13–103. [Ritchie, "Louisiana Campaign"]

Stephen, Walter W. "Andrew Jackson's Forgotten Army." *Alabama Review* 12 (Apr. 1959):126–31. [Stephen, "Forgotten Army"]

Tatum, Howell. "Major Howell Tatum's Journal." Edited by John Spencer Bassett. *Smith College Studies in History* 7 (1921–22), nos. 1–3.

Tousard, Louis de. "Letters re Battle of New Orleans." *Magazine of History* 25 (July, 1917):40–42.

Trussel, John B. B., Jr. "Thunder by the River." *Field Artillery Journal* 39 (July–Aug. 1949):173–75.

Ventura Morales, Juan. "Juan Ventura Morales to Alexandro Ramirez, November 3, 1817." *Boletín del Archivo Nacional* 13 (Jan.–Feb. 1914):9–21.

Wellesley, Arthur, Duke of Wellington. "Letter of Duke of Wellington (May 22, 1815) on the Battle of New Orleans." *Louisiana Historical Quarterly* 9 (Jan. 1926):5–10.

West, Elizabeth Howard, ed. "A Prelude to the Creek War of 1813–1814." *Florida Historical Quarterly* 18 (Apr. 1940):247–66. [West, "Prelude"]

Wilkinson, Norman B. "The Assault on New Orleans, 1814–15." *Louisiana History* 3 (Winter 1962):43–53. [Wilkinson, "Assault"]

Wright, J. Leitch, Jr. "A Note on the First Seminole War as Seen by the Indians, Negroes, and Their British Advisers." *Journal of Southern History* 34 (Nov. 1968):565–75.

———. "British Designs on the Old Southwest: Foreign Intrigue on the Florida Frontier, 1783–1803." *Florida Historical Quarterly* 44 (Apr. 1966):265–84. [Wright, "British Designs"]

Newspapers

Augusta Chronicle, Augusta, Georgia

Mississippi Republican, Washington, Mississippi Territory

Mobile Gazette, Mobile, Alabama Territory

National Intelligencer, Washington, D.C.

New Orleans Gazette, New Orleans, Louisiana

Niles' Weekly Register, Baltimore, Maryland

The Republican and Savannah Evening Ledger, Savannah, Georgia

Royal Gazette and Bahama Advertiser, Nassau, New Providence

The Times, London, England

Unpublished Works

Eckert, Edward K. "William Jones and the Role of the Secretary of the Navy in the War of 1812." Ph.D. dissertation, University of Florida, 1969.

Harrison, Frances Kathryn. "The Indians as a Means of Spanish Defense of West Florida, 1783–1795." Master's thesis, University of Alabama, 1950. [Harrison, "Indians"]

Lengle, Leland. "Harry Toulmin." Master's thesis, Duke University, 1967.

Index

DATE DUE

FEB 02 1983			
2-16-83			
DEC 1 4 1995			

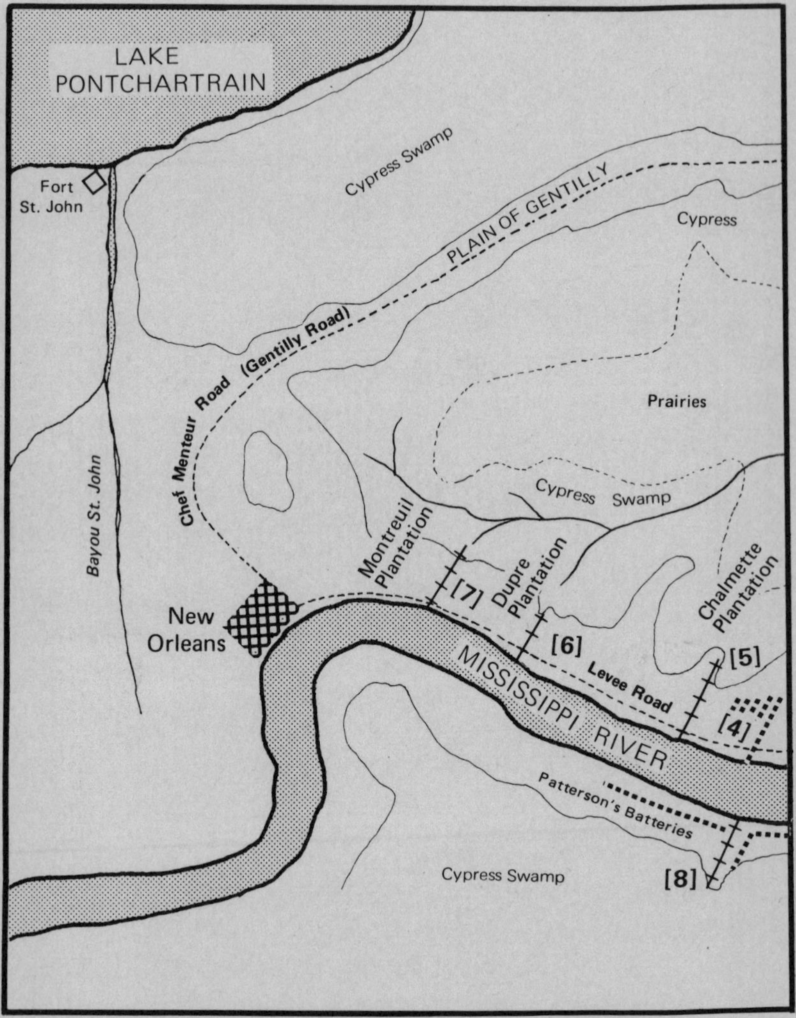

British attack on the Gulf Coast, December 23, 1814, to January 8, 1815. (1) Battle of December 23. (2) Coffee's attack. (3) Jackson's attack, December 23. (4) Pakenham's British attack,

← Card + Pocket

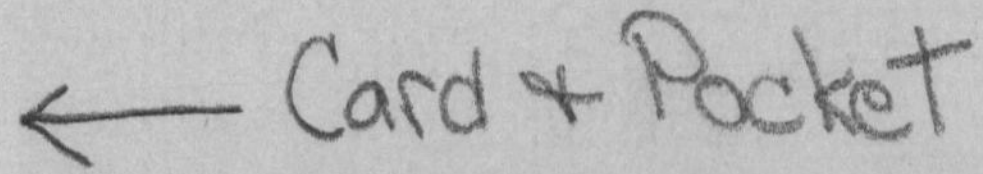